Performing Americanness

Performing Americanness

*Race, Class, and Gender in Modern
African-American and Jewish-American Literature*

Catherine Rottenberg

DARTMOUTH COLLEGE PRESS
Hanover, New Hampshire

Published by University Press of New England
Hanover and London

Dartmouth College Press
Published by University Press of New England,
One Court Street, Lebanon, NH 03766
www.upne.com
© 2008 by Dartmouth College Press
Printed in the United States of America

5   4   3   2   1

Library of Congress Cataloging-in-Publication Data
Rottenberg, Catherine.
Performing Americanness : race, class, and gender in modern African-American and Jewish-American literature / Catherine Rottenberg.
p.   cm.
Includes bibliographical references and index.
ISBN-13: 978–1–58465–682–1 (cloth : alk. paper)
ISBN-10: 1–58465–682–4 (cloth : alk. paper)
1. American literature—Minority authors—History and criticism. 2. American literature—20th century—History and criticism. 3. American literature—21st century—History and criticism. 4. National characteristics, American, in literature. 5. Race in literature. 6. Religion in literature. 7. Sex role in literature. 8. Minorities in literature. 9. Passing (Identity) in literature. I. Title.
PS153.M56R68   2008

810.9'3552—dc22   2007037125

University Press of New England is a member of the Green Press Initiative. The paper used in this book meets their minimum requirement for recycled paper.

To Ariel and Neve

Contents

Acknowledgments

I would like to thank Shlomith Rimmon-Kennan and Louise Bethlehem, who both, in their own ways, helped me to find my voice and allowed me to travel my own course. I waited anxiously and impatiently for Shlomith's early morning phone calls when she would gave me her verdict on my chapters (usually on my answering machine). For her unwavering support, I am profoundly grateful. I wish to thank Shuli Barzilai for her steadfast encouragement and wise advice, Carola Hilfrich for her amazing help over the years and, most of all, for her friendship, and Shira Wolosky for her guidance as well as for teaching me to read poetry. Gabi Motzkin made three years of funding possible, and I would like to express my deep appreciation to him. Many, many thank-yous to Maya Barzilai, Cheryl Greenberg, Gina Rucavado, Amritjit Singh, Jacinda Swanson, and Niza Yanai, who all gave me invaluable feedback over the years. Niza Y. and Nitza B. went to bat for me when I most needed it, and I feel extremely indebted to them both. Barbara Hochman never allowed me to lose hope, and I have admired her ever since we first met. My gratitude also goes to Ayelet Ben-Yishai, Yinon Cohen, Amit Yahav, and Amalia Ziv.

A very special thank-you goes to Dan Caspi, Henriette Dahan-Kalev, and Jimmy Weinblatt, as well as to Donald Pease for agreeing to read my introduction, introducing me to the University Press of New England, and for his constant and enthusiastic support for my project. I could never have made it this far without the extraordinary generosity of Judith Butler. She made a post-doctoral year at Berkeley possible — a year that changed my life in many expected and in some unexpected ways — and always encouraged me to believe in myself as an academic. Her work has been a continued source of inspiration and her friendship has buoyed me during difficult times.

I would also like to note that the journal *American Studies* has allowed me to publish a modified version of "*Salome of the Tenements*, American Dream Discourse and Class Performativity," which appeared in Vol. 5, No. 1 (2004): 5–29. An earlier version of Chapter Two appeared in *Criticism*, Vol. 45, No. 4 (2003): 435–52; and a shortened version of Chapter Four was first published as "Race and Ethnicity in *The Autobiography of an Ex-Colored Man* and *The Rise of David Levinsky*: The Performative Difference" in *MELUS*, Vol. 29, Nos. 3–4 (2004): 307–23.

Last but never least, I want to express my love and gratitude to family: To Elizabeth, my sister, whose alternative readings and provocative questions have never stopped challenging me; to my parents, David and Shelly, who have rejoiced with me; to Neve, without whom I probably never would have graduated from college let alone finished a book; and, finally, to my beautiful Ariel, who has taught me the meaning of wonder.

Performing Americanness

Introduction

Performing Americanness

W HY ARE READERS still so fascinated by narratives of "racial passing" and the "one-drop rule"? Why does the literature depicting first-generation immigrants to the Jewish Lower East Side continue to feel pertinent and one might even go so far as to say revelatory? What is it about such early-twentieth-century African- and Jewish-American fictions that has ensured their status as modern "ethnic" classics? The fascination with the novels produced by the emergent African-American middle class and the newly arrived Jewish immigrants, two groups located on the periphery of US society during the Progressive Era and Harlem Renaissance, seems to persist because these literary texts raise questions about what it means to be American with particular force. The narratives not only confront the topical issues of gender, race, class, and ethnicity with important insight, but they also address marginalization and social stratification with an urgency difficult to ignore.

It is perhaps not surprising that many "ethnic" novels written in the first decades of the twentieth century are preoccupied with what "Americanness" signifies.[1] After all, the Progressive Era and the Harlem Renaissance were periods of tremendous upheaval in the United States, and thus periods that profoundly queried accepted notions of American identity.[2] If, prior to the Civil War, the country could have been described as rural and agrarian-based, by the end of World War I only one-third of Americans lived on farms, and over one-half of the entire population lived in approximately a dozen cities. Independent production on farms and in small businesses was giving way to corporate capitalism, dramatically altering the domestic economy. In addition, trans-Atlantic immigration and internal migration were on the rise. The postbellum United States was fast becoming a heavily industrialized, diverse, and urban-centered society.[3]

As many cultural historians have documented, these years witnessed significant demographic shifts in the African- and Jewish-American populations. Nearly half a million African Americans left the South for northern cities between 1910 and 1920, and in the following decade this trend not only continued but intensified. By 1920, the black presence in New York City had increased by at least 60 percent. Along similar lines, approximately two and a half million Eastern European Jews arrived in the United States between 1880 and 1920, radically transforming the makeup of Jewish communities. Prior to this massive immigration from Eastern European, most of the Jews in the United States had been in the country for at least one generation and had arrived from Western and Central Europe. By 1915, the majority of U.S. Jews were first-generation immigrants from Russia and Poland and lived in the eastern metropolises.[4] Together with the historic social changes taking place within these minority communities, there was also a marked expansion of an African-American as well as a Jewish-American literary culture. And many of the texts written by African Americans and Jewish immigrants during this period were meditating on the desirability of fitting into hegemonic U.S. society.

While the publication of Phillis Wheatley's poetry in the eighteenth century usually is invoked as marking the beginnings of an African-American literary tradition, most critics agree that African-American literature "came into its own" or experienced an "aesthetic flowering" at the turn of the twentieth century.[5] This is one reason that the literature produced during the Harlem Renaissance has been the site of so much critical interest in recent years.[6] In contrast to the pre–Civil War United States, in which the greater part of black Americans were slaves and denied access to education, the post-Reconstruction years witnessed the growth of a small black middle class and an attempt to create a particularly African-American literature.

Lewis Fried's edited volume *Handbook of American-Jewish Literature* (1988) similarly dates the emergence of a particularly Jewish-American literary tradition to the turn of the twentieth century and the massive waves of immigration.[7] The volume, in fact, only begins its genealogy with the 1880s. Other scholars also have argued that this literature came of age during the Progressive Era. Published as a book in 1917, Abraham

Cahan's *The Rise of David Levinsky,* for instance, has long been considered the first classic Jewish-American novel written in English.[8]

Not only did these two minority literatures undergo a transformation at around the same time, but both the African- and the Jewish-American fiction produced at the turn of the last century describe the rapidly changing historical landscape and highlight how such changes created and stimulated certain conflicts vis-à-vis notions of Americanness. This literature is acutely aware of the liminal position of African and Jewish Americans at the time; and quite a few of the novels dramatize the ways that these minority groups attempted to move from margin to center by carving out a niche for themselves in mainstream U.S. society as well as the mechanisms by and through which these groups were excluded from sites of power.

Reading African- and Jewish-American Literature Side by Side

The particular texts that I have chosen to focus on in this book — *Arrogant Beggar* (1927), *The Autobiography of an Ex-Colored Man* (1912), *Passing* (1929), *Quicksand* (1928), *The Rise of David Levinsky* (1917), and *Salome of the Tenements* (1923) — engage in contemporaneous political and social polemics, such as how to define "blackness" and "Jewishness," and explore some of the potential "identity effects" of marginalization. The six novels expose how subjects have been both *compelled* and *encouraged* to emulate dominant U.S. norms, and reveal that precisely those subjects who have not been able to assume privilege in relation to gender, class, race, or ethnicity — crucial components constituting Americanness — often have redoubled their efforts to emulate the hegemonic mores associated with these categories. Consequently, the texts under consideration become powerful sites for exploring the very complex modes through which dominant norms have helped to produce and sustain social stratification in the United States.

Although there is a considerable amount of literary criticism on the different novels I examine, only a handful of scholars have attempted to compare African- and Jewish-American literary texts.[9] This is quite surprising given the complex, fraught, yet nonetheless intertwined history of these two minority groups. The majority of scholars who have analyzed the relationship between these two literary traditions have focused on black-Jewish relations and the way each minority group has "imagined" the other through literary representations.[10] However, these scholars have not addressed how issues of gender, race, class, and ethnicity get played out in these "ethnic" fictions, nor the way the literature positions the two groups *differently* vis-à-vis dominant society and hegemonic notions of Americanness. In addition, almost all of the comparative studies that have been written look at post–Harlem Renaissance literature while I focus on early-twentieth-century African- and Jewish-American fiction.[11]

There are many reasons for doing such a comparative study. By juxtaposing these two sets of early twentieth-century literary texts, it becomes clear, for instance, that the construction of race and the construction of ethnicity have had very different historical trajectories in the United States and that the two cannot be collapsed. This kind of comparative analysis therefore sheds new light on the category of ethnicity, since the texts gesture toward the historical *difference* between the racialized status of African Americans and the racial in-betweenness of other minority groups, many of which "became white" by the end of World War II. The development of the category of ethnicity during the interwar period, then, has to be understood in relation to the changing racial landscape in the United States. Ethnicity as a category of identity, I propose, has evolved out of a discourse of race, which has itself revolved around the poles of whiteness and blackness. Moreover, in Chapter Four I show that "being Jewish" and identifying as "ethnic" in the United States historically has not interfered with identifying as an American, whereas historically "being black" has. Reading these narratives side by side reveals that the very intelligibility of ethnicity in the U.S. context depends on the prior construction of the black-white divide.

Another benefit of juxtaposing African- and Jewish-American texts concerns the elusive but important concept of privilege. The notion of "privilege" gained currency following the civil rights and the feminist movements, and in recent years it increasingly has been invoked as a means of unveiling unequal and exploitative power relations: between men and women, whites and people of color, heterosexuals and homosexuals, and upper and lower classes. Comparing minority narratives from the early twentieth century allows for a multi-layered examination of privilege, not least because Jews and African Americans were positioned differently vis-à-vis the existing social hierarchies. Whereas the African-American novels, not surprisingly, tend to emphasize racial issues, early-twentieth-century Jewish immigrants were relatively privileged in relation to race. Thus, the Jewish-American narratives dwell more on questions of class and the possibility of upward mobility. By pushing questions of class to the forefront, however, the Jewish-American texts can be seen to reinforce the privilege that comes from or with "being white," or, as we will see, almost white.

In Chapter Five, I propose that when one specific category, that is, gender, race, class, or ethnicity, is a site of "privilege," there tends to be a rendering invisible of that category. This may, in turn, have the effect of bringing into focus the other categories in relation to which a subject is not "privileged." In *The Autobiography of an Ex-Colored Man*, for instance, the ex-colored man examines questions of race and even class, categories in relation to which he cannot easily assume privilege. However, maleness continues to serve as his standard. There is no examination of the privilege that comes with "being a man" in the United States.

Since all six texts in my study depict protagonists who are able to assume privilege in relation to at least one category, examining the different novels reveals the way in which privilege works through an interplay of "presence" and "absence" of gender, race, class, and ethnicity. This interplay tends to reinforce existing social hierarchies by naturalizing the norms connected to each category as well as by producing degrees of privilege and a "divide and conquer" effect. Reading these early-twentieth-century African- and Jewish-American narratives together thus allows for a critical analysis of "privilege," a concept which has yet to be theorized adequately.

These are not the only advantages of juxtaposing African- and Jewish-American literature, however. Another important advantage has to do with what such a project can tell us about the relationships among dominant norms, desire, and identity.

Performativity

In the following chapters, I not only bring the novels of Abraham Cahan, James Weldon Johnson, Nella Larsen, and Anzia Yezierska together and offer a critical comparative analysis, but I also read these texts through the lens of performativity. The existing literary criticism reads these specific African-American and Jewish-American texts separately, and quite a few scholars still tend to gauge a character's "successful" or "unsuccessful" assimilation according to whether there is recognition and acceptance of some kind of "authentic" Jewish or black self.[12]

Even when critics have attempted to avoid essentialist arguments (where Jewishness or blackness is understood to consist of identifiable, trans-historical, and/or inherent qualities), commentaries on Yezierska and Cahan's texts are still read through an "assimilationist" paradigm, and Larsen's and Johnson's passing narratives continue to be caught within a subversive/recuperative opposition.[13] I question the use of assimilation as an analytical framework for reading these Jewish-American novels because the concept retains an essentialist notion of the self as well as a static and monolithic notion of U.S. and Jewish culture. As will become clear, I prefer to read the Jewish-American texts as passing narratives of sorts rather than as tales of assimilation. In addition, the subversive/recuperative binary becomes less relevant in my readings of the African-American passing narratives — passing is not understood to be either necessarily subversive or necessarily reinforcing of existing race relations; rather, passing becomes the point of entry into a discussion of race as performative reiteration.

Performativity, it is important to underscore, is not conceived here as the subject's freedom to choose or "play at" a variety of identities, but rather as both constitutive of identity and a constraining manifestation of dominant norms. In this book, I closely follow Judith Butler's groundbreaking work on gender performativity. According to Butler's formulation in *Bodies That Matter* (1993), gender performativity is constituted by two kinds of performatives that are inextricably connected and interdependent. On the one hand, the iteration of gender norms operates like a performative speech-act where the discursive repetition of norms acts to constitute or produce that which it enunciates.[14] The repetition of gender norms necessarily precedes the emergence of the subject and initiates the subject into the dominant social order.[15] That is, in any given society, a subject's gender identity only becomes recognizable and coherent to her/himself and to other members of society *through* specific gender norms. On the other hand, gender performativity refers to social comportment. The iteration of norms actually compels bodies to act, gesture, and behave in certain ways — ways that constantly attempt to embody the fantasy of a coherent and natural gender core. To remain viable within a given society, the subject *must* cite and mime the very norms that created his/her intelligibility in the first place.

When I speak of norms, then, they are to be understood, again following Butler, as *regulatory ideals* that circulate and operate in the service of particular power relations, such as heteronormativity and white supremacy. Thus, according to a theoretical framework based on performativity, dominant norms help shape who we are and what we desire, and subjects are compelled to identify with these norms if they wish to maintain a non-marginal existence.[16] Of course, this compulsion has very real "effects" on our bodies and psyche, since bodies are compelled as well as encouraged to strive to embody certain attributes associated with the categories of gender, race, class, and ethnicity. And if subjects only become intelligible by "passing through," as it were, and "taking up" regulatory norms (where the "taking up" can even be non-normative), then this constitutive and simultaneously compelled identification with regulatory ideals is an inescapable part of subject formation.[17]

I stress the compelled aspect of performativity because performativity all too often gets conflated with the notion of an autonomous agent who can choose identities at will or with rather simplistic notions of identity as fluid. But even though subjects are forced to identify with regulatory ideals that "guarantee a recognizable and enduring social existence," subjects are never fully determined by these norms and resistance is always possible.[18]

One key advantage of reading African- and Jewish-American literature through the lens of performativity relates to what the notion of performativity can illuminate in this fiction. All of the narratives that I discuss are overtly concerned with and explicitly thematize the power of the hegemonic norms that have been linked to gender, race, class, and ethnicity, and therefore to dominant notions of Americanness. Since performativity is a theoretical framework that understands norms to be constitutive of identity and allows for an examination of the "identity effects" of dominant norms, bringing the notion of identity as performative to bear on the texts can make intelligible certain features of the novels that have not yet been sufficiently discussed. For instance, these narratives dramatize the compelled aspect of gender and race identification as well as how the American Dream discourse has helped produce non-essentialist class identities, in which class status is understood to be transformable in ways that gender, race, and ethnic identities are not. Moreover, while many critical theorists have claimed that race and class are irreducible to gender, as far as I am aware, few theorists have tried to map out the differences among these categories. The novels actually highlight the irreducibility of the categories, and the notion of performativity provides me with the theoretical tools for charting the ways in which these differences get played out in the texts.

Once the work of outlining the differences among the categories has begun, other crucial issues emerge as well. Using performativity as the point of entry into an analysis of the texts sheds new light on some of the power relations that have helped shape social stratification in the United States during the past century, such as white supremacy. If race and ethnicity are not interchangeable categories but are both constituted differently by and through performativity and thus by hegemonic norms, then we can begin to trace and comprehend Jewish Americans' successful "morphing" of race into ethnicity. As I mentioned above, the texts narrativize how the concept of ethnicity developed out of a carefully policed racial hierarchy that positioned "whites" on top and "blacks" on the bottom. Race, as a category of identity, has proven to be a real obstacle to acceptance and success in mainstream U.S. society. Ethnicity, on the other hand, has not. The Jews' position on the white side of the increasingly entrenched black-white divide — precarious though this position was in the early part of the last century — allowed for their transformation into an ethnic group. And as an "ethnic" rather than a racial group, Jews could (and did) move up the social hierarchy more easily. Differences among "ethnic" groups thus worked in conjunction with the black-white dichotomy to create an intricately stratified racial hierarchy in the United States.

Furthermore, by showing how class has operated differently from gender and race due to its particularly non-essentialist discourse, the novels draw attention to some of the reasons why the enormously unequal distribution of resources has caused little mass protest in the United States in the past century. The American Dream discourse has helped to erase or at least camouflage systemic sources of class inequality, since it has promoted the belief that anyone can move up the class ladder if only he/she works hard and maintains a certain level of integrity; in this way, it has helped (re)produce, justify, and excuse class inequalities by linking them to individual effort. As a result, failure is more likely to be attributed to some flaw in the individual subject rather than to iniquitous social and economic structures.

Moving back and forth between text and theory, *Performing Americanness* also argues that the African- and Jewish-American texts can help expand the notion of performativity, which has been either limited to discussions of gender or invoked as a buzzword to describe every and all aspects of identity. In fact, there has been a lack of sustained theoretical discussion in the literary criticism that utilizes Judith Butler's notion of (gender) performativity.[19] Although quite a few literary scholars employ the notion of performativity to read early-twentieth-century African- or Jewish-American literature, they do not offer a theoretical explanation of performativity, which is crucial if we are to go beyond reductive notions that conflate performativity with a chosen or playful performance.[20] The novels under consideration provide me with the tools for giving a theoretical yet textually informed account of performativity, one which I believe is faithful to Judith Butler's work.

More importantly, though, the literary texts help complicate the notion of performativity not only by drawing attention to the performative "nature" of other categories, but also by concurrently highlighting that the norms linked to gender, race, class, and ethnicity have not been identical; this, in turn, suggests that one cannot simply transpose Butler's notion of gender performativity onto the other categories. Each set of regulatory ideals has had its own particular genealogy in the United States, and therefore each category can be said to produce a different and unique modality of performativity. Race performativity is irreducible to gender or class performativity, and as I show in the first four chapters, the novels dramatize the specific operations of each one.

One last crucial advantage of reading these texts as a dramatization of the performative "nature" of identity that I will mention here has to do with agency and the possibility of resisting hegemonic norms. The novels underscore that regulatory ideals do not operate as monolithic entities. For instance, as I demonstrate through an analysis of *The Rise of David Levinsky* (Chapter One), conflictual gender ideals (that is, femininity as docility/submissiveness versus the New Woman or femme fatale) circulate simultaneously alongside dominant norms linked to other categories, such as race and class. Both among the different categories as well as within each one, there are always a series of incompatible and divergent norms. The key point is that the fractured and competing nature of the norms circulating in society opens up potential spaces for subjects to "perform differently." The texts thus point to the way that agency materializes in the interstices of competing norms—some dominant, others not—where the conflictual nature of norms open up spaces of negotiation. The narratives, in sum, meditate on this question of agency in very interesting ways, and a nuanced conception of resistance can be culled from a reading of the novels, one that derives, in large part, from the characters' ability to negotiate *between* divergent norms and therefore between different possible configurations of identification and what I term the desire-to-be.

Identification and Desire-to-Be

As mentioned above, the six novels reveal that the norms linked to gender, race, class, and ethnicity respectively have their own particular history (which, in turn, suggests that the mode of performativity each category has created is both unique and changes over time); yet such a study also underscores that the different modalities of performativity cannot simply be reduced to the varying norms attached to each category. Rather, in order to understand the way each modality of performativity has operated, it is necessary to examine the way different regulatory ideals function on the level of identification and the desire-to-be.

I understand identification as being constituted, initially, by the primary address or interpellation through which a subject is initiated into the dominant social order as a gendered, raced, classed, and "ethnicized" being. Judith Butler's now famous example of the way in which we greet newborns: "It's a girl!" or "It's a boy!" is a good illustration of what I mean by primary interpellation. This preliminary interpellation both inaugurates the subject qua subject and imposes an initial identification with a specific gender, race, class, or ethnicity; in other words, this interpellation *entails* an enforced primary identification.[21] As Michel Pecheux has argued, interpellation is achieved by the identification of the subject with the discursive formation, i.e., in which he is constituted as subject.[22] And although a subject's identification is *never determined* once and for all by the primary interpellation, all subsequent disidentifications are understood to be mediated by this primary address.

Norms wield the power to form and regulate the subject, but they are not simply internalized; rather, there is always a chance that the subject will "twist" norms and identify in unpredictable ways. But, regardless of how a subject identifies, whether in normative ways—as a "feminine" woman, as uncritically white or middle class—or in non-normative ways, such identifications are never seamless or without ambivalence.[23] Moreover, identifying in terms of gender, race, class, or ethnicity is never a discrete occurrence, but rather these identifications cross, crisscross, and are interwoven, leading to potential fissures. The desire-to-be, which is my neologism, is conceived as the subject's desire to live up to the norms associated with a particular category, and as will become clear in the following chapters, it too is always multifaceted and riddled with ambivalence.[24]

Notwithstanding the complexities of identification and desire, however, this book ultimately endeavors to understand the way in which *dominant* norms of gender, race, class, and ethnicity have operated and to consider some of the conditions of possibility of resisting these norms. I therefore make a methodological and theoretical distinction between the way that norms operate on the hegemonic level (e.g., as mechanisms that (re)produce *dominant* U.S. culture) and thus as *regulatory ideals* and the way these norms are "taken up" on the level of social praxis and within communities. On the one hand, I do think it is possible and important methodologically to speak about each set of hegemonic norms associated with the different categories separately as well as in isolation from actual social practices. Only by identifying and isolating the dominant norms operative in a given society can we begin to analyze how they work to shape who we are, what we desire, and the ways we might resist them. On the other hand, I am also convinced that in praxis things are always much more complex. On the level of social practices, gender, race, class, and ethnic norms operate simultaneously, contaminating one another as well as producing multiple cross-identifications that are often conflictual. Furthermore, the attempt to embody a norm is always incomplete — norms are *ideals* that can never be embodied or accomplished once and for all. Yet, since the novels I examine depict their protagonists' desire to live nonmarginal lives and their attempts to emulate dominant regulatory ideals, they allow for both an examination of the operation of norms on the hegemonic level *and* of how the process of "emulation" is always partial and at times even characterized by noncompliance.

Nella Larsen's *Passing* and *Quicksand*, as well as James Weldon Johnson's *The Autobiography of an Ex-Colored Man*, for instance, disclose how dominant U.S. race discourse has created and encouraged a distinct bifurcation between identification and desire, such that certain subjects who have been (at least initially) forced to identify as "black" simultaneously have been encouraged to privilege and consequently desire to live up to attributes associated with "whiteness." This contrasts with the dominant heteronormative discourse in the United States, which has functioned by creating two disparate and ideal gender identities (although one is privileged and defined over and against the other), and created and compelled desire in subjects to conform to either one. "Being a woman" within this matrix is not necessarily undesirable, even though it is conceived to be lower on the hierarchical ladder. Heteronormativity, unlike white supremacy or class stratification, requires two separate (but unequal) *ideals*. In a white supremacist society, however, blackness is not constructed as desirable on the hegemonic level. Larsen and Johnson's texts accordingly reveal that while there have been two idealized genders under heteronormativity, historically there has been only one hegemonic and ideal race under the United States's white racist regime. As I argue in Chapter Two where I analyze *Passing*, subjects who have been interpellated as black and who have wished to maintain a nonmarginal existence have been compelled and encouraged to privilege and thus desire to be "white," that is, to live up to attributes associated with whiteness. Larsen's novella underscores that the de-linking of identification and desire-to-be is key to understanding the particular mechanisms by and through which *race* performativity has operated on the level of the dominant U.S. social order.

Anzia Yezierska's *Arrogant Beggar* and *Salome of the Tenements*, as well as Abraham Cahan's *The Rise of David Levinsky*, all illustrate, in different ways, how U.S. class norms have discouraged identification with the lower classes and urged subjects to live up to regulatory ideals linked to the middle class. Unlike gender and race, which historically have been conceived of as biological facts that cannot be altered, the novels suggest that class in the United States has *not* been conceived of historically as an essence. Therefore, the norms linked to class have not been construed as natural attributes. As I propose in Chapter Three through a discussion of Yezierska's *Salome of the Tenements*, while initial identification with a particular class is necessary as part of the functioning of class societies—otherwise the upward mobility and American Dream discourse would cease to be meaningful—it does not signify in the same way as it does in either gender or race discourse.

In contrast to both U.S. white supremacist and heteronormative discourses, in U.S. class discourse, climbing from one class to another and actually disidentifying with one's initial lower class status has been posited as something desirable; that is, disidentifying with one's initiation into society as lower class is not only allowed, but may even be encouraged actively. This is clearly not the case with either gender or race, for in both identification with the initial interpellation is carefully regulated. One only has to think of the one-drop rule to understand just how closely racial identification has been policed in the United States. In *The Autobiography of an Ex-Colored Man*, it is not the protagonist's financial success and his disidentification with his previous class status but his "passing" as white that is understood, both in the novel and in the ex-colored man's mind, as a transgression.

Thus, if performativity is understood as the power of the dominant social order to create certain repetitive effects on a subject through the discursive reiteration of its regulatory ideals, then these Jewish- and African-American texts point to the ways in which *each* category (and here I will shift from referring to gender, race, class, and ethnicity as categories of identity to categories of *identification*) has produced a unique and irreducible modality of performativity. By using the literary texts as reference points, I show why identification and the desire-to-be are important methodological terms for understanding how individuals have come to be gendered, raced, classed, and "ethnicized" in the United States, and how these categories are both inextricable from hegemonic notions of what it means to be American and important axes along which social stratification has developed.

Resistance

This book does not attempt to address the oppositional terms and debates that have, until recently, plagued criticism on Harlem Renaissance texts.[25] For instance, I do not enter into the discussion about whether the Harlem Renaissance succeeded or failed in creating an independent cultural movement. Nor is this book an effort to outline a "black" aesthetic (whether conceived in essentialist or non-essentialist terms) or what constitutes a Jewish-American literary tradition. Rather, in the following chapters, I am interested in looking at representations of gender, race, class, and ethnicity in specific African- and Jewish-American texts in order to see what they can tell us about the ways these categories of identification have operated to circumscribe identity in the United States during the early part of the twentieth century.

There is a tension throughout—a productive one, I hope—between the need to contextualize my argument, since, as the literary texts reveal, different norms circulate in different localities and change over time, and an effort to come up with certain theoretical tools for understanding how power has operated differently in relation to various categories of identification. The novels I have chosen to work on are particularly valuable for such an endeavor because they enable me to offer ways of theorizing the difference or "irreducibility" among categories of identification and to show how this irreducibility, alongside competing norms within each category, might open up spaces for negotiating different kinds of performances. If I manage to draw attention to and stimulate further debate about what constitutes this elusive "irreducibility," then I will deem this project a success.

And while the texts certainly gesture toward the way that identification and desire are always mediated through dominant norms, they also underscore again and again that mediation is not determination. Subjects can and do negotiate *between* the different possible configurations of identification and desire-to-be. In fact, all of the novels can be said to point to the fissures and gaps that emerge from within the dominant social order itself, and to dramatize the productive and contestatory possibilities these spaces create. Yet the literary texts simultaneously highlight the difficulty, or perhaps even the impossibility, of predicting when and how a subject will resist or attempt to undermine regulatory ideals; moreover, the effects of such resistance are never straightforward or necessarily subversive. The ex-colored man's complete disidentification with blackness constitutes a resistance to the hegemonic injunction to identify as black (or else), but does this resistance in any way manage to undermine existing racial hierarchies? In *Salome of the Tenements*, the millionaire philanthropist John Manning attempts to throw off class privilege, and yet how successful is he in abjuring class norms or in trying to do away with his privilege? Helga Crane's "choices" in *Quicksand* may derive from a certain kind of agency, but can her choices be seen to subvert the normative attributes associated with race and gender? And what does it mean to "choose" to disidentify with a set of regulatory ideals or to "give up" privilege if the subject is not conceived to be an autonomous self-determining agent? Abraham Cahan, James Weldon Johnson, Nella Larsen, and Anzia Yezierska do not provide ready-made or simple answers to these inquiries. Rather, their novels probe these issues with particular depth, drawing our attention to the immense constitutive power of hegemonic norms as well as to the seemingly infinite ways that social subjects might perform differently.

More importantly, perhaps, these Jewish- and African-American texts bring to the fore what "Americanness" has signified in the past, while urging us to think about how Americanness might come to signify differently in the future, in ways that would encourage contestatory norms to remain continuously in circulation. If agency does indeed emerge from a subject's ability to negotiate among divergent norms, then guaranteeing the existence of alternative regulatory ideals is absolutely vital to a democratic society. One might even argue that the novels dramatize a certain moral imperative — the necessity of ensuring that, at any given historical moment, there are always *many* possible, socially sanctioned, and thus normative ways of performing Americanness.

Chapter One

Performativity in Context

"AND YET WHEN I take a look at my inner identity it impresses me as being precisely the same as it was thirty or forty years ago. My present station, power, the amount of worldly happiness at my command, and the rest of it, seem devoid of significance."[1] So declares the protagonist of Abraham Cahan's *The Rise of David Levinsky* (1917) in the novel's opening paragraph. Whether read as a *bildungsroman*, a rag-to-riches narrative, a story recounting the difficulties of assimilation, or some combination thereof, commentators usually concur on one fundamental point. This book, considered one of the first Jewish-American classics written in English, is preoccupied with the question of identity. Moreover, most critics agree that the novel investigates the difficulty of forging a coherent and stable sense of self. In his introduction to the 1993 Penguin Twentieth-Century Classics edition, for example, Jules Chametzky discusses David Levinsky's unsuccessful search for "a true, unfragmented self."[2] Other scholars similarly have understood the text as an exploration of the protagonist's attempt to negotiate between Old and New World subjectivities.[3]

The Rise of David Levinsky undoubtedly queries identity claims. This chapter, however, contends that the theoretical and ontological assumptions informing many of the existing critiques are problematic. By framing David Levinsky's identity crisis as a conflict between "the impulse to assimilate" and the "spiritual desire to maintain contact with Jewish culture and community," critics create and uphold a binary opposition between the Old and New Worlds that ultimately essentializes both American and Jewish culture, assuming monolithic and self-identical entities.[4] This kind of critique, as I have noted in the introduction, is prevalent not only among Cahan scholars, but also among literary critics who read early-twentieth-century Jewish-American literary novels through the lens of assimilation more generally. The ontological assumptions lurking in the background of such analyses often remain unexamined; concepts such as "desire" and "impulse" are invoked without any theoretical discussion, and frequently the desirability and/or possibility of a "secure sense of self" is taken for granted.

The following pages consequently underscore some of the limitations of this kind of analysis and attempt to offer an alternative reading of *The Rise of David Levinsky*. As will become clear, I do not understand this novel as a "classic immigrant narrative," where assimilation is shown to have its benefits and costs. Rather, the text's trajectory is conceived as laying bare the performative constitution of gender identity in particular and of identity categories more generally. Therefore, I will be reading the novel as a radical feminist critique, not only because the text exposes the performative aspect of identity, as Magdalena Zaborowska already has argued, but also because it demonstrates the impossibility of any subject ever fully inhabiting hegemonic gender ideals. If a radical feminist project is conceived of as the critical investigation of the processes that produce and destabilize identity categories, and, more particularly, the categories man and woman, masculine and feminine, then Abraham Cahan's novel certainly fits the feminist bill.

While I employ Judith Butler's theoretical framework as a point of reference, I also suggest that the novel complicates Butler's notion of gender performativity by revealing the way in which gender norms, and norms more generally, neither operate as monolithic regulatory ideals nor in tandem and unproblematically with other categories of identification. In other words, the text dramatizes how conflictual gender ideals circulate simultaneously (i.e., femininity as docility/submissiveness versus the New Woman) alongside competing categories of identification, such as ethnicity and class. The performative reiteration of gender ideals is always complicated by the existence of competing norms.

The Old World

The Rise of David Levinsky is divided into two major sections. In the beginning or first section, the reader is introduced to the protagonist, David Levinsky, in the Old World, where the grid of intelligibility is made up of certain categories of identification, such as gender, race, and class. Linked to each regulatory category are a set of specific, prescriptive, and culturally determined practices, attributes, rules, qualities, and traits; these categories with their prescriptive practices and traits, in effect, comprise the Old World's norms. These norms, in turn, constitute the Old World's dominant social order, and, as the novel suggests, subjects are always recognized, known, and acknowledged in reference to — and through the lens of — this existing grid of intelligibility.

While race, gender, and class dominate as categories that make sense of the personae dramatis in Antomir, they are constituted differently from the norms circulating in Abraham Cahan's fictive United States.[5] The early chapters of *The Rise of David Levinsky* resonate with Daniel Boyarin's description of the model male in rabbinic culture as the Torah scholar. According to Boyarin, the traditional, ideal, East European male was "gentle, timid and studious."[6] In the Jewish community of Antomir, the Torah scholar is indeed the model for masculinity, and men are urged to live up to ideals of modesty, humbleness, and simplicity. Acts of violence, demonstrations of pride, courage, and competition are frowned upon and punished. When David ends up in a brawl with his bitter enemy, the talented Polish Talmudist, for instance, he is admonished by other Talmudists for acting just like Gentiles.

Although there is more overlap between the norms of femininity in Antomir and America, some differences stand out. While expressions of female sexuality are policed, especially outside of marriage, women's active participation in the public sphere is not only acceptable but expected in the traditional life of the town. The Talmud scholars of Antomir are "supported either by the congregation or by their own wives, who kept shops, stalls, inns, or peddled, while their husbands spent sixteen hours a day studying Talmud" (29). Enabling men to study Torah by working for money in the public sphere is, in many ways, encouraged. David's mother not only works her fingers to the bone "peddling pea mush or doing odds and ends of jobs" to enable her son's studies (4), but is portrayed as an active agent; she is described by her son — admiringly, as it were — as "a leader in most of the feuds that often divided the whole Court into two warring camps" (12). Her final act is one of retribution on the Gentiles who have beaten her son, and her pugilistic intentions are lauded by the community.

Although these norms of female activity cannot be separated from the ubiquitous ideal of female sacrifice for man or child — for even

David's mother's activity is indissoluble from norms of maternity—the positive valence attached to women bread-earners *who support their husbands* is relatively unique to this community. This, I believe, serves to underscore that technologies of domination have to be interpreted within their own systemic structure: "Within the structure of rabbinic Judaism it is the 'indoor,' somewhat private realm of the House of Study that defines the social prestige and power of men over women, and not the estate of getting and spending, of economic power, that produces such distinction in bourgeois society."[7]

However, if performativity is construed as the power of the dominant social order to produce certain repetitive effects on subjects through the discursive reiteration of its laws, then an examination of the regulatory ideal that constitute that order, that is, the norms of masculinity and femininity circulating in Antomir, is not enough. We must also clarify what it means to claim that performativity is constitutive of identity.

Performativity

As Judith Butler has argued in her landmark books, *Gender Trouble* (1990) and *Bodies That Matter* (1993), laws or norms necessarily precede the emergence of the subject. These norms, in effect, create the condition of possibility for the emergence of the subject and initiate or interpellate that subject into the dominant social order. In Butler's parlance, "[S]ubject formation is dependent on the prior operation of legitimating . . . norms."[8] In order to remain viable within a hegemonic system subsequent to the initial interpellation—which, as I will argue in the next chapter, imposes certain primary identifications—the subject must, in its turn, incessantly cite and mime the very norms that created its intelligibility in the first place.[9] The process of signification therefore occurs through the constant performative reiteration of norms, and this reiteration actually materializes a set of effects on the matter of bodies.

The reader is immediately inducted into Antomir's dominant gender and social order. David recalls in the first pages of the novel how, as a little boy growing up alone with his widowed mother, he was ever awake to the fact that other little boys had fathers, and "that most married women had husbands" (4). Moreover, early in the narrative, David describes the punishment meted out to a married woman who strays from the path of "virtuousness." It is through the description of the encounter between David's mother and an errant wife that an image of correct female behavior emerges. Not long after, the ideal of the studious male is introduced through the initial "discovery" of David's "good head" and the importance attached to this discovery. The narrator's invocation and repetition of ideals of masculinity, femininity, and heterosexuality thus help to demonstrate the way that the dominant social order is actually created, reproduced, and upheld by and through reiteration, and how, through such repetition of dominant norms, identities and interests are constituted. The establishment of this hegemonic order is the necessary condition for the subjects' intelligibility.

If norms are understood to be regulatory ideals, and the subject's identification and identity qua subject is irrevocably intertwined with emulating extant norms, then identification with these norms actually compels bodies to act, gesture, and behave in ways that strive continuously and repetitively to embody the fantasy of a coherent and natural self.[10] Power, I will be arguing throughout this book, alongside Michel Foucault and Judith Butler, operates *primarily* in a positive fashion by producing objects of inquiry and knowledge, constituting norms, and consequently creating and shaping the subject's identity, preferences, aspirations, and behavior. Negative power then, in its Foucauldian sense, ensures, through prohibitions and restrictions, that subjects conform to constructed norms. Norms or regulatory ideals that constitute and make social practices possible (and are the condition of possibility of the emergence of the subject) are produced, according to a Foucauldian analysis, through an "artificial unity" composed of a series of disparate attributes. For instance, a series of traits linked to masculinity in Antomir (gentle/studious/modest/penis) and femininity (active/willing to sacrifice/pious/vagina) are concatenated artificially in the service of specific social hierarchies.

In Antomir, as in America of the later section, the configuration of power includes male dominance, although a very particular kind of dominance. Male domination, Daniel Boyarin contends, has been for rabbinic patriarchy the "central moment in the construction of gender."[11] As mentioned, in contrast to other societies, the social hierarchy in the town of David's birth places the Torah scholar at its zenith. Whereas turn-of-the-century U.S. manhood "constructed bodily strength and social authority as identical," ideal masculinity according to Antomir standards is embodied in the gentle, passive, and modest Talmudic scholar or *yeshiva buchor*.[12] The particular attributes constituting masculinity in Antomir, in turn, materialize *specific* effects on the matter of bodies: "The stylized repetitions that produce gender differentiation within Jewish praxis were the performances of Torah study."[13]

This clearly plays itself out in David's attempt to emulate Nephtali. Nephtali is portrayed as embodying the desirable traits that a good *yeshiva buchor* should possess; he initially represents the model Talmudists — and thus model male — for David. Nephtali is studious, considered "one of the noted 'men of diligence' at the seminary"; he is also described as reticent, modest, and emotional: "Nephtali had little to say to other people, but he seemed to have much to say to himself. His sing-songs were full of meaning, of passion, of beauty" (35); and he meets flattery with self-deprecation. On the one hand, then, David's preferences, desires, aspirations, and ideals have been shaped and created by Antomir's dominant social order. His desire to be a model *yeshiva buchor* is not coincidental, but rather produced and encouraged by the Jewish community. On the other hand, his attempts to approximate this masculine ideal are described as a kind of performative reiteration or what I would term bodily speech acts: "I strove to emulate his cleanliness, his graceful Talmud gestures, and his handwriting. At one period I spent many hours a day practicing calligraphy with some of his lines for a model" (35). David attempts to mime, through repetitive imitation, the bodily gestures and movements of Nephtali, the paradigm of masculinity. And by depicting how the "essential" traits of Antomir "manhood" can be mimed, the text begins to unveil the way in which "being a man" is always constituted by repeating and citing a set of social conventions produced and instituted by the ruling hegemonic order. In sum, David's desire to emulate Nephtali is, I believe, a manifestation of performativity as positive power.

The New World

The transition that occurs in the novel's second major section reveals two crucial facets vis-à-vis performativity. First, the configuration of regulatory ideals is specific to particular historical moments and geographical locations. Although many times norms of femininity and masculinity retain traces crossculturally or of past configurations — such as the ideal of the maternal instinct continued to hold force even in twenty-first-century America — the disparate attributes linked to a specific category of identification are liable to shift. In the New World, the site of the novel's second section, the traits linked to and held together under the rubric "masculinity" are no longer gentle/studious/ modest/penis, but rather something more like assertive/competitive/ ambitious/penis. Norms, the novel suggests, vary quite significantly historically, geographically and crossculturally. From the moment David debarks and sets foot on U.S. soil, he recognizes that the timidity of the Talmudists that once elicited accolades now places him at a disadvantage in relation to dominant U.S. society. His first experience in the synagogue also teaches him that in the New World a man must earn his own living. Since the interpellation into U.S. society occurs immediately, though unevenly, the protagonist has to learn quickly what it means and what it takes to be a viable subject in the New World.[14]

Soon after he arrives in the United States, David is forced to undergo a make-over. His side-locks are cut off and his traditional Jewish garb, made of a long-skirted coat, is discarded; both appurtenances serve to feminize the "traditional Jew" in the New World. David emerges with short hair and a new suit, and describes this initiation in the following way: "It was as though the hair-cut and the American clothes had changed my identity," thus underscoring the way in which gender identity manifests itself most obviously in and through outward appearance (101). Yet Abraham Cahan discloses, through his depiction of David Levinsky's "rise," that dressing is not enough for the performance of masculinity; one must also act the part—through bodily gestures, aspirations, tastes, and recognizable discourse.

Assertiveness and competitiveness are attributes that David slowly assumes, and, in many ways, he has to unlearn his earlier socialization. As Magdalena Zaborowska points out, David learns to connect manhood with sexual conquest and prowess.[15] However, Zaborowska appears to suggest that the masculinity circulating among the Jewish vendors on the Lower East Side is somehow ethnically particular: "Unable to reject or resist this model of *ethnic* masculinity, young Levinsky pretends to be a quiet accomplice of his elder fellow vendors and learns quickly the rules of performance that a marginal bystander needs to embrace to appear one of the group."[16] This claim seems to me to be mistaken. The norms of manhood invoked and reiterated by this group of Jewish vendors are in no way particular to these "ethnics." In her seminal book *Manliness and Civilization*, Gail Bederman traces the changing discourse on masculinity in turn-of-the-century America. Whereas "Victorian ideologies of manliness urged civilized men to restrain—especially selfish aggressiveness and sexual predation," by the 1890s, a very different kind of norm was emerging.[17] The ideal of masculinity linking such attributes as virility, violence, and competitiveness was becoming increasingly entrenched in U.S. society as a whole.

Using the motto he has picked up from the "smutty" conversations with his co-vendors, "Every woman can be won, absolutely every one," David sets out to perform the role of American male. Unlike his sexual initiation with Matilda in Antomir, in which she had to instruct the young Talmud scholar on what to do and where to place his hands, in his first sexual encounters in America he has already assumed the role of initiator. His attempts to "win" his landladies are full of clichés that he undoubtedly has picked up from the aforementioned "smutty" conversations. For instance, after deciding to "conquer" Mrs. Levinsky, he begins his discourse by praising her singing and her good looks. "Beautiful singing!" and "I dreamed of telling you that you are a good-looking lady," serve as his opening lines. It is not surprising that Mrs. Levinsky responds with: "What has got into that fellow . . . He is a greenhorn no longer . . ." (118). She seems to be suggesting that David has been initiated into dominant U.S. culture; he is, in effect, invoking and reiterating a certain masculinist discourse and striving to embody the male lover by appropriating and repeating a certain recognizable language of sexual courtship and conquest. A similar scene ensues with Mrs. Dienstog, although this time he is a bit more "successful" for his pains.

Throughout the second half of the novel, Cahan depicts David as patterning himself on men whom he thinks embody some aspect of the New World masculine ideal. Although his English teacher initially is described as somewhat effeminate, as soon as Bender begins to impress on his student the importance of assertiveness and discloses his successful courtship of a young woman, David begins to pay heed. Bender's stories and anecdotes introduce the new immigrant to "detail after detail of American life. It accelerated the process of 'getting me out of my greenhornhood' in the better sense of the phrase" (135). Jake Mindels, the handsome young immigrant who desires to become a doctor, serves as a temporary model as well, and David adopts traits that will help him assume his role of American male more easily: "I adopted many of the English phrases he was in the habit of using and tried to imitate his way of dressing" (163).

Eventually, however, David Levinsky performs masculinity well enough that he depends less on particular Jewish role models and more on Anglo-Saxon ones:

> I sought to dress like a genteel American, my favorite color for clothes and hats being . . . dark brown . . . The difference between taste and vulgar ostentation was coming slowly, but surely, I hope . . . I was forever watching and striving to imitate the dress and ways of the well-bred American merchants with whom I was, or trying to be, thrown. All this, I felt, was an essential element in achieving business success; but the ambition to *act* and *look like a gentleman* grew in me quite apart from these motives. (260)

Genteel and Gentile, it is important to note, are synonymous in the narrative. The novel describes, *in great detail*, the pains David takes to emulate this American manhood. He confesses that he would watch "American smokers and manner of smoking as though there were a special American manner of smoking and such a thing as smoking with a foreign accent" (326). Eliminating his Talmudic gesticulations, "a habit that worried [him] like a physical defect," also becomes a crucial element in his Americanization (327). These gesticulations seem to David to be "so distressingly un-American," and he narrates the means he devises to keep them from participating in his speech. Here we also begin to see how norms of "race" are interrelated with the regulatory injunctions concatenated to masculinity. All marks of Jewishness must be extirpated in the performance of ideal U.S. manhood, for in turn-of-the-century America the body of the Jew was often seen as "interchangeable with the body of the gay man—physically different, exotic, feminine."[18]

In many ways, the scenes with Dora, Fanny, and later Anna Tevkin demonstrate David's (seemingly) complete and successful identification with and assumption of American hegemonic ideals of masculinity. His relationship to women is one of subjugator and vanquished, stalker and prey. His discourse overflows with images of conquest and victory—feats of virility. The narrator tells us that he idolizes Dora, but never ceased to "dream and to seek her moral downfall" (291). Fanny is the potential trophy wife, good-looking and respectable, but not particularly intelligent: "She is expected to be a wife, a mother, and a housekeeper. Everything else is nonsense" (397). And later in the narrative, when David pauses to think about his possible marriage with Anna

Tevkin, he tells himself, "As for her 'radical' notions, they really don't matter much. I could easily knock them out of her." He is confident that he can "win her," that "she shall be [his], whether she wants it or not" and this confidence arouses "the fighting blood in [his] veins" (483). But it is precisely the moment in which David thinks he is embodying the masculine ideal that he has sought after tirelessly that the gap between normative ideals and actual social behavior is revealed. Anna's simple answer that marriage is out of the question leaves David sick and defeated.

Impossible Ideals

In one of the few scholarly articles that reads *The Rise of David Levinsky* through the lens of performativity, Magdalena Zaborowska contends that David Levinsky's fragmented identity is a result of his failure to be Americanized successfully "as a Jew and a male who is rejected by the dominant culture."[19] But this explanation, even if it were accurate, does not account for the identity trouble David experiences in Antomir. Put differently, if Zaborowska's assertion is correct, then how are we to understand the problems of identity raised in the first section of this chapter? Identity fragmentation, as Zaborowska terms it, is present throughout the novel, and not exclusively in the section dealing with the United States. In the aforementioned quote, Zaborowska seems to collapse back into an unintentional essentialism. As I already have argued above, the novel itself exposes that to "be a Jewish male" even in traditional Antomir is not something inherent and/or given, but rather comprised of performative reiteration. Thus, I believe Zaborowska fails to underscore the way in which performativity constitutes identity at all times; on the contrary, she appears to be following David Levinsky himself, who claims (in the passage that opens this chapter), "when I take a look at my inner identity it impresses me as being precisely the same as it was thirty or forty years ago." Despite David's declaration, however, I believe the narrative dramatizes the way in which the notion of a coherent, stable, and "essential" inner identity is illusory.

Zaborowska's oversight is critical, since two of the most important consequences deriving from the notion of identity as performativity are, as a result, glossed over. First, subjects cannot escape performativity; each and every subject in a particular social order is always constituted by and through the existing grid of intelligibility. In order to remain viable and nonmarginal in that given social order, subjects *must* attempt to approximate dominant norms. Second, *no* subject can ever fully embody a specific norm once and for all. Due to historically specific configurations of power in a given society, certain ideals are upheld as normative; but even those subjects who can assume privilege due to their position within the power hierarchy are not exempt from the rigors of performative reiteration. I believe that Cahan exposes this early on in the novel as he describes, again in great detail, David's incessant attempts to embody the *yeshiva buchor*. According to Zaborowska's reading, David should be able to approximate the ideal successfully and seamlessly in the Old World, David, due to his privileged position as Talmud scholar. But this does not seem to be the case. The norm of the "true Talmud scholar," just like the "true American" — Anglo-Saxon heterosexual upper-middle-class male — is also an impossible-to-embody ideal.

When David first enters the Preacher's Synagogue, we are told that he must constantly remind himself that he is an "independent scholar." He cannot fully inhabit this role, and he finds himself, much to his own dismay, indulging in actions not fit for a pious scholar: "If I caught myself walking fast or indulging in some boyish prank I would check myself" (37). His "bursts of piety" are inevitably punctuated by periods of apathy, which were then sure to be "replaced by days of penance and a new access of spiritual fervor" (39). This last passage suggests, among other things, that the potential for lapse is ever-present, and the attempt to approximate norms is *never* a smooth or uncomplicated process. Repetitive endeavors to embody or demonstrate once and for all true "masculinity" prove a failure. Even in the days of his seemingly unproblematic identification with the *yeshiva buchor* norm, David discloses that he was never so diligent as at the hour when he expects the arrival of his mother with his dinner-pot. As soon as he notices her in the synagogue, he takes to "singing and swaying to and fro with great gusto" (33). These hyperbolic acts also can be seen as the site of a "dissonant and denaturalized performance that reveals the performative status of the natural itself."[20] Or, as David himself puts it: "We are all actors more or less. The question is only what our aim is, and whether we are capable of a 'convincing personation'" (194).

One of the most interesting moments in the New World narrative is the final scene between Anna and David, in which David proposes marriage. Throughout this scene, David struggles to invoke and reiterate what he assumes to be the "correct" love-making discourse. When Anna demurs the first time, David announces that her rejection does not discourage him. He continues by asseverating that he cannot and will not give her up. However, in the middle of this pronouncement, a fascinating interjection is made by the first-person narrator. In parentheses, David acknowledges the fact that he is utilizing and trying to live up to a certain discourse, "That's it," he says to himself, "now I am speaking like a man of firm purpose" (497). But, at this crucial moment in which his maleness is at stake, the text underscores that David cannot embody the norm of masculinity once and for all. In order to "be" a man of firm purpose, he must *incessantly* repeat the discourse that allows one to be perceived as a man of firm purpose. Masculinity's dependency on reiteration disputes and undermines its claim to naturalness and/or originality. Moreover, the danger of a slip-up or a wrong move or gesture is ever-present. In this case, any "softening" of his discourse and comportment would jeopardize his tenuous claim to "being" a masculine man. And at the end of the scene, David does indeed lose his composure: "The room seemed to be in a whirl. I felt the cold perspiration break out on my forehead . . . I was sick at heart" (497). Thus, by setting up dominant social orders, both in the Old World and the New World, and then providing us with a character who constantly fails to live up to their normative demands, the text dramatically illustrates the impossibility of any subject ever fully embodying regulatory ideals.[21] As we will see in the next section, though, Anna's rejection of David can be read as having little to do with his failure to embody ideal American masculinity, but rather as helping to uncover the conflicting nature of the dominant social order.

The final scene between David and Anna also brings to the fore a relatively undertheorized aspect of performativity. More specifically, the use of drag or cross-dressing has for too long been a privileged site for investigating the way in which "hyperbolic norms are dissimulated as the heterosexual mundane."[22] Examining certain moments in "everyday" performances of heterosexuality and masculinity in which fissures emerge, like the one examined above, proves just as illuminating, since they highlight how identity is constituted by and through performativity even for the most "normalized" and norm-identified subject; the social practice of attempting to embody hegemonic gender norms is shown *not* to be *substantively* different from cross-dressing—*both* are imitative and consist of repetitive citation. This kind of analysis underscores that it is not only the excluded and radical abnormal—in the case of heterosexuality, homosexuality—which always threatens to expose the self-grounding presumption of the sexed subject as not natural.[23] The performance of the quotidian social practice of heterosexuality serves as its own potentially disruptive site. I do not believe that theorists have emphasized or exemplified this crucial point enough.

Competition in Context

According to a Butlerian framework, performativity, as the most efficacious form of positive power, tends to reinforce the hegemonic order and upholds existing hierarchal power relations. Reiteration produces the illusion of an identifiable and stable referent for regulatory ideals, making norms seem natural and normal. However, as Judith Butler has underscored time and again, since the dominant social order is dependent on reiteration for its very existence, it is also—necessarily—open to variation. The irreconcilable space between normative roles and actual social practices creates a continuous dissonance; gaps and fissures necessarily emerge within any hegemonic order as subjects strive to embody regulatory ideals. And this space is one of the sites where the possibility of agency and subversion open up:

> There is no subject prior to its constructions, and neither is the subject determined by those constructions; it is always the nexus, the non-space of cultural collision, in which the demand to resignify or repeat the very terms which constitute the "we" cannot be summarily refused, but neither can they be followed in strict obedience. It is the space of this ambivalence which opens up the possibility of a reworking of the very terms by which subjectivation proceeds—and fails to proceed.[24]

The questions then become: when and where is the gap between the ideal and social practices exposed? And when does the exposure result in a disruption of the "normal" course of things?

These questions have generated much debate in recent years. Moya Lloyd, in her article "Performativity, Parody, Politics" (1999), argues that it is easy to overemphasize the discontinuities in gender performance and to present them as indicative of disruptive behavior. What is occluded, as a consequence, is the space within which performance occurs, as well as the others involved in or implicated by the production. Lloyd stresses that only some performances in certain contexts urge categorical rethinking.[25] Similarly, Lois McNay contends that the concept of agency that "underlies Butler's notion of a politics of the performative remains abstract and lacking in social specificity."[26] Both critics, in effect, point to the importance of context in determining whether the fissures come to light and whether the chain of signification, that is, performative reiteration, continues to reinforce, or alternatively, short-circuit, choke up, and/or redirect the dominant social order.

I fully concur with McNay and Lloyd that social context is crucial when thinking about the possibility of subversion and agency; a reconceptualization of context serves as a crucial intervention in and an important supplement to Butler's work on performativity. However, I have some reservations about the aforementioned theorists' conception of context. On the one hand, Lloyd warns us that we must center our discussions of subversion and agency on particular occasions in determinate locales. Yet she neglects to give us theoretical tools for understanding the constituent aspects of context. It is not enough to state that parodic performances are likely to have their greatest effect within communities predisposed to the dissolution of stable norms. This does not address the conditions of possibility of the emergence of such communities or of such parodic performances. On the other hand, McNay claims that Butler privileges an idea of structural indeterminacy over that of praxis, and thus cannot account for the way in which the performative aspects of gender identity are lived by individuals in relation to the web of social practices in which they are enmeshed.[27] In order to help conceptualize the *context* of social practices and supplement Butler's theoretical insights, she invokes Pierre Bourdieu's notion of the field.

The field, according to McNay, "potentially yields a differentiated and dynamic model of power relations where each field has its own historicity and logic which may reinforce or conflict with those of other fields."[28] Interestingly, McNay herself falls into abstraction exactly at this critical juncture, for she does not outline or specify what those other fields might consist of in praxis. A return to Butler's conception of the field or grid of intelligibility, and the norms that constitute this grid, may prove useful in beginning to chart a working theory of context. Although her critical work is concerned for the most part with the operations of heteronormativity, I believe Butler's notion of the grid of intelligibility can be used to reconceptualize the idea of "fields" in terms of categories of identification, such as class, gender, race, and ethnicity. In the fifth chapter, I explore in greater depth the possibility of using Butler and Bourdieu as correctives to one another.

Here, I would like to return to the Anna-David scene, which highlights the crucial significance of context. The scene reveals that fissures, gaps, and the "non-spaces of cultural collision" emerge not only due to the gap between the ideal and social practice intra-subjectively (i.e., as any given subject attempts to remain viable in the specific cultural context by emulating norms), but they also emerge inter-subjectively— between subjects—as a result of the complex makeup of the hegemonic order. In other words, confrontations or interactions between subjects who identify with different gender ideals can potentially lay bare the disjunctions and contradictions within the nexus of force relations. Anna's conception of the ideal male, for instance, is not equivalent or reducible to David's; she, it seems, prefers what might be termed the "residual" ideal of Victorian masculinity. The norm of the virile, competitive, and assertive male, epitomized in the successful businessman, is not the only one circulating in Cahan's America, although it does serve as the hegemonic one. Thus, the grid of intelligibility is not a "realm of uniform normativity," but rather is traversed by a "multiplicity of heterogeneous power relations" and competing normative injunctions.[29] Within any given hegemonic order, more than one set of gender norms circulate, alongside different and competing categories of identification that complicate these sets of norms.

A masculinity comprised of attributes such as assertiveness, competitiveness, and ambition therefore competes with its other forms. And what we witness in the Anna-David scene is, I believe, a clash of ideals, a confrontation that, in effect, undermines the dominant norm's claim to uniformity, and therefore naturalness. It is no coincidence that Anna rejects David and eventually marries a high school teacher, a man whose profession can be seen to symbolize intellectuality, gentility, and restraint—a quite different ideal of masculinity. Although Anna remains within the heterosexual matrix, the contradictory and, in many ways, irreconcilable sets of norms circulating within her society, allow a certain space for performing femininity and heterosexuality differently. She ends up married, but on terms, though not of her own making, that twist and resist the hegemonic ones. The family life and the femininity she aspires to are not the traditional domestic middle-class wife and mother. Rather, she is depicted as actively engaged in the public sphere, through her work as a stenographer and as a publisher of a modernist magazine. Her portrayal brings to mind the emergent ideal of the New Woman, which I will discuss in later chapters in some detail. Although the kinds of occupations open to women are clearly circumscribed, alternatives to the domestic model of femininity are present in Anna and David's world. As Gail Bederman points out, "only certain possibilities for action are imaginable" under the terms of the existing grid of intelligibility. "Yet because so many potential ambiguities and contradictions exist . . . many possibilities for dissent and resistance remain."[30]

The Rise of David Levinsky brings to the fore and exposes both how the social practice of attempting to embody gender norms operates by repetitive citation and the ineluctable gap that emerges as subjects try to approximate these ideals. As I have argued above, however, this novel gestures toward yet another gap that emerges in the context of specific dominant social orders. This is the space, or perhaps the non-space, of cultural collision, which is engendered by competing sets of norms and conflicting categories of identification. It may be that in order for the exposure of the first kind of gap (between ideal and social practice) to gain political currency and efficacy, the second fissure must also be forcibly present, for this space appears to be crucial in enabling subjects to perform differently, at least in the framework of the novel. For instance, David's exposure to a different set of competing norms in Antomir—to the young "modern Jew," the barishnaya and the young gymnasist—is what appears to facilitate and ultimately enable his disidentification with the *yeshiva buchor* ideal, and his ability to entertain the possibility of other futures for himself.

To complicate matters even further, though, Cahan depicts David's own recurrent and intra-subjective struggle to negotiate between the two seemingly incompatible ideals of American masculinity. On the one hand, he wants to "be a cultured man" and receive an education (167); on the other hand, he gives this up to make money and to acquire the kind of power that accrues to great wealth. This indicates, once more, that identification with norms is always a complex and unstable process. The uneasiness David occasionally expresses about his success as a businessman may stem, at least in part, from his recognition of alternative normative injunctions that have been attached to the category of "male." Perhaps this negotiation between the two forms of masculinity discloses that once other norms are deemed potentially legitimate, a subject's identification with the hegemonic norm linked to a given category is forever after incomplete and problematic, suggesting that gaps surface intra-subjectively not only due to the ineluctable dissonance that emerges between the ideal and social practice, but also due to possible incomplete, ambivalent, and vacillating identifications. I explore these complex aspects of identification, disidentification, and performativity in the following chapters.

Whether the exposure of gaps leads to a critical examination of how ideals of gender gesture toward a referent they can never capture or to "systematic recuperation of seemingly radical practices" does indeed seem to be contingent on context.[31] The confrontation of conflicting sets of norms does not necessarily result in subversive performances or critical rethinking, yet it does seem to be one of conditions of possibility of performing differently. Cahan demonstrates the way in which David's uneven identification with U.S. norms does not really lead him to critically rethink the processes that produce and destabilize identity categories. But the depiction of the character, David Levinsky, does urge the reader of *The Rise of David Levinsky* to do so. An emphasis on context, that is, the space within which performance occurs and *the others involved in or implicated by the production*, may therefore enable critics to understand more fully the operations of performativity as well as the possibility of agency, since the conditions for performing differently appear to derive both from the constitutive instabilities of performativity itself as well as from the complexity of the social orders within which performatives gets "played out" and witnessed.

This chapter has focused almost exclusively on the representation of gender in *The Rise of David Levinsky*; yet, as I have argued, the novel seems to complicate Judith Butler's theoretical insights into gender as performative reiteration by gesturing toward the complexity and non-monolithic "nature" of the dominant social order. In the following chapter, I examine the representation of race in passing narratives, and more specifically in Nella Larsen's *Passing*, which today is considered a classic African-American text. My reading of *Passing* pushes Butler's concept of performativity in yet another crucial direction, since I argue that we must understand race as a category of identification and thus as a unique and irreducible modality of performativity.

Chapter Two

Passing

Race, Identification, and Desire

IN THE SECOND HALF of the nineteenth century, African-American writers such as William Wells Brown and Frances Harper began invoking the phenomenon of passing in their texts as a way of investigating the complexities and contradictions of the category of race in the United States.[1] The light-enough-to-pass Negro (but usually Negress) would play a central role in the imagination of African-American writers for the next fifty years. Interestingly, the majority of early-twentieth-century African-American writers have at least one novel or story that revolves around the issue of race "transgression." Charles Chesnutt's *The House behind the Cedars* (1900), Jessie Faucet's *Plum Bun* (1928), and James Weldon Johnson's *The Autobiography of an Ex-Colored Man* (1927) are perhaps the best-known examples. Nella Larsen's 1929 novel, *Passing*, the text under discussion in this chapter, thus can be seen as inheritor and perpetuator of a long tradition of such narratives. In recent years, Larsen's text has become the most celebrated instance of passing in African-American literature, eclipsing the tradition that preceded it.[2] This is not coincidental, for Larsen is a master of ambiguity and intrigue, and the enigmatic finale of her novel has generated heated debates and countless interpretations.

Following the "rediscovery" of Nella Larsen's *Passing* in the 1970s, many scholars attempted to determine whether Larsen's use of passing can be seen as a subversive strategy[3]; that is, whether the narrative serves to reinforce hegemonic norms of race or whether it ultimately posits passing as a viable survival strategy, which has the potential to disrupt "the enclosures of a unitary identity."[4] While this question still informs many critiques, in the past few years commentators have been concentrating more and more on the ways in which passing interrogates and problematizes the ontology of identity categories and their construction. Rather than trying to place passing in a subversive/recuperative binary, these articles and books use passing as a point of entry into questions of identity and identity categories more generally. In the 1996 book entitled *Passing and the Fictions of Identity*, Elaine Ginsberg claims that "passing is about identities: their creation or imposition, their adoption or rejection, their accompanying rewards or penalties. Passing is also about the boundaries established between identity categories and about the individual and cultural anxieties induced by boundary crossing."[5]

Many contemporary commentators concur that Larsen's novel exposes — through the characterization and depiction of Clare Kendry in particular — that the notion of an "essential self" is problematic, if not illusory. Martha Cutter, for example, asserts that Clare "founds her identity not on some sense of an essential self but rather on a self that is composed of and created by a series of guises and masks, performances and roles."[6] The use of performance and performativity as a way of understanding passing is not unique to Cutter; quite a few articles on *Passing* utilize Judith Butler's notion of (gender) performativity as a means of conceptualizing the way that identity gets played out in the text.[7] In addition, critics such as Martin Favor and Jennifer DeVere Brody have attempted to theorize the relationship between the different categories of identification such as race and gender in *Passing* so as to complicate Judith Butler's emphasis on *gender* performativity. And while Favor and Brody provide convincing arguments regarding how gender and race norms are articulated through one another in Larsen's fiction, neither scholar has managed to offer a sustained theoretical analysis of race as a unique *modality* of performativity, one that is different from gender.

In this chapter, I contend that Larsen's text can help critics understand the specific and, as I will argue, *irreducible* features of race performativity. That is, I believe the novel can help us begin mapping out the differences between the categories of gender and race, since it uncovers the way in which regulatory ideals of race produce a specific modality of performativity. *Passing* is especially conducive to interrogating the modality of race performativity because, unlike other passing narratives of the period, Larsen presents us with two protagonists who can pass for white; yet, only Clare "passes over" into the white world. The depiction and juxtaposition of these two characters reveal the complexities and intricacies of the category of race. While Irene can be seen to represent the subject who appropriates and internalizes the hegemonic norms of race, Clare's trajectory dramatizes how dominant norms can be misappropriated and how disidentification is always possible.

At least one qualification is needed at this point, however. This chapter attempts to uncover the ways in which power, in the Foucauldian and Butlerian sense, operates on the hegemonic level; it does not presume to make a claim about the multiplicity of social practices per se. Thus, as I emphasized in the Introduction, when I speak of norms, they are to be understood as *regulatory ideals* that circulate and operate in the service of particular relations of power. Hegemony, though, as many theorists have already argued and as we will see in the last section of this chapter, is never complete, indicating that counterdiscourses and alternative norms are always circulating within any given society.[8]

Race as Performative Repetition

According to Louis Miron and Jonathan Xavier Inda, race is not the effect of biological truths but is a historically contingent, socially constructed category of knowledge. In their article, "Race as a Kind of Speech Act," they argue that "race does not refer to a pre-given subject. Rather, it works performatively to constitute the subject itself and only acquires a naturalized effect through repeated or reiterative naming of or reference to that subject."[9] Moreover, there is no biological basis for dividing "the human species into groups based on the idea that certain physical traits, such as skin color, are tied to attributes of behavior, intellect, and morality."[10] The norms that constitute the dominant social order and create "the grid of intelligibility" are produced and circulated by the relations of power existing within a given society. In a white supremacist society, for example, norms work by constructing a binary opposition between white and black (or nonwhite), in which white is always privileged over black. Or, in Miron and Inda's words, "[S]ocial groups impose meaning on their world by ordering and organizing matter, often through the construction of binary oppositions."[11] Subjects are interpellated into the hegemonic social order as gendered and raced beings, and are recognizable only in reference to the existing grid of intelligibility. For Miron and Inda, the interpellation "Look, a Negro" famously addressed by Frantz Fanon is parallel to "It's a girl!"[12] And once interpellated, subjects must, in turn, incessantly cite and mime the very race norms that created their intelligibility (and thus their condition of possibility) in the first place. In short, according to Miron and Inda, race performativity is the power of discourse to bring about what it names through the citing or repetition of racial norms.

The two critics cogently point out that norms or regulatory ideals that constitute and make social practices possible are produced through an artificial unity composed of a series of disparate attributes: "Physical features, namely skin color, are linked to attributes of intellect and behavior, establishing a hierarchy of quality between white and black."[13] Accordingly, a series of traits linked to whiteness (civilized/intelligent/moral/hardworking/clean) and blackness (savage/instinctual/simple/licentious/lazy/dirty) have been concatenated artificially in the service of specific social hierarchies.[14] In *Passing*, Clare recounts how her white aunts, who took her in after her father died, thought that hard labor would be good for her: "I had Negro blood and they belonged to the generation that had written and read long articles headed: 'Will the Blacks Work?'"[15] The "lazy black worker" has a long history in American race discourse.[16] Jack Bellew, Clare's racist husband, also invokes and reiterates this kind of discourse when he tells Irene that black people are "always robbing and killing. And . . . worse" (172). The concept of race, like that of gender, does not denote a natural phenomenon, but rather "groups together attributes which do not have a necessary or natural relationship to one another in order to enable one to make use of this fictitious unity as a causal principle, an omnipresent meaning," according to Michel Foucault.[17] And insofar as the performative repetition of norms is the condition of possibility for viable subjects, race performativity compels subjects to perform according to these artificial unities, thus shaping their identity and their preferences. Performativity is, indeed, one of the most fundamental manifestations of the Foucauldian notion of positive power.

While "Race as a Kind of Speech Act" is one of the few articles that offers a sustained and rigorous theoretical analysis of the way in which race is subtended by performativity, I have serious misgivings about the simple transposition of Butler's notion of gender performativity onto race.[18] Although I agree with Miron and Inda that we need to begin understanding race as performative reiteration and see my intervention as a supplement to their important work, critics must be careful not to ignore the specificities of race norms. Otherwise, we run the risk of eliding the particular mechanisms through which the subject comes to be raced.

Heterosexual normativity functions by creating two disparate and ideal gender identities, and while one is privileged and defined over and against the other, hegemonic society both compels and creates desire in subjects to conform to either one. "Being a woman" within this matrix is not necessarily undesirable, even though it is conceived to be lower on the hierarchical ladder. In a white supremacist society, however, blackness is not (and perhaps never) constructed as desirable. This statement is to be understood *from the point of view of hegemony, that is, the dominant culture* and is not a description of all social practices. In a white racist society, the construction of blackness as undesirable is one of the mechanisms employed to control subjects, both black and white.

Jack Bellew, for example, invokes and reiterates racial norms that concatenate blackness with immorality and undesirability. He does so while simultaneously admitting that he has never "known" any black people (172). At the infamous tea party organized by Clare, both Gertrude and Clare repeat the undesirability of bringing "dark" babies into the world. Irene herself also invokes and reiterates this discourse. At the N.W.L. dance, she is asked whether she considers a guest—a particularly dark man—handsome. She replies, "I do not!" She goes on to say that people find unusually dark people attractive because they feel they are in the presence of something a bit repugnant (205). Thus, in order to understand the mechanisms that operate in race performativity as it manifests itself in the context of the turn-of-the-century United States, both the specific history of race relations and racism must be examined as well as the modality of performativity they produce.

Assumption of Whiteness and the Contradictions of Race

The scene in which Clare Kendry and Irene Redfield re-encounter one another after twelve years of separation serves to initiate the reader into the strange phenomenon of passing. When Irene initially escapes the searing heat of an August day in Chicago and enters the Drayton, there is no hint in the text that she is doing the forbidden, that is, ingressing white-only space. It is only once Irene becomes aware of another woman's stare that the reader understands Irene has been "passing herself off as white." The other woman continues to survey Irene, and it is this unwavering look that forces Irene to wonder whether the other woman knows that "here before her very eyes on the roof of the Drayton sat a Negro" (150). Irene's fear of detection generates an inner monologue in which she admits that the other woman couldn't possibly "know" she is a Negro.

Clare's stare causes Irene to question her own (successful) attempt to pass as white. She is surprised by the possibility of being caught in the act of performing whiteness, for, as she tells us, she has never been found out. However, the stare does not cause her to question whether the "languorous black eyes" of the other woman are part of a "black" and not "white" body. Irene takes it for granted that the other woman is white. Even after Clare approaches her old acquaintance and insists that she recognizes Irene, Irene asks herself, "What white girls had she known well enough to have been familiarly addressed as 'Rene by them?" (151). Both Irene's admission that she has never been questioned when passing, and her failure to register the possibility of the other woman "being" something other than she seems, suggests that race norms work through assumptions of whiteness. As Sara Ahmed has argued, in a society in which white is the ideal or norm, one is assumed to be white unless one looks black: "'[L]ooking black' becomes a deviation from the normalized state of 'being white.'"[19] The invisibility of the mark of whiteness is exactly the mark of its privilege.

This assumption of whiteness is also dramatically (and disturbingly) exposed when Irene first encounters Jack Bellew, Clare's white racist husband. The tea party to which Clare invites Irene after their re-encounter includes three women: Clare, Irene, and Gertrude. All three women are light enough to pass, although Clare is the only one who has completely "passed over." Bellew, who claims to know a "nigger" when he sees one, does not for a moment entertain the idea that one of the women sitting with his wife might be "black." He therefore feels perfectly comfortable acknowledging that he doesn't dislike niggers but rather hates them. "They give me the creeps," he admits, adding, "the black scrimy devils" (172). It appears that American racial classification assumes "that racial identity marks the subject in the form of absence or presence of color."[20] In other words, racial identity and classification seem to be constituted through skin color.

But the category of race, it turns out, is much more complex, and these scenes bring to the fore the contradiction at the heart of race definition in the United States. On the one hand, as we have seen, race is assumed to manifest itself in the visible, that is, skin pigmentation, and seems to operate in an "optical economy of identity."[21] But as Nella Larsen makes very clear in her text, the visible markings or lack thereof are not enough to tell the "truth" of race. After all, the three women at the tea party are not "white" but "black." One of the most rudimentary lessons of passing, as Amy Robinson argues and Larsen dramatizes, is that "the visible is *never* easily or simply a guarantor of truth."[22] Irene herself is aware that optics are not enough to gauge race as it is defined in the United States, averring that "[w]hite people were so stupid about such things for all they usually asserted that they were able to tell; and by the most ridiculous means, finger-nails, palms of hand, shapes of ears, teeth, and other equally silly rot" (150). Jack Bellew also articulates the contradiction. His pet name for his wife is Nig, a strange nickname given that Clare has passed successfully into white society. He tells Clare that she can get as black as she pleases, since he "knows" that she is not a "nigger" (171). Once there is an assumption of whiteness, pigmentation does not signify in the same way. Melanin, it seems, is not the manifest truth of race, although it has played a crucial part in the construction of racial thinking in the United States.

Race, as a category, has a specific history and genealogy in the United States, and its definition has never been a stable one. F. James Davis claims that it was during the 1920s that the "one-drop rule" was cemented, which stipulated that any person with *any* black ancestry was defined as black:

> In 1870 and 1880, for example, mulattoes were officially defined to include "quadroon, octoroons, and all persons having any perceptible trace of African blood." In 1890 enumerators were told to record the *exact* proportion of the "African blood," again relying on visibility. In 1900 the Census Bureau specified that "pure Negroes" be counted separately from mulattoes, the latter to mean "all persons with some trace of black blood." In 1920 the mulatto category was dropped, and black was defined to mean any person with any black ancestry, as it has been ever since.[23]

Not only does this kind of very brief historical analysis disclose the way in which race definition has shifted and fluctuated since the Civil War, but as Ann Pellegrini puts it: "Racial thinking does not neutrally find and record the 'truth' of race, but produces it."[24] The category of race has never been about skin color; rather, it has been about social differentiation and demarcation, power and control.[25] For example, no necessary relationship exists between one drop of African ancestry and the defining of a subject as black, although due to the specific historical conditions in the United States — that is, anxiety about passing, which originated during slavery and later received powerful reinforcement under the Jim Crow system — this classification has prevailed. In *Who is Black?* Davis brings in other countries' definitions of race in order to substantiate this claim. In Brazil and Puerto Rico, for example, "a substantial proportion of racially mixed [people] are considered white."[26]

The "assumption of whiteness" begins to reveal the specificity of race norms. In heteronormative regimes, one is assumed to be *either* woman or a man, even if the standard and privileged position is male. The lack of visual markers "indicating" whether a given subject is male or female is destabilizing. In white racist regimes, the lack of visual markers is not destabilizing in and of itself. Rather, since whiteness is always privileged and the only desirable color, or, in other words, since there is only one ideal race, subjects are immediately assumed to be white in the absence of any telling marks of "color." But again, as *Passing* makes very clear, race construction is about much more than visibility.

The Specific Operations of Race Performativity

Juxtaposing Homi Bhabha and Judith Butler can help critics conceptualize some of the differences between race and gender as performative reiteration. Although Bhabha does not mention performativity explicitly in his influential article "Of Mimicry and Man," it seems that mimicry does indeed operate through performative reiteration, that is, through the colonized subject's incessant attempt to mime and inhabit the colonists' authority and hegemonic ideals. While Butler tends to concentrate on gender, Bhabha many times isolates issues of race ("white but not quite"). My goal, therefore, is to read these two theorists as potential correctives to one another, once again using "passing" as a point of entry into the question of race as performative reiteration.

In his now classic *The Location of Culture*, Bhabha states that, in the colonial situation, mimicry emerges "as one of the most elusive and effective strategies of colonial power and knowledge."[27] The mimic man, the nonwhite native, does not "re-present" but rather repeats and imitates the discursive effects of colonial (or racist) discourse; mimicry is an effect of colonial discourse. On the one hand, the colonizer demands that the other approximate, through mimesis, the norms of the colonizing power, norms associated with whiteness.[28] On the other hand, in order to continuously naturalize, justify, and authorize his power, the colonizer must constantly maintain the difference between himself — as a white man — and the other. In other words, colonial discourse moves between the recognition of cultural and racial difference and its disavowal.

According to Bhabha, there is an ambivalence, a difference, at the "origins" of colonial discourse's authority. By rearticulating colonial "presence in terms of its otherness, that which it disavows," the mimic man potentially can disrupt the self-grounding assumptions of whiteness (and colonialism itself), disclosing the way in which otherness inheres in presence.[29] Mimicry can always turn to mockery; it is a hybrid site and can lay bare the way in which the colonial presence "is always ambivalent, split between its appearance as original and authoritative and its articulation as repetition and difference."[30] While Bhabha invokes psychoanalytic concepts such as paranoia and narcissism in order to explain the ambivalence that "grounds" racist identification, I would like to reposition his insights (even further) within a Foucauldian framework in the context of 1920s United States.

I believe that the ambivalence that Bhabha points to in colonial discourse is similar to the contradiction that *Passing* exposes as being at the "origins" of race definition in the United States. The novel manages to reveal the paradox embodied in racist discourse, and lays bare how racist discourse attempts to produce desire in the black other — or nonwhite — to mime the ways of the whites (thus, there is really only one norm), while at the same time this discourse assumes that "nonwhiteness" has inherent characteristics that preclude black subjects from ever really becoming "white." In order to maintain the fiction of its own racial purity and superiority, racist discourse must constantly invoke and reinforce the "nonwhiteness" of the other subject, whom it concomitantly encourages to live up to norms of whiteness.

Insofar as this is the case, white racist regimes create a particular bifurcation between identification and desire, one that is distinct from the divide characterizing heteronormativity. Taking the little boy as the standard measure of how the bifurcation of identification and desire operate, Sigmund Freud, in his *Group Psychology and the Analysis of the Ego*, states that: "In the first case one's father is what one would like *to be*, and in the second [i.e., the little girl] he is what one would like *to have*." The little boy exhibits special interest "in his father; he would like to grow like him and be like him, and take his place everywhere ... At the same time as this identification with his father, or a little later, the boy has begun to develop a true object-cathexis toward his mother."[31] Identification and desire to have are therefore "two psychologically distinct ties"; desire to have is a straightforward sexual object-cathexis while identification "endeavors to mould a person's own ego after the fashion of the one that has been taken as a model."[32] Identification, in other words, turns out to be not a sexual tie, but rather an emotional one. As Diana Fuss points out, "For Freud, desire for one sex is always secured through identification with the other sex; to desire and to identify with the same person at the same time is, in this model, a theoretical impossibility."[33]

On the one hand, I argue that the difference between the desire to be and the desire to have is an ambiguous one, but one which is carefully maintained in the service of heteronormativity. Subjects are encouraged *to desire* to live up to the norms of a specific gender while concomitantly encouraged (and compelled) to desire the other. Thus, to complicate the usual psychoanalytic schema, in which identification and sexual object-choice typically are seen to be necessarily and essentially distinct for "normal" sexual development, and to build on Diana Fuss and Ann Pellegrini's insights that desire and identification are always implicated in one another, I argue that desire in heterosexual regimes operates by *engendering, encouraging,* and *compelling* a specific type of relationship between two forms of desire: the desire-to-be, which induces the subject to live up to hegemonic *norms*, and a desire for, which induces a desire for sexual intimacy with the other gender.[34] On the other hand, I would like to complicate further this schema by arguing that the conflation of identification with the "desire-to-be" needs to be rethought. My comparison between the way in which identification and desire operate in heteronormativity and racist regimes will focus only on the identification/"desire-to-be" axis, since I believe this is where the crux of the difference lies.[35]

Like norms of gender, race norms operate by compelling subjects to assume or identify with certain identity categories; in the case of gender, subjects are interpellated into the dominant social order as either men or women and compelled to identify as either one or the other; in the case of race, subjects identify as either black or white. As Michel Pecheux has argued, interpellation is achieved by the identification of the subject with the discursive formation, i.e., in which he is constituted as subject.[36] But this is where the similarity between gender and race ends, since white racist regimes create a distinct bifurcation between identification and desire-to-be, such that certain subjects are encouraged to privilege and thus desire attributes associated with whiteness, but concurrently these same subjects are *forced* to identify as black (which has gained its specific signification due to white supremacist discourse such as the one-drop rule).[37]

The assumption of whiteness that I outlined in the previous section is an effect of the way in which whiteness circulates as the ideal, while the one-drop rule and all of the prohibitions linked to trying to identify differently help ensure that subjects do not transgress the boundaries. The ambivalence or contradiction underlying the assumption of whiteness actually can be restated in the following way: identify as black (or else) but aspire to be white. This contradiction, which actually constitutes the hegemonic category of race, proves to be a very effective way of policing its borders.[38] The particular modality of the bifurcation, in other words, is simultaneously a product of power relations in a given society and that which allows power to operate effectively. This analysis diverges from a Freudian analysis not only because it underscores the different relationship between identification and desire in heteronormativity and racist regimes, and posits that identification and the "desire-to-be" cannot be collapsed, but also because in both regimes desire and identification are understood to be constituted by and through Foucault's conception of power.

Irene identifies as black, despite the fact that she can pass as white. Due to the one-drop rule that was operative in the United States and inscribed in law at the time, it is no wonder that she does so. Irene's identification with blackness is described as a "bond," "tie of race" (182), "the strain of black blood" (192). Although these descriptions can be read as having a positive valence, Irene's relationship to her identification with blackness is revealed, I believe, when she suspects that her husband is having an affair with Clare. She describes herself caught between two allegiances — herself or her race: "Race! The thing that *bound* and *suffocated* her . . . [T]he *burden* of race" (225, emphasis added). Race identification is ultimately described as something imposed.

Interestingly, all of the major narratives of passing from this period underscore, in one form or another, how the category of race is forced upon the subject. All of these light-enough-to-pass characters, from Rena Walden to the first-person narrator in *The Autobiography of an Ex-Colored Man* to Angela Murray in *Plum Bun*, are interpellated into the symbolic world as black. The impact of the initial interpellation into the dominant social order is seemingly so great that the passing subject never can free him or herself of it psychic effects. Attempts to identify differently are always in relation to that first initiation into subjecthood. However, many of the protagonists in these texts take the risk of identifying differently in order to access the privileges of whiteness, and most of them pay a high price or are punished for this "transgression."

Punishment was an ever-present threat for subjects who attempted to identify differently. The "passing" mention of lynching in *Passing* is deceptive (231), for despite Larsen's description of Irene's staid middle-class lifestyle, the threat of violence against black Americans who over-stepped certain racial boundaries was ever-present in the 1920s United States. Lynching, as Robyn Wiegman points out, served as an effective "disciplinary practice for racial control."[39] It should be remembered that the Ku Klux Klan was revived during this period and began spreading into the North. Powerful white supremacy currents, which included incitement to race riots, also reemerged in the 1920s. Brian's answer to his son's question about why "they" only lynch colored people, "Because they hate'em . . . Because they are afraid of them, son," reveals some of the simmering racism that (actually) saturates Larsen's novel.[40] Through prohibitions and restrictions—again, the Foucauldian notion of negative power—the one-drop rule ensured that subjects conform to these constructed norms by compelling people with any African ancestors to identify as black. In many ways, Irene is compelled to identify as black, although, as we will see shortly, her desire "to be" lies elsewhere.

If *Passing* discloses that identifying as black (historically) has been a compelled identification, and not about the *desire* to usurp the other's place (to be or appropriate and thus become the other), then some of psychoanalysis's most basic assumptions about identification are called into question. Identification no longer can be understood simply as "an endless process of violent negation, a process of killing off the other in fantasy in order to usurp the other's place, the place where the subject desires to be."[41] Nor can it be understood as the psychological process whereby the subject assimilates an aspect, property, or attribute of the other, and is transformed."[42] For identification with blackness under white racist regimes historically has been not only coerced, but it also has been coded as *undesirable*.[43]

Desire and identification are not free-floating entities, since "we must understand power as *forming* the subject . . . , as providing the very condition of its existence and the *trajectory of its desire*."[44] I would argue that the identification-desire dichotomy and its effect on subjects, such as a compelled primary identification, must be understood as one of the necessary productions of hegemony, that is, one of the most effective mechanisms of positive and negative power. As Butler herself says in her earlier writings, heteronormative and racial discourse are *formative* of desire and identification, and there is no reference to some prediscursive libido or amorphous desire that does not further produce the contours of that desire.[45] The "effective" operation of the dominant social order *requires* the production, encouragement, and compelling of certain kinds of identifications and desires-to-be, since in order for dominant norms to continue operating effectively as regulatory ideals, subjects must understand and define *themselves* through these norms. A compelled primary identification thus ensures that subjects recognize themselves in and through regulatory ideals, while the desire-to-be shapes and regulates subjects' preferences and aspirations.[46]

It might seem that power should work in such a way as to encourage black-identified subjects to approximate blackness as defined by the hegemonic order. This would operate as a mechanism of control because the subject's attempt to approximate these norms would ensure that subject's subordination. But herein lie the paradox and complex workings of positive and negative power. If a regime privileges certain attributes, then it must also encourage subjects to desire and strive to embody them. It can and does attempt to bar certain subjects from accessing privilege and positions of power through race differentiation and classification or, in other words, compelling race identification, but it cannot completely control the effects of its own discourse. So long as blackness is coded as undesirable under white supremacist regimes, only those black-identified subjects who strive to embody attributes associated with whiteness will gain admittance to some of the benefits of privilege and power.[47]

Thus, in racist regimes, a concatenation that is very different from heteronormativity takes place. In heteronormativity (again, on the hegemonic level), identification with "being a woman" almost always implies (and is inextricably intertwined with) the desire to "be a woman," that is, a desire to live up to the norms of femininity in a particular social order. Femininity is posited as desirable and as something that "women" should approximate; wanting to "be a woman" is coded as positive. The forced identification with blackness, however, is not linked with a desire to live up to norms of blackness. Rather, black-identified subjects, *in order to sustain a nonmarginal existence*, are compelled and encouraged to privilege and consequently desire to be "white," that is, to live up to attributes associated with whiteness. As a consequence of the trauma of colonialism, Frantz Fanon claims that "the black man wants to be white," while Stuart Hall argues that "blacks could gain entry to the mainstream — but only at the cost of . . . assimilating white norms of style, looks, and behavior.[48] This again is in stark contrast to heteronormativity, where women are not encouraged to live up to norms of masculinity, nor are men urged to live up to feminine ideals. Whereas female-identified subjects (subjects interpellated into the dominant social order as women) who desire to approximate masculinity (active, aggressive, etc.) are threatening to the powers that be, black-identified subjects who attempt to approximate whiteness often have been embraced by hegemony.

Although *Passing* is ostensibly about the dangers of passing over to the white world as manifested in the enigmatic death of Clare, I would argue, along with many other critics, that the novel is just as much about Irene's attempting to approximate norms of whiteness.[49] Despite — or perhaps due to — her black identification, Irene is depicted as desiring a civilized and cultured life. "Irene didn't like changes, particularly changes that affected her smooth routine of her household" (188). Brian's dream of leaving the United States for Brazil is thus disturbing to Irene on (at least) two counts. It represents a change that would disrupt the "pleasant routine of her life" (229), and Brazil, according to Irene's assessment of things, is decidedly not a civilized place. Irene's routine, it is important to underscore, consists of maintaining the appearances of white middle-class prosperity. She occupies herself with mothering, social obligations, and "uplift work"; and despite her declaration to Clare that she is "wrapped up in her boys and the running of her house," it seems that black maids do most of the arduous housework. As Jacquelyn McLendon points out: "Irene Redfield, in her strict adherence to bourgeois ideological codes, strives to mask any feelings or behavior that appears to be uncivilized or unladylike, measures herself by white standards, and lives in constant imitation of whites."[50] Irene strives to obtain "marginal acceptance and security in American society," and this desire to be a viable and accepted subject in the United States forces her to "imitate the prejudices of the dominant society."[51]

Security—being a wife and mother, living in New York's Harlem—is the most important and "desired thing in life" for Irene Redfield (235). Any and all attributes linked to hegemonic ideas of blackness—"the open expression of emotion and feeling rather than intellect, a lack of 'civilized refinement in sexual and social life'"—are carefully policed by Irene.[52] Her occasional outbursts of temper and impetuosity are followed by self-admonishment. Even when Irene first suspects that Brian is having an affair with Clare, she refuses to display her emotions. Despite the shock and horror, Irene throws her already-planned tea party. She keeps up appearances: "Satisfied that there lingered no betraying evidence of weeping, she dusted a little powder on her dark-white face and again examined it carefully" (218). Rather than show any signs of distress, Irene "went on pouring. Made repetitions of her smile. Answered questions. Manufactured conversation . . . So like many other tea-parties she had had" (219). Interestingly, it is during this tea party that Larsen underscores the way in which the norms of civility are dependent on their reiteration.

Irene also ensures that any semblance of overt sexuality is checked; the stereotype of the lascivious, over-sexed black woman was still very much in circulation during the period Larsen depicts.[53] At one point, she suddenly admits to herself that Clare is "capable of heights and depths of feelings that she, Irene Redfield had never known." But the clincher is in the next admission. Irene has "never cared to know" these feelings (195). Brian is her husband and the father of her sons, but as she ponders what to do with the suspicion of Brian's affair with Clare, she also tells us that she has never truly known love. The desire to approximate norms of civility is so powerful that Irene is willing to "hold fast to the outer shell of her marriage, to keep her life fixed, certain. Brought to the edge of distasteful reality, her fastidious nature did not recoil" (235). To dissolve the marriage no doubt would bring the kind of notoriety that Irene tries so hard to avoid. Moreover, if the marriage is already more about striving to embody the ideals of the white middle class, then it is not at all clear that the "substance" of the marriage would change after Brian's affair; the two already sleep in different rooms. In short, Irene strives to be as prim, as proper, and as bourgeois as (ideals of) white middle-class ladies.[54]

This desire to approximate norms of whiteness is reiterated in the other two major passing novels of this period.[55] As we will see in Chapter Four, the protagonist in James Weldon Johnson's *The Autobiography of an Ex-Colored Man* clearly exposes the "compelled desire" to embody attributes associated with whiteness. After witnessing a black man being lynched, he decides to pass. He abandons his ragtime career, which is associated with "black" culture, marries a white woman, and becomes a successful businessman. He expresses his anxiety of "being found out," but decides to take his chances anyway. And whereas Johnson's protagonist takes his chances as a white man, Angela Murray in *Plum Bun* finds the strain of passing too much for her and ends up married to a light-enough-to-pass black man. And while both sisters, Angela and Virginia (who is not light enough to pass), ultimately are compelled to identify as black, they — just like Irene — are also depicted as striving to live up to white middle-class norms of respectability. In order to access privilege, it seems, subjects interpellated into the social order as black must constantly endeavor to embody attributes associated with whiteness.

Thus, *contra* Miron and Inda, I would like to emphasize that the raced subject, in order to remain *viable* and *nonmarginal* in a white supremacist power regime, must constantly and perpetually attempt to embody norms that historically have been associated and concatenated with whiteness. Although white racist regimes help create black subjects, the racial norms that this regime produces, promulgates, and compels subjects to approximate are invariably norms associated with whiteness. I believe that the delinking of identification and "desire-to-be" is key to understanding the particular mechanisms by which and through which norms of race operate under racist regimes. Moreover, desiring to approximate blackness — as it comes to be defined by this regime — means disidentifying with the dominant norms, can be dangerous, and can sometimes even lead to death.

Identification Trouble

By way of conclusion, I would like to introduce some additional complicating factors and qualifications. As mentioned, in white racist regimes, attributes associated with whiteness are always privileged. While such a regime would not necessarily discourage marginal black-identified subjects from striving to embody blackness—although I would argue, once black-identified subjects access privilege, most if not all attempts to glorify attributes associated with blackness are punished—the splitting of identification and desire-to-be actually serves as one of the most efficacious mechanisms of control. This delinking ensures that the desirability of whiteness is reinforced, while black-identified subjects simultaneously are prevented from accessing many of the privileges that "true" whiteness grants.

Clare, however, disrupts this schema to a certain extent. Through her characterization, the reader is exposed to an interesting process of identification, disidentification, and a further disidentification. Interpellated as a black woman, Clare "chooses" to pass over into the white world. Her marriage to a white racist who does not know that she is passing in many ways underscores the risk that this kind of disidentification carries. In her first identification crisis, Clare "decides" to perform race norms differently. Rather than remain a black-identified woman who strives to approximate norms of whiteness, Clare begins not only to approximate white norms, but also to identify as a white woman. In the letter that Clare sends to Irene after meeting her at the Drayton, Clare indicates that she had been on her way to "freeing" herself from her identification with blackness (145). We learn early on that Clare's decision to pass is inextricably intertwined with her determination to "be a person and not a charity or a problem . . ." (159). In contrast to Angela Murray, the protagonist of *Plum Bun*, Claire has no loving family with whom she has to break ties and disown in order to pass. The risks she takes, like the ones taken by the protagonist in *The Autobiography of an Ex-Colored Man*, are, according to Clare herself, "worth the price" (160), for performing whiteness confers status and allows one to assume privilege.

Clare's desire to reclaim her initial identification as a black woman, however, is one that cannot be explained according to the logic of privilege. For this very reason, Larsen's description of this further disidentification is fascinating. Clare knowingly courts danger and punishment when she shows up in Harlem; in many ways, she can be seen to be putting her social existence into jeopardy. In sharp contrast to the "status" she gains by performing whiteness, her appearance in black Harlem does not confer privilege.

Larson's portrayal of Clare thus suggests that my preceding discussion did not fully capture the complexity of race performativity and of performativity more generally. Hegemonic regimes, as I argued above, cannot completely control the effects of their own discourse. Even though whiteness is privileged over and against blackness in white supremacist regimes, the very repetition and circulation of different, and, at times contradictory, racial norms create the possibility of subversion. As Judith Butler has reminded us time and again, because the dominant social order is dependent on reiteration for its very existence, it is also necessarily open to variation. As we saw with the depiction of David Levinsky, subjects must *incessantly* attempt to embody norms, which, in turn, creates a continuous (and potentially discernable) dissonance; gaps and fissures can and do emerge within the dominant social order as subjects strive to embody regulatory ideals.[56] Due to the non-coincidence of ideals and social praxis, there is always the possibility that subjects will repeat norms in unpredictable and potentially contestatory ways.

In a sense, this is what Clare is depicted as doing when she attempts to approximate certain hegemonic norms of blackness. Unlike Irene, Clare does not police overt signs of sexuality. Her "shade too provocative" smile that she gives the waiter at the Drayton is one of the first things Irene notices about her old acquaintance (148), and when the reader is first introduced to Clare, she is with an unknown and never-named man; we find out later that he is not her husband. This linking of Clare and sexuality occurs throughout the text, from the gossip that Clare's disappearance from her aunts' house elicits through the way she dresses in clothing meant to deliberately attract attention to her beauty, to Irene's suspicion that she is having an affair with Brian. It seems that Clare herself cultivates and performs this image; for example, during Clare's first visit to Irene and Brian in Harlem, she admonishes Irene for not writing by describing how she waited, in vain, for a response to her correspondence: "Every day I went to that nasty little post-office place. I'm sure they were all beginning to think that I'd been carrying on an illicit love-affair . . ." (194).

Clare is associated consistently with theatrics, excess, and danger. Irene describes her as having a "strange capacity of transforming warmth and passion, verging sometimes almost on theatrical heroics" (144). There is a constant emphasis on her "having way," her selfish disregard of others when attempting to attain something for herself. Clare, who describes herself as lacking any "proper morals or sense of duty" (210), is depicted as presenting a danger to the white middle-class conventions that Irene strictly adheres to.

Although constituted through and circumscribed by norms, the fractured and competing nature of the ideals circulating in society, as I suggested in the first chapter, also seems to open a space for subjects to perform differently. Clare's second disidentification trouble, for instance, appears to be precipitated by her re-encounter with Irene. In the letter Clare sends to Irene after their meeting at the Drayton, she indicates that once she was glad to be free of her identification with blackness, but now she has a "wild desire" to associate with black people. Clare adds that it's Irene's fault, for if she hadn't seen the other woman in Chicago, the thought of escaping her "pale life" would never have occurred to her (145). What this points to, I believe, is that confrontations or interactions between subjects potentially can lay bare the disjunctions and contradictions within the nexus of force relations. Clare, who initially had attempted to "perform race" by identifying and desiring to be white at the risk of "being found out," is suddenly confronted by Irene, who has "chosen" not to "pass over." This encounter, in turn, opens up a space of negotiation. It is not that Clare wishes to trade places with Irene, but rather that Clare, like Anna Tevkin in *The Rise of David Levinsky*, recognizes that other *configurations* of identification and "desire-to-be" are possible. Thus, a nuanced conception of agency very similar to the one we encountered in Abraham Cahan's text emerges, one that emerges from the subject's ability to recognize and negotiate *between* the different possible configurations of identification and "desire-to-be" that help constitute the field of intelligibility.

Racial norms are spawned by a particular configuration of power relations, and these norms are both the condition of possibility of viable subjects, and help produce and shape the subject's very preferences, aspirations, desire, and identification. Larsen's portrayal of Irene reveals just how powerful and effective these racial norms can be. This does not mean, however, that subjects are merely docile bodies; rather, subjects can and do "perform differently." The depiction of Clare gestures toward the way in which identification and desire-to-be can be misappropriated and "assumed" in potentially subversive ways. Although Clare's enigmatic death ultimately precludes an unambiguously subversive or celebratory reading of the novel, tracing her identification and subsequent disidentifications can give us insight into how power can be challenged through contestatory performances.

In both this chapter and the preceding one, I have isolated gender and race respectively in order to outline some of the *specific* ways subjects come to be gendered and "raced." This "isolation" has allowed me not only to trace and examine the identification/desire-to-be nexus, but also to argue that both gender and race need to be rethought as unique modalities of performativity. I continue this methodological move in the following chapter by isolating class; this is, I contend, a necessary step if we are to understand the mechanisms that have produced classed subjectivities in the United States.

Chapter Three

American Dream Discourse
and Class Performativity

AT LEAST FOR THE PAST CENTURY, the American Dream has been an important feature of class discourse in the United States. Jennifer Hochschild defines the Dream as the promise held out to each and every American that he or she has a reasonable chance of achieving success through his or her own efforts. Achievement, therefore, translates into reaching "some threshold of well-being, higher than where one began."[1] *Salome of the Tenements*, Anzia Yezierska's 1923 novel, brings to the fore and dramatizes various aspects of the American Dream. Success, as the protagonist Sonya Vrunsky defines it, means leaving poverty—"the prison of . . . soul-wasting want"—behind; Sonya is described as wanting more than anything else to move away from the "blackness of poverty" and to reach the "mountain-tops of life."[2] The image of upwardness, whereby poverty is presented as low and wealth as high, is a central trope in the novel. In this way, Yezierska portrays the United States as a society with clear class stratifications, but also a society in which individuals are capable of changing their location in the hierarchical formation—that is, they can rise above want and need, and enjoy the "higher life," where the "luxuries of love, beauty, plenty" abound (68).

Class takes on an urgency in Yezierska's writings that has not been addressed sufficiently by her critics. Many critics have read Yezierska's work through the lens of "assimilation" and "liminality," contending, for example, that Yezierska's narratives give voice to the "misread, the marginalized, [those] who are attempting to work out a relationship between their birth-culture and a mainstream America."[3] Similarly, Ellen Golub argues that Yezierska's fiction is "one of balked desires and lost homes," as the female protagonists find that their attempts to become "truly" American are complicated in various ways.[4] However, as I argued in Chapter One, by framing their analysis through a binary opposition between American and Jewish culture, critics reinforce the idea that each term constitutes a monolithic, homogeneous, and self-identical entity; they do so without examining questions of power and hegemony. The few critiques that have specifically addressed issues of class in Yezierska's novels do not offer a theoretical analysis of the way U.S. class discourse operates in her texts.[5]

In the following pages, I argue that *Salome of the Tenements* explicitly queries and dramatizes the logic of upward mobility and provides a fascinating staging of class "conflict" in (Yezierska's fictive) Progressive Era America.[6] The novel tells the story of Sonya Vrunsky, an orphaned child of Jewish immigrants working as a columnist on the Lower East Side, who falls in love with the millionaire and progressive philanthropist John Manning. Sonya is determined to get what she wants, and she finds a way into Manning's life. Things fall apart soon after Sonya and Manning's marriage, though, and Sonya eventually leaves Fifth Avenue and returns to the Lower East Side. Here, she works as a dressmaker, and, through her hard work and talent, makes a name for herself as a fashion designer. At the end of the novel, Sonya re-encounters Jaky Solomon, who also has worked himself up from a lowly tailor to a Fifth Avenue designer, and the two ultimately become partners, both in work and in love.

Yezierska's flamboyant and sometimes hyperbolic narrative style, alongside her constant invocation of class norms, make this text a particularly suitable site for investigating the way in which class status is constituted by and through performativity.[7] Concentrating on the functions of class *discourse* in the novel, I contend that the narrative reveals many of the ways that this discourse has operated in the United States, and how class, *as a category of identification* — similar to gender and race — is constituted by and through certain regulatory ideals or norms.[8]

In this chapter, I am thus moving away from the traditional Marxist conceptions of class as an already-existing social group defined by its relation to the means of production. Drawing on the insights of twentieth-century Marxist theorists such as Antonio Gramsci, Raymond

Williams, and Louis Althusser, among others, I problematize the econ-
omist conception of the relationship between the material base and the
ideological superstructure. Ideology and hegemony, as all of these theorists have argued in different ways, help *produce* our perception and
definition of the world in general, and therefore of class more specifically. Class discourse, in other words, is not unlike racial (and gender) discourse, which generates "a field of ethics, knowledge, and power
that contributes its unique order of truths to the processes that produce
and regulate individual subjects, conditioning the intimate consciousness through which they come to know and understand and indeed
constitute themselves as racial beings."[9] Drawing on such insights,
I go one step further, contending that Yezierska's narrative discloses
how class is constituted by and through certain regulatory ideals or
norms and needs to be rethought as a unique modality of performative
reiteration.[10]

The American Dream

Many American authors both before and after Yezierska have dramatized the power of the upward-mobility discourse. But due to the historical moment in which Yezierska was writing—as part of the first
generation of Jewish-American authors writing in English and specifically about the process of "Americanization" after the major waves of
Eastern-European Jewry immigration—her corpus helps bring into
sharp focus how the American Dream helped shape U.S. identity in the
early twentieth century.

The American Dream is informed by a very specific notion of the
social subject as an individual.[11] As Gillian Brown has pointed out, the
term "individualism" only came into use in the United States in the late
1820s, when market society and forms of the modern liberal state were
well established. By the mid-nineteenth century, though, the notion of
individual rights—promulgated much earlier in the political philosophy of John Locke—comprised an article of cultural faith.[12] The idea
that individuals are proprietors of their own person (and any capital
they may own), for which they owe little or nothing to society, alongside
the conviction that an individual's freedom should be limited only by
the requirements of the freedom of other individuals, rapidly became
cornerstones of American liberal democracy.[13] In addition, since the

passage of the Nineteenth Amendment in 1920, the United States increasingly has emphasized the formal equality of all of its citizens; that is, not only is every subject "guaranteed" equal rights, but every citizen also can potentially govern. The American Dream, with its central tenet of upward mobility, depends both on the emphasis of individual rights and on the formal recognition of individual equality.[14]

The social subject of American liberal democracy also has been conceived of as an agent of choice. As we will see in the next section, *Salome of the Tenements*, through its depictions of the two main protagonists, Sonya and Jaky, in many ways echoes and reinforces liberalism's most basic assumptions — assumptions that prioritize a self understood to be "an active, willing agent, distinguishable from [his/her] surroundings, and capable of choice" even in the most difficult situations.[15] The individual subject becomes the locus of agency, for he/she is presented as having the opportunity and ability to climb within the class hierarchy. In addition, the notion of success that the American Dream promulgates, while not necessarily reducible to acquiring great wealth or even to attaining upper-middle-class status, is certainly inextricably related to moving *up* the class hierarchy.

The conviction that one can ascend the class ladder actually points to an interesting tension within American class discourse. On the one hand, the American Dream seems to suggest that America is not a class society of the traditional European type (because anyone potentially can move up the ladder), while on the other hand, the discourse assumes the existence of some kind of class formation, otherwise the very notion of moving up within the hierarchy would be nonsensical. It could be argued that the difference between the traditional European class society and the one in the United States is that the latter does not posit structural class limitations that unfairly hinder the individual. Even Karl Marx argued that "[in] the United States of North America ... classes, indeed, already exist," but they have not become fixed; rather they "continually change and interchange their elements in a constant state of flux."[16]

In *Salome of the Tenements*, Sonya's relationship to John Manning's class position reveals this interesting tension within the American Dream and class discourse.[17] According to Sonya, Manning is the one of the "American-born higher-ups"; he belongs to a particular social milieu, a different "class where there were social rules and regulations to be observed" (36). There is a very clear recognition of class difference and social barriers between classes. But, throughout the novel, Sonya also invokes the ideal of formal equality and the lack of structural limits on individual upper mobility. "You and I, com[e] from the opposite ends of society," she tells Manning, "[b]ut here, in America we come together and eat by the same table like born equals" (36). Moreover, Sonya is depicted as believing in the possibility of individual class transformation, and the narrative actually has her realize this possibility: first by marrying Manning, but then, perhaps more importantly, by becoming a successful designer who lives far above want and need.

Performing Upward Mobility: Willpower, Hard Work, and Moral Uprightness

As the novel discloses, the possibility of climbing the class hierarchy is contingent upon the individual's readiness to emulate certain norms that are produced, reinforced, and circulated by the American Dream. More specifically, the norms of determination, hard work, and moral uprightness are revealed to be regulatory ideals or normative injunctions that the protagonists constantly must endeavor to approximate and embody if they wish to "better themselves." The text dramatizes the idea that without a will of steel, hard work, and some kind of moral sensibility, individuals will be unable to take advantage of the opportunities that America offers; and, if they fail to make good on the American Dream, they have only themselves to blame.

The potential powers of the individual will, for instance, play a crucial role in the text from the moment we are introduced to Sonya. Sonya's first meeting and interview with John Manning, the millionaire and philanthropist, is described as a result of her perseverance and ingenuity: "[T]he force of her will had materialized her desire into flesh and blood" (3). And, as obstacles arise during her daring and spectacular courting of Manning, Yezierska has Sonya constantly invoke the liberal conception of the will, in which the autonomous subject's determination to do or change something is translated immediately into a deed, as a way of motivating herself. Whenever she feels her plan is faltering, Sonya reminds herself that where there is a will there is a way, and though she occasionally is cowed by the difficulties that seem to frustrate her grand plan, she does not give up. Against all odds, Sonya convinces a famous Fifth Avenue designer to create a thousand-dollar dress—gratis—for her lunch date with Manning. She also persuades her rapacious "Essex Street tyrant" landlord to paint and renovate her dilapidated apartment. In the end, "her indomitable will" wins the day, and Manning and Sonya get married (97).

While the narrative of Sonya's success usually is described in terms of her desire and constant attempt to live up to the norm of unswerving determination, Yezierska's depiction of Jaky Solomon's rise to fame stresses the potential benefits of hard work. From his early days, Jaky recognizes that he is no "common tailor," but he works in factory after factory, saving his money for the day when he can sail to Paris (18). His determination finally bears fruit when a rich customer invites Jaky to be her private designer; he then is able to realize his dream of developing his talent in Paris—"At last after years of struggle!" (20). He "worked himself up from a Division Street tailor to a Paris designer" (22, emphasis added). The narrative exposes how, in order to live up to the norm of the hard-working subject, one must, among other things, adopt a certain conception of time where nonproductive activity is perceived to be wasteful. That is, in order to "be" a hard-working subject, subjects must incessantly repeat and endeavor to approximate the norms that come to define what a hard-working subject "is" in a given context.

Following her decision to leave Manning, Sonya forces herself to work as a waitress: "Much as she hated the work of the restaurant, she was determined to stick it out at all costs until by strictest economy she had saved up enough to go to a school of design" (167). And as soon as she sees her opportunity, she grabs it; she convinces a manufacturer to take her on as machine hand. Given that she has a goal in front of her, she is not afraid of grueling labor: "After the shop closed, she sat up half the night reading fashion books, poring over designs. At lunch time, she hurried through a scant meal and greedily spent every moment . . . studying how the more exquisite gowns were made" (169). Sure enough, through her hard work and resolution, she proves herself to be a talented dressmaker. When the reader takes leave of her, Sonya has become a successful and sought-after designer.[18]

Jennifer Hochschild and J. Emmett Winn both have argued convincingly that moral uprightness has been an important aspect of American cultural discourse vis-à-vis class.[19] Historically, there has been a subtle but very real equation of "failure" to move up the class hierarchy with lack of virtue, while "success" often is identified with goodness. Moreover, only individuals who capitalize on the (supposed) lack of class structural barriers in America and work hard can move up the ladder. As we will see in the next section, those who do not take advantage of the promises that the American Dream holds out to them are coded as pathetic or failures. Mobility is thus moralized, and success "is associated with virtue."[20] Fame, power, and wealth in and of themselves are not necessarily enough to warrant respect. Rather, the motives and the way in which a person transforms him/herself are important and must correspond in some way to the dominant perception of moral uprightness. Honesty, or honest economy and toil, integrity, charity, and realizing one's aims and purposes in ways compatible with an equal liberty for others are some of the virtues that traditionally have been attached to moral uprightness in the United States.[21]

Sonya's desire to return to her Lower East Side roots in order to democratize beauty plays a crucial part in countering her image as willing to do anything to get what she wants: "I'll rob, steal or murder if I got to," she tells Gittel at the beginning of the novel (8). Once she thought she could reach the "higher up place" through dissimulation and marriage, through grabbing "love" and "power" by force (162). Sonya initially is described as "an egoist with driving force that will carry her anywhere" (21). Later in the novel, she changes course and succeeds in reaching the "mountain-tops of life" through hard work and by selling the promise of democratization by opening an inexpensive boutique on the Lower East Side. In other words, Sonya's return can be seen as yet another attempt on her part to embody and approximate the norms that allow for upward mobility.

We have seen how Sonya constantly attempts to embody the ideals of hard work and determination. Here, I argue, she is performing the norm of moral uprightness. Yezierska, wittingly or unwittingly, both exposes how and, in some ways, helps (re)produce the notion that upper mobility is permitted and applauded "with the moral proviso that one does not abandon one's personal and spiritual values in harvesting the rewards of the materialistic myth of the American Dream."[22] Whereas her marriage and life with Manning is described as undermining Sonya's personality and her belief in "true" democracy, her success as a designer coupled with her future store seem to reinscribe the various aspects of the myth, wherein subjects may, "with proper motives, enjoy social mobility and moral well-being."[23] Sonya cannot reap the benefits of a higher class status until two criteria are met: One, she has to achieve material well-being through her own efforts and not vicariously through Manning; and two, her newfound success must include some form of "charity," which will signify, in turn, her newfound moral probity. It should not be forgotten, however, that Sonya and Jaky plan to open a little shop on Grand Street "*on the side*" (178, emphasis added).

Class Discourse and the Lack of Assumption of Essence

If upward mobility is posited as something possible and desirable, as indeed it is in the novel, then class status is something one can change; it is not a determining attribute. In stark contrast to other categories of identity, such as race, gender, and perhaps even ethnicity, in the twentieth-century United States, class was not constructed—even in hegemonic discourse—as an essence. In fact, the lack of assumption of essence in class discourse constitutes the very condition of possibility of the discourse of upward mobility, and I believe that it is here that the unique and irreducible modality of class performativity lies.

The conception of class status as transformable has important and far-reaching consequences. Since, in the United States, gender and race historically have been conceived of as essences by the dominant social order, as biological facts that cannot be altered, the norms concatenated to these categories of identification have been construed as natural attributes. According to hegemonic conceptions of gender, women *are* feminine—they *are* nurturing and emotional and the like; blackness, in the United States' white racist regime, has been equated with lack of intelligence, laziness, licentiousness. By contrast, hard work, willpower, and moral uprightness are not so much attributes that are naturally concatenated to (social) groups but rather have been understood in the United States as characteristics that can be acquired by particular and individual subjects. Michael Sandel highlights this point through his distinction between attributes that one *has* and attributes that one *is*.[24] This distinction informs the notion of possessive individualism operative in hegemonic U.S. class discourse and underlies the liberal subject. "The possessive aspect of the self . . . means that there must always be some attributes I have rather than am."[25] Twentieth-century American class discourse not only has tended to emphasize the acquisitive aspect of the self, but also has helped produce the very notion of possessive individualism. Hegemonic race and gender discourses (which in many ways actually undermine or contradict the paradigm of the liberal subject), by contrast, rely on essence: One does not *have* certain attributes; one is understood *to be* those attributes.

As a result of Yezierska's constant (and often hyperbolic) invocation and reiteration of Progressive Era class norms, her text becomes a very useful site for investigating the ways in which hegemonic discourse has tended to enforce a belief that *certain* attributes are manifestations of individual determination and not biologically determined characteristics. Consequently, the narrative suggests that norms associated with class status can be wielded in a way that gender, race, and ethnicity cannot; as Sonya's performance of "being a lady" suggests, they can be donned and doffed more easily and with fewer repercussions.

After having approached her landlord in her everyday clothes and failed to convince him to fix up her apartment, Sonya dons the suit Jacques Hollins (Jaky Solomon's trade name) has made for her. Instantly, it seems, she is transformed into a "lady."[26] The stenographer in the landlord's office as well as the landlord himself do not realize that Sonya is the same woman who unsuccessfully pleaded her case the day before. The stenographer is obsequious, and when Sonya enters the restaurant in which the landlord is eating, he is described as feeling that "a superior being from another world had dropped down from the sky" (50). Sonya not only dresses the part of the lady, but she adopts the mannerisms associated with this class. That is, she assumes a haughtiness and a "commanding confidence" (59). And, after she sees how easy it is to "pass" as a "lady," she uses her performance in various situations. Her assumption of privilege convinces others that she is privileged. In this way, Yezierska not only highlights the way in which "being a lady" is constituted by performativity, but also reinforces the idea that class identity can be changed.

The novel, in effect, dramatizes the way class has functioned as one of the regulatory categories of identification through which a subject's identity becomes recognizable and coherent to her/himself and to other members of society. Subjects, the text reveals, are interpellated into the dominant social order as classed subjects, just as they are concomitantly interpellated as gendered and raced subjects. As we have seen in previous chapters, in the case of gender, subjects are interpellated into the dominant social order as either men or women and thus (initially) compelled to identify as either one or the other; in the case of race, subjects historically have been forced to identify as black, nonwhite, or white. In the case of class, the preliminary interpellation imposes an

initial identification with a specific class, compelling subjects to identify as under- or working-, middle- or upper-class. But this, I suggest, is
where the similarity ends.

While there are two idealized genders under regimes of compulsory
heterosexuality, this hierarchy has postured as "difference" rather than
as good/bad or high/low. By compelling and encouraging "women" to
live up to norms of femininity, heteronormative regimes reinforce their
hegemony. The linking and consequent collapsing of identification and
"desire-to-be" is fundamental to the operations of heteronormativity.
The operation of identification in relation to class, however, is different.
Unlike gender discourse (and to a great extent race discourse), which
historically has camouflaged hierarchy by employing the euphemism of
difference, class discourse posits a clear hierarchy without any attempt
to conceal the social stratification. Class is, I believe, necessarily rather
than contingently a hierarchical concept precisely because the discourse
that constitutes it does not assume essential distinctions among individuals. Given the hierarchical nature of class discourse, norms that are
associated with the positions higher up on the ladder have been patently
privileged — privileged without the disguise or mask of difference.

In the United States, the initially compelled identification with the
lower or under classes historically has not been linked with a desire
to live up to the norms connected with these classes. Rather, *in order
to sustain a nonmarginal existence,* subjects who are initially interpellated into a lower class are urged to privilege and strive to live up to
norms associated with the middle and upper-middle classes. Dissimilar
to heteronormativity (but comparable to white racist regimes), American liberal discourse has created and encouraged a distinct bifurcation
between identification and desire-to-be, such that certain subjects who
(initially) are forced to identify with the lower classes are simultaneously encouraged to privilege and desire attributes associated with the
classes that are higher up on the ladder. Identification with the lower
classes, like identification with blackness, historically has not only been
imposed, but also has been coded as *undesirable.* Thus, the delinking of
identification and "desire-to-be" once again emerges as a crucial nexus
of power, yet here it helps lay bear the particular mechanisms by and
through which norms of *class* operate.[27]

When Sonya bursts into Jaky Solomon's (now Jacques Hollins) Fifth
Avenue shop by saying she wants to see her old friend, Jaky is surprised.
He does not recognize himself in the old name: "[H]e had buried his

Division Street pedigree under five years of Fifth Avenue success and was puzzled as to who this 'old friend' might be" (22). Jaky Solomon is described as having almost completely disidentified with his initial interpellation as lower-class tailor. Moreover, he is not punished for changing his name to Jacques Hollins; rather, his transformation into wealthy designer is posited in the text as inevitable given his genius. This lack of sustained identification with class status makes sense, since class in the United States has not been understood in ontological terms. Because individuals can and are even encouraged to acquire attributes associated with a higher class and to appropriate that class's belief system, there is nothing very subversive or disruptive about class passing. By stark contrast, race passing and gender passing—when exposed— are much more threatening to the powers that be than class passing, because class "passing" or, more precisely, potential class transformation is one of the key promises of the American Dream. Furthermore, given the historical development of American society in the twentieth century, in which individualism increasingly has been promoted, any kind of sustained class identification has been extremely threatening to hegemonic society, since it potentially can lead to class solidarity and a disruption of capitalist development. I return to this in the next section.

Interestingly and importantly, Sonya's failure to approximate upper-middle-class norms during her wedding reception is ascribed to her "ethnicity" rather than her "class" by Manning's upper-class friends. Sonya's inability to pass as a "higher up" is described as being due to Sonya's Jewishness and not to the fact that she is from the working class (128). "Astonishingly well-dressed," the wealthy guests admit, but "[h]er gesticulating hands show her origin" (121). This scene reveals how class status, while present as a social force, becomes unarticulated and rendered invisible—insuperable difference is deflected away from class and projected onto ethnicity. If the American Dream is to retain its powerful hold and creative force on subjects' imaginations and desires, limitations vis-à-vis mobility must be explained away by "essential" differences and not class status. It is not that one cannot move from the lower to upper classes, but rather that a Jew cannot become an Anglo-Saxon. In this way, the possibility of upward mobility is maintained, structural limitations based on class are denied, and a glass ceiling based on ethnicity (and race and gender) is created.

In contradistinction to both white racist and heteronormative regimes, climbing from one class to another and thus potentially dis-identifying with one's initial interpellation is posited as something desirable.[28] Rather than the doctrine "identify as black (or else) but aspire to be white" that has been operative in race performativity under white racist regimes, as I have argued in the second chapter, a different kind of injunction seems to operate regarding class. Perhaps it can be stated in the following way: "This is who you are now, but you can be something better if only you persevere, work hard, and maintain some kind of socially recognized moral probity." While initial identification with a particular class is necessary as part of the functioning of class societies — otherwise the upward-mobility discourse would cease to be meaningful — this identification does not signify in the same way that it does in either gender or race discourse. In U.S. liberal discourse, there is the promise and therefore the possibility of complete transformation, including the subject's very identification. As Rita Felski suggests, "One can change one's class in a way that one cannot change one's sex or race . . . [I]f one has become upper-middle-class as a result of social mobility, then one really is upper-middle-class."[29] Felski's comment simultaneously reveals just how entrenched the notion of essence has become within race and sex discourse as well as the difference that the lack of assumption of essence makes regarding the construction of class. Thus, disidentification with the initial interpellation actually may be encouraged rather than punished. I would even go so far as to argue that in the United States the initial interpellation vis-à-vis class is less powerful psychically, and that any kind of lasting identification with this or that class may even be actively *discouraged*.

Individualism Versus Class Consciousness

The emphasis on the individual, as we have seen, subtends the norms of hard work, willpower, and moral uprightness. But what the success stories of Jaky and Sonya also bring into sharp focus is that upward mobility depends on a rejection of any notion of class solidarity or identification along class lines, as well as an embrace of what Pierre Bourdieu has termed the "cult of the self."[30] This cult of self celebrates and consequently reinforces the belief in subjects as autonomous agents. Individual personalities with their set of unique properties, gifts, and talents are valorized, creating a culture that privileges the private and intimate as against the public and the collective.[31] The corollary of the orientation toward individual mobility and the cult of self is the break-up of solidarities.

In his *German Ideology*, Marx famously argues that separate individuals form a class only insofar as they have to carry out a common battle with another class; otherwise they are "on hostile terms with each other as competitors."[32] The cult of self tends to negate any possibility of "common battle," suggesting that the American Dream serves to individuate subjects by holding out the promise of upper mobility to *individuals* who endeavor to live up to certain norms, while simultaneously encouraging society to blame "unsuccessful" *individuals* for their own failure. Whereas gender and race discourse homogenize subjects by insisting on similarities or dissimilarities across groups, hegemonic American class discourse actually has operated as a heterogenizing force.

Perhaps one could even go so far as to assert that class subjects gain much of their intelligibility as individuals through and by this discourse. Class discourse therefore can be seen to operate as one of the modalities of power "in which each individual receives as his status his own individuality."[33] In other words, American class discourse has *helped* produce, circulate, and reinforce the idea and reality of the individual and of individuality. Consequently, the possessive individualism underpinning twentieth-century American class discourse, whereby individuals have been encouraged to "acquire" and perform a variety of characteristics that potentially can distinguish them from the masses, alongside the cult of self that stems from the same source and lionizes individual personalities and attributes, have assisted in spawning the individuated subject and in making him/her recognizable qua individual.

It is in large part due to Sonya's belief in upward mobility and the American Dream that she is able to say, "*I* am *I* . . . In me is my strength. I alone will yet beat them all" (162, emphasis added). Sonya's belief in her own strength, in the power of her own will, enables her to differentiate herself from her acquaintances. Her project of bettering herself entails leaving acquaintances such as Gittel Stein and Lipkin behind. Gittel, resigned to poverty and unable to take her fate into her own hands, is not a desirable companion for Sonya, who does everything she can in order to change and overcome her circumstances. The text points to the entrenched U.S. belief that resignation is something one chooses; things might have been different for Gittel had she empowered herself with a belief that she could change her lot. "[W]hy should I hate [Sonya] simply because she stretches out her hands to life as I'd like to do, if I only had it in me!" Gittel is described as asking herself (11). Gittel, on the one hand, is described as envying Sonya, which points to her desire to become more like her colleague and thus highlights the way in which the "desire-to-be" helps shape and comes into play even with subjects who fail to live up to middle-class norms. On the other hand, her lack of "willpower" seems to warrant and justify her static and gray existence.

In Sonya's eyes, the poet Lipkin is also a pathetic character: "Try as she would to be sympathetic, he only exasperated her" (69); she has no patience for his acceptance of poverty and his general submissiveness. "Everything comes to him who goes to fetch it," is Sonya Vrunsky's motto; people who do not manage to "pull themselves up by the bootstraps" have only themselves to blame (41). Here we see not only the intricate ways in which individualism is linked to hard work, willpower, and thus to upper mobility, but also the moral tinge of this linkage. People who fail are presumed to lack talent, will, or moral uprightness. The American Dream discourse very clearly helps to "recode social problems as individual problems with individual solutions."[34] Success or failure to live up to the norm of the "higher life," where the "luxuries of love, beauty" abound, accordingly, is contingent on the individual, thereby bringing not the group but the individual—with all of his/her talents, abilities, and attributes or lack thereof—into sharp focus. Interestingly, Gittel and Lipkin are only individuated to a certain extent in the story. The narrative intimates that their failure to rise above the prison of poverty is due (at least in large part) to their own personal and individual failings. However, unlike Sonya, Jaky, and even John Manning, their personalities are indistinct, and the narrative has them fall back into the anonymous depths of poverty.

As we have seen, hegemonic discourse seems, on the one hand, to hold out the promise of upward mobility to all and sundry. With determination and hard work, there does not seem to be any reason why one cannot better (and individuate) oneself. The possibility of moving into the middle class is something that seems to be realizable even to the newest and poorest immigrant. On the other hand, the cult of the self also encourages the belief in individual talent and genius, and emphasizes the need to "fulfill individual potential."

All three of Yezierska's major novels from the same period incorporate these contradictory strains of dominant U.S. class discourse, which is another reason that her texts can be seen to provide important insights into the operation of such discourse in the twentieth century. Sara Smolinsky of *Bread Givers* and Adele Lindner of *Arrogant Beggar* are poor working-class Jewish protagonists (Sara is an immigrant while Adele is the child of immigrants) who, due to their hard work *and* undeniable talent, succeed in "making it." Sara is a gifted writer and becomes a public school teacher, while Adele turns out to be a very talented cook and businesswoman.

In *Salome of the Tenements*, Sonya and Jaky work hard and have the will to succeed, but they also are described as having redoubtable talent, Jaky as a "virtuoso" and Sonya as an "unfolding genius" (17, 174). This tension, I believe, has played an important part in preserving the status quo and effectively serves to explain why, at the end of the day, many people like Gittel and Lipkin find themselves trapped in and by their class. For, while the discourse has circulated the belief that it is possible for anyone to move up the class hierarchy, the caveats on exceptional talent alongside the emphasis on personal qualities that make an individual worthy of upward mobility work to help justify why certain subjects manage to "better" themselves while most people are unable to do so. Hard work and determination are necessary but insufficient conditions for transforming oneself into an outstanding individual—one also needs talent.

Sonya's dislike of the settlement house project accordingly is related not merely to its attempt to enforce "the Gospel of Simplicity" and the emulation of Anglo-American upper- and middle-class norms. Rather, it also is connected intricately to her objection to the project's attempt to socialize the "worthy poor" in ways that counter the American belief in and desire for individuality.[35] In the novel, all of the institutions for the working poor are described in terms of their lack of "human warmth," of any "touch of individuality" (134, 162). Settlement work, it seems, actually undermines the cult of the self and discourages the notion of unique personalities; it homogenizes the poor rather than encouraging individual self-expression. Charity, which is attached to endless codes of conduct, is opposed to Sonya's individual vibrancy and desire to make it on her own in her own way.[36]

Following Meredith Goldsmith, I contend that Sonya's success and her desire to make beautiful clothes accessible and affordable to working-class women points to Sonya's "internalization of the subtlest, and most insidious, principles of Americanization."[37] By inculcating working-class women into American ideals of beauty, Sonya "unwittingly conscripts" the factory girls into the same repressive ideology. In contrast to Goldsmith, though, I believe the norms that Sonya and Jaky have "internalized" are the ones linked to the "cult of self," in which the ideal of beauty constitutes only one dimension. By returning to the Lower East Side in order to open up a "little shop on Grand Street . . . [B]eauty for those that love it, beauty that is not for profit" (178), Sonya and Jaky are reinforcing—in a subtle but very effective way—the class system and all of the norms associated with it. First, Jaky and Sonya are described as American success stories, and as such their presence on the Lower East Side can be seen to buttress the notion that anyone can live out the American Dream. Second, the democratization of beauty through the creation of a clothing store offers the working class a chance to make *themselves* more beautiful, even while they continue to be exploited in their everyday lives. This democratization diverts attention away from structural inequalities in the United States and allows working men and women to concentrate on their individual self-expression. As we have seen, the idea that each citizen can and should choose and express her/himself as an individual is not only consistent with but foundational to liberalism.

This "cult of self" and emphasis on individuality also manifests itself in Sonya and Jaky's obsession with beauty and aesthetics. Throughout the novel, Sonya rejects the "cheapness of the[se] ready-mades," that is, the mass-produced clothes of the Lower East Side (15). She hungers for clothing that will express her personality, her self. When she convinces Jaky Solomon to design a dress for her lunch with Manning, Yezierska describes Sonya as being intoxicated by the sense of "release from the itching shoddiness of ready-mades—the blotting out of her personality in garments cut by the gross" (33). Jaky shares and reinforces Sonya's belief in the transformative power of clothing. He tells Sonya that she "don't have to be a second-hand pattern of a person—when [she] can be [her] own individual self" (26). Nothing, according to both Jaky and Sonya, is beautiful but "what's intensely personal" (112). Sonya and Jaky's desire for individuated beauty is a clear rejection of mass production and the homogenization process that goes along with it.

By way of conclusion, I would like to address the manner in which these two processes—mass production and individuation—that seem so much at odds, actually reinforce and undergird one another in the

American twentieth-century context. There appears, at first glance, to be a major contradiction in U.S. liberal class discourse, with its particular historical fusion of republicanism, the Protestant ethic, and capitalist accumulation. On the one hand, American class discourse has encouraged capitalist mass production (and settlement work), which tends to produce homogeneity and commonality. On the other hand, the remnants of the Protestant ethic and republicanism have tended to stress the importance of individual self-reliance and accomplishments. Mass production, as Sonya's description of the ready-mades indicates, creates sameness. In many ways, it also offers — parallel to the American Dream — the promise of material well-being to all and sundry, since items are sold at very affordable prices. In other words, it feeds into and reinscribes the notion of "formal" equality. Anyone, it seems, can buy the basic and necessary commodities that allow for the "good life." The leveling aspect of mass production, however, prompts those subjects who wish to distinguish themselves to reject the "shoddiness of the ready-mades" and strike out on their own; obviously, individuation assumes that there is something from which one must distinguish oneself.

This cycle is reminiscent of the tension that I discussed above involving the simultaneous and contradictory claim circulated by American class discourse that there are no classes per se in the United States and that anyone potentially could move up the class ladder. Homogeneity and individuation, upper mobility and classlessness are part and parcel of the same "relationships of force" that Foucault has described. Homogeneity is the condition of possibility of individuation, just as the assumption of the lack of essence vis-à-vis class is the condition of possibility of upper mobility. These tensions operate productively within the same discourse and effectively spawn and manipulate subjects' "desire-to-be." Where sameness is coded as undesirable, individuation and the desire to be exceptional will be encouraged by the hegemonic order. And what all of this teaches us, I believe, is that in order to understand the process of class materialization, we must continue to emphasize the *productive* and *material* nature of discourse.

Chapter Four

Race and the Making of Ethnicity

NELLA LARSEN'S *Passing*, as we saw in Chapter Two, presents us with a fascinating scene in which Irene Redfield "passes" for white so that she can enjoy the cool breezes of the Drayton's roof café. The stare of another woman suddenly makes Irene uncomfortable, and she wonders whether the "rude observer" could possibly know that "before her very eyes on the roof of the Drayton sat a Negro."[1] Irene, however, immediately assures herself that people "always took her for an Italian, a Mexican, or a gipsy." Never when she was alone "had they even remotely seemed to suspect that she was a Negro" (150). While this scene is important for a number of reasons, many of which I already have discussed, here I would like to concentrate on Irene's reflective comment, made as an aside in the text, since it actually brings to the fore some crucial questions concerning the ways in which race and ethnicity have been constructed in the United States and how they have operated as categories of identification. Although Nella Larsen wrote *Passing* in 1929, before "ethnicity" had emerged as an important cultural category to mark difference, the clear distinction that Irene Redfield makes between the Negro and the Italian, Mexican, and gipsy can be seen to presage the development of the term.

The division made between the Negro and other minorities points to at least three aspects of American race discourse that I will be discussing in this chapter. First, racial discourse in the United States has evolved, to a large extent, around an *ideology* of a binary opposition — the black-white divide. The Negro, and not the Italian, the Jew, or even the Mexican, as Irene tells us, has represented the Other of whiteness. Second, racial discourse has created a very patent racial stratification;

while black and white have for the most part served as the reference points and the defining terms, there have been "intermediary" or in-between racial groups. People may have mistaken Irene for an Italian or a Mexican, but they never appeared to suspect she was a Negro. What this suggests, then, is that Italians and Mexicans have been situated differently in the racial hierarchy and have had access to things and places that the Negro has not. As an Italian or Mexican, it seems, Irene would be granted entry to the exclusive Drayton hotel. As a Negro, she would be ejected from the premises. Third, Larsen, wittingly or unwittingly, illustrates how the construction of race and the construction of ethnicity have had very different historical trajectories in the American context. In contradistinction to Werner Sollors' claim that race is merely one aspect of ethnicity, Irene's comment gestures toward the historical *difference* between the racialized status of African Americans and the racial in-betweenness of other minority groups.[2] What have come to be understood as ethnic and racial identities are not ontological essences, but rather, as Robyn Wiegman put its, "powerful fictions that have developed as a result of historical specificities and contingencies which have served as a profound ordering of difference."[3]

Using Larsen's opening scene as a point of entry into the contentious discussion regarding the ways in which the categories of race and ethnicity have operated in the United States, in what follows I compare and contrast Abraham Cahan's *The Rise of David Levinsky* and James Weldon Johnson's *The Autobiography of an Ex-Colored Man*. Written just a few years apart, both novels explicitly query what it means "to be American," and they do so by exploring how "race" affects one's chances of success in Progressive Era America.

As we saw in Chapter One, Cahan's protagonist, David Levinsky, is a poor Jewish immigrant from Russia who continuously strives to "become an American"; he quickly sheds his Orthodox ways, and although he initially aspires to be a man of letters, he eventually abandons this dream to become a cloak manufacturer in New York City. When the reader takes leave of him, he is a millionaire who is acquainted with "hundreds, if not thousands, of merchants, Jews and gentiles, throughout this country and Canada."[4] Johnson's narrator is the "unsanctioned" offspring of a wealthy "white" Southerner and a "black" sewing woman, who only discovers he is "black" during a traumatic experience in grade school. He, too, decides against going to college and travels to New York, where he discovers both ragtime and his ability to make a career playing this nascent form of music. Ultimately, though, after witnessing a man being lynched in the South, the narrator chooses to give up ragtime and "pass" as a "white" man. At the end of the novel, he is also a wealthy and established "white" man in New York City.

Werner Sollors, one of the few critics to do a comparative study of these two novels, sums up the similarities between them in the following way: "Both books depict the externally upward journeys of protagonists from poverty to material success, from ethnic marginality to a more 'American' identity, and from a small-town background to the urban environment of New York."[5] While Sollors underscores the affinities between the two novels, in the subsequent pages I will highlight the differences by culling out and juxtaposing specific scenes from each text — scenes that have certain narrative and/or structural similarities. In this way, I highlight the distinctive modalities of the categories of race and ethnicity as they manifest themselves in these Progressive Era texts.

The Black-White Divide

Law and blood are crucial terms if one wants to understand the particular construction of race in the United States. In *Who is Black?* F. James Davis claims that, "Before World War I it was clear that . . . the one-drop rule would . . . prevail in social practice and in the courts, and in the North as well as the South."[6] He also points out that no other "ethnic" population or minority has ever been defined according to the one-drop rule: "The definition of a black person as one with any trace at all of black African ancestry is inextricably woven into the history of the United States. It incorporates beliefs once used to justify slavery and later used to buttress . . . the Jim Crow system of segregation."[7]

Going back even further in American history, one discovers that already at the end of the eighteenth century the terms of the racial debate were being inscribed into law. The 1790 Naturalization Act stipulated that only "free white persons" could become American citizens. Accordingly, from the very beginning, "the processes of becoming white" and "becoming American" were interconnected. In 1875, ten years after the end of the Civil War, this act was amended in order to allow immigrants and "aliens" to argue for naturalization on the basis of African nativity or descent, thus codifying the increasingly binary racial logic. Sarah Gualtieri points out, however, that during the Progressive Era not one single applicant in the racial prerequisite cases attempted to naturalize on the basis of African nativity or descent[8]; all of the immigrant groups—such as Chinese, Filipino, Japanese— attempted to naturalize as whites.[9]

Contemporary critics have questioned the reliance on the black-white binary as the defining paradigm of racial formation in the United States. In his article, "The Unstable Other: Locating the Jew in Progressive-Era America," Eric Goldstein contends that, despite the black-white dichotomy's power, "it was never a sufficient framework for understanding the much more complex set of categories through which Progressive-Era Americans understood and spoke about race."[10] In addition, Susan Koshy warns us of the dangers of leaving untheorized "the intermediary racial groups" such as Asian Americans.[11]

I certainly agree that racialization has been a complex, uneven, and contingent process in America and that the black-white divide is in no way sufficient to explain how racial categories have operated on the level of social practices. However, I do think we need to understand this binary as part of the workings of cultural hegemony. In effect, the black-white axis has operated to secure the tenuousness of race to a framework of stable boundaries, which in turn provides the necessary grounding for the ideology of white supremacy.[12] As Stuart Hall has argued famously, "The binary is the form of the operation of power, the attempt at closure: power suturing language. It draws frontiers: *you* are inside, but *you* are out."[13]

It is not coincidental that Goldstein and Koshy continue to invoke the black-white divide as a way of *distinguishing* the other discourses surrounding the racial categorization of Asian Americans and Jewish Americans; this, I believe, is revealing. In her article "Category Crisis: South Asian Americans and Questions of Race and Ethnicity," Koshy states, for example, that: "In the United States . . . the history of slavery had developed the meanings of the black-white binary prior to the arrival of immigrant groups." She adds that new immigrants usually have been positioned on an intermediary level in the racial hierarchy and have had to negotiate their racial status, invoking but also changing the signification of whiteness.[14] Goldstein also states that "the black-white discourse was . . . the most central, powerful discourse of otherness employed by white Americans" during the Progressive Era.[15] Moreover,

David Roediger, Noel Ignatiev, Karen Brodkin, Sarah Gualtieri, and others have shown convincingly how different immigrant groups, such as the Irish, the Jews, the Chinese, and the Syrians, endeavored to utilize the hegemonic discourse on race, that is, the black-white dichotomy, in order to position themselves on the white side of the divide.[16] Some, as we know, were more successful than others.

The Train Ride

In what follows, I extract two scenes from *The Autobiography of an Ex-Colored Man* and *The Rise of David Levinsky* in an attempt to illustrate some of the ways in which the black-white divide has operated. Both texts, I argue, reveal the power of the dichotomy, pointing to the ways that it has circumscribed racial logic and categorization. However, they also dramatize the uncertainty surrounding the racial position of the Jew at the turn of the century, which, I believe, can be seen to represent the way in which the hegemonic discourse on race imposed (and produced) ideals of whiteness while simultaneously barring "not-quite-white" minority groups from the privileges of *Anglo-Saxon* whiteness. The binary opposition thus can be seen to serve as a nexus that not only circumscribes racial logic but also spawns what Susan Koshy has termed "stratified minoritization."[17]

In the latter part of the novel, the narrator of *The Autobiography of an Ex-Colored Man* decides that he is interested in pursuing a career as a ragtime musician and travels to the South in order to gather "authentic" material from the rural folk. During one of his train journeys, the narrator describes an interesting encounter among four men in the smoking car. The men — a Jewish cigar manufacturer, a professor from Ohio who teaches in Alabama, an old Union soldier, and a Texan cotton-planter — begin to discuss the "Negro question." The conversation eventually develops into a dialogue between the old Union soldier and the Texan. The Southerner vehemently argues that "[t]he Anglo-Saxon race has always been and always will be the masters of the world" and that the Civil War was a "criminal mistake."[18] The Northerner upholds the "essential rights of men" but simultaneously admits that he wouldn't consent to having his daughter marry a "nigger" (163).

This scene is interesting, I believe, not so much because of the way in which the stereotypical attitudes of the Northerner and the South-

erner are depicted, but rather for what it fails to disclose *and* for the way
the Jew and the narrator himself are positioned as the scene unfolds.
What the narrator does not reveal in his description of this scene is
that the smoking-compartment is, undoubtedly, for whites only. This
is, after all, a portrayal of the Deep South at the turn of the twentieth
century, the heyday of Jim Crow. The narrator is clearly "passing." As a
"black" man, he would be denied access to such a space — a (purport-
edly) all-white and all-male site that can be seen as representative of
hegemonic space. It is only by virtue of his "light skin" and the assumption of whiteness that he is privy to the discussion at all.

In this scene, the white men take center stage, and, as the narrator
indicates, define the terms of the debate: the overt white supremacist
views held by the Texan versus the liberal white paternalism the old
Union soldier advocates. The Jew is present in the compartment and
thus seems to be accepted as white, and, interestingly, he also feels he
has a right to speak. That is, he participates in the discussion, at least
initially, and is even described as commendable in his ability to agree
"with everybody without losing his allegiance to any side" (158). His
position vis-à-vis the dominant culture, though, is not an altogether
unproblematic one, and the Jew's diplomatic introjections reveal his
somewhat precarious situation. He cannot side totally with the white
racist, for this also seemingly would sanction anti-Semitism: "He knew
that to sanction Negro oppression would be to sanction Jewish oppression" (158). On the other hand, the narrator also suggests that the Jew
attempts to differentiate himself from the Negro by agreeing to the
Negro's natural inferiority. The Jew appears to be able to assume a certain kind of white privilege, yet he cannot assume white *Anglo-Saxon*
privilege. His "Jewishness," which he does not attempt to conceal, seems
to stand in the way.[19] The narrator, in stark contrast, not only must conceal his "blackness" but is also silenced; he watches and listens as "the
Negro" is discussed. Moreover, he would not even be present physically
if it were not for his ability to "pass."

It is also on a train ride that Jew meets black in Cahan's *The Rise of
David Levinsky*. After David Levinsky begins to succeed in the manu-
facturing business, he decides to travel cross-country to find additional
buyers for his wares. The description of one of these trips to the Midwest
bears some structural resemblance to the one described above. Again,
the scene unfolds in the smoking car, in which a group of men, both
Jews and gentiles, are discussing a variety of topics. Loeb, a "drummer"

from one of the larger manufacturing outfits, suddenly turns the conversation to the Russian Jews and commences to poke fun at their "foreign" mannerisms. David, who is himself a gesticulating Russian Jew, laughs "with the others," but is described as inwardly writhing with discomfort and anger. He confronts Loeb, asking him why he is making fun of the Jewish people when Loeb himself is a Jew. Loeb readily admits that he is a Jew and a "good one, too," but he doesn't understand what his being Jewish has to do with anything (328).

Both train scenes, I argue, expose that the Jews' position on the white side of the divide cannot yet be taken for granted. The ex-colored man's description of the Jew's equivocation on the "Negro question," and thus his lack of assumption of privilege vis-à-vis the dominant culture, is one indication of his still in-between status. The parallel assumed between anti-black racism and anti-Semitism illustrates that questions of Jewish acceptance into mainstream American culture still revolved around the issue of "race." Loeb's jibes at the Russian Jews due to their marks of difference alongside the scene's description of David's attempt to hide his gesticulating hands and his desire to emulate the "well-dressed American Gentiles" also point to the still precarious or unsettled position of the Jew in relation to the hegemonic white American culture. As Eric Goldstein has argued, the Jew in Progressive-Era America was (still) an unstable and unreliable other.[20]

The train scene in *The Rise of David Levinsky*, however, can be understood as a dramatization of how becoming "American" in turn-of-the-century America required jockeying for a position in relation to the racial reference points.[21] Unlike the Jew in the first scene, who fails to take a stand on the "Negro question," Loeb, who is American born (though the descendent of earlier Jewish immigrants), not only seems to have no trouble revealing his "Jewishness," but also makes a point of ridiculing the Russian Jews in the presence of gentiles. This, I argue, can be read as kind of "white" bonding, an attempt on the part of Loeb to differentiate himself clearly from the more recent arrivals and prove that he is part of the higher echelons in the racial hierarchy. Loeb is simultaneously positioning himself and other American-born Jews closer to the side of the gentiles *and* initiating David into the dominant "white" society, showing him what needs to be done in order to gain not only *admittance* but also *acceptance* into the hegemonic culture. The retention of any kind of Jewish particularism is branded as atavistic. However, as I will discuss below, this scene also reveals that

the embrace of whiteness does not necessarily entail a total disidentification with "Jewishness."

Alongside the "white" bonding, there is also male bonding in the
smoking car scene. Loeb and the other men begin to tell each other
"smutty" stories and "there ensued an orgy of obscenity that kept" the
men shouting (328). The sexualized interaction between Jew and non-
Jew is striking and in stark contrast to the train scene with the old but
"liberal" Northern soldier who would not consent to have his daughter
marry a "nigger," thereby underscoring the way in which white racist
discourse has produced and reinforced a fear of "black sexuality" —
especially black male sexuality — and outlawed miscegenation.[22]

In this all-male hegemonic space, the Jew is literally and metaphori-
cally both inside and outside. David listens and laughs at the others'
stories, but he does not participate actively. Loeb's more secure relationship to the dominant white and Gentile culture seems to suggest
that once the Jews leave their foreign ways behind, there is a great likelihood that they will be recognized as "full-blooded whites." It is no
coincidence that the "deformity" that Loeb believes marks the Russian
Jew is a form of gesticulation, one that Loeb himself claims to be free
from. That is, the Russian Jew is being made fun of not so much due to
any kind of perceived natural or essential inferiority, but rather due to
his outward and therefore dispensable signs of foreignness.

Toward the end of this scene, the men — Gentiles and Jews — enter
the dining car together. David describes this repast as filling him with
pleasure: "The electric lights . . . The easy urbanity of the three well-
dressed Americans . . . [T]he whiteness of the table linen, [and] the silent
efficiency of the colored waiters . . . gave me a sense of uncanny gentility and bliss" (330). This is the first and last time a black man appears
on the scene. The presence of the silent and silenced black servant is
contrasted with the whiteness of the table linen — and thus metonymi-
cally with the four or five "white" men eating at the table. This contrast,
(which may be incidental but is certainly fraught with meaning), serves
as a background for, and I would argue, *facilitates* the Jew's negotiation
of his racial positioning. In other words, this scene is a dramatization
of the way in which "Negroes" historically have served as the "other"
against which a "popular sense of Whiteness, which cut across ethnicity . . . could be generated."[23] Whereas the Jew is portrayed in both
scenes as a "middleman minority," it seems that his acceptance into
symbolic whiteness is well on the way.

Career Crises and American Identification Scenes

The two novels also portray the historical *difference* between the racialized status of African Americans and the racial in-betweenness of other minority groups, many of which "became white" by the end of World War II. Certain scenes suggest that the "racial" history of European immigration is irreducible to African-American "racial" history. Although I would hesitate to reduce the development of the United States' particular race regime to the history of slavery, scholars such as Vilna Bashi and Antonio McDaniel and A. Smedley are right to point to slavery as *one* of the major causes that has spawned a specific regime of racial knowledge and categorization, one that enabled turn-of-the-century European immigrants to carve out an alternative "racial" category that became what we understand today as ethnicity.[24] The concept of ethnicity, I argue, emerged out of the carefully policed hegemonic racial hierarchy that positioned "whites" on top and "blacks" on the bottom.[25] Susan Koshy argues that while the morphing of race into ethnicity has been possible for intermediary racial groups and has functioned to open up an avenue and affiliation with whiteness, "this transformation has been less possible for blacks."[26] I would go further and say that morphing race into ethnicity has not been possible for African Americans at all, since the intelligibility of ethnicity depends on the prior construction of black-white binary opposition. This point is crucial.

In both novels, the protagonists decide to abandon their dreams of attending college due to fortuitous circumstances. David blames his decision on spilt milk: "One day, at the lunch hour, as I was opening a small bottle of milk, the bottle slipped out of my hand and its contents were spilled over the floor and some silk coats" (187). This incident, "a mere trifle," the narrator tells us, "gave a new turn to the trend of events, changing the character of my whole life" (187). At the time, he is working for a German firm as a cloak operator. And when one of the employers sees the spilt milk, he flies into a rage. David is resentful of both the abusive language that his employer uses and the pay cut that he is forced to take. It is at this juncture that David begins contemplating setting up shop on his own.

The ex-colored man's decision, on the other hand, is all but made for him. The day before he is to begin attending classes at Atlanta University, he discovers that someone has stolen all of his money. He is left "in a strange city without money or friends" (63) and is forced to leave for Jacksonville that very night, abandoning forever his dream of obtaining a college degree. It is in the course of the pursuit of careers that the narratives diverge; and it is the description of the trajectories of these two protagonists that dramatizes some of the ways in which the historical construction of race and the construction of ethnicity have differed in the U.S. context.

David Levinsky's path to material success is not without its hardships and obstacles. As he endeavors to find both wealthy sponsors and firms willing to buy his samples, he encounters different forms of anti-Semitism. On the one hand, he is discriminated against by his German-Jewish employers, who tend to treat the more recent arrivals as "an inferior race" (187). On the other hand, the gentile cloak-manufacturing world "had not yet learned to take the Russian Jew seriously as a factor in advanced commerce" (206), and David's Russian name and his appearance work against him. According to David's description of his world, there is a very clear "racial" hierarchy: Russian Jews curry favor with the German Jews because the older immigrants are higher up on the ladder. "But then German-American Jews curry favor with Portuguese-American Jews, just as we all curry favor with Gentiles" (528). None of these setbacks or prejudices, however, keep him down for long. He is determined to make it, and he is willing to do almost anything to succeed, including waylaying potential buyers and exploiting his workers.

The scene that I would like to discuss in this context is one that occurs toward the end of the novel. David is already a successful businessman, and he is about to be married. However, on his way to visit his bride-to-be's family in the country, he stops overnight at a Jewish resort in upstate New York. The Jews who are present at the resort are "people who had blossomed out into nabobs in the course of the last few years." And the "bulk of the boarders . . . was made up of families of cloak-manufacturers, shirt-manufacturers, ladies'-waist-manufacturers, cigar-manufacturers, clothiers, furriers, jewelers, leather-goods men, real-estate men, physicians, dentists, lawyers" (404). Presumably most of the visitors are also Russian Jews. In her *How Jews Became White Folks*, Karen Brodkin point out that:

Compared with other immigrants, Jews were upwardly mobile. But compared with nonimmigrant whites, that mobility was . . . circumscribed. The existence of . . . anti-Semitic barriers kept the Jewish middle class confined to a small number of occupations. Jews were excluded from mainstream corporate management and corporately employed professions, except in the garment and movie industries, in which they were pioneers. Jews were almost totally excluded from university faculties. Eastern European Jews were concentrated in small businesses, and in professions where they served a largely Jewish clientele.[27]

Cahan's depiction of these immigrants is evocative, for he describes them as both upwardly mobile *and* as holding very specific and non-corporate jobs. In this way, he is (wittingly or unwittingly) buttressing the notion that Jews were upwardly mobile in the Progressive Era and — through the detailed listing of the various occupations — laying bare which professions were open to Jewish immigrants at the time. Thus, if we read this scene for a moment as a slice of social history, we see that acceptance into mainstream America for these immigrants was partial and that clear hierarchies existed not only between black and white, but also among whites and not-quite whites. This system of differences among the "white" and "off-white" groups worked in conjunction with the black-white dichotomy to create a complex and contingent hierarchy that was not only based on "race" but would come to be based on "ethnicity" as well.

During the evening meal, the conductor who is playing music for ambiance suddenly strikes up the "Star-Spangled Banner." The reader is told that "[t]he effect was overwhelming. The few hundred diners rose like one man, applauding . . . Men and women were offering thanksgiving to the flag under which they were eating this good dinner, wearing these expensive clothes." David describes the reaction of the Jewish diners in the following way: "It was as if they were saying: 'We are not persecuted under the flag. At last we have found a home'" (424). And it is David himself who asks the musicians to play "America," and when they do, all of the diners are portrayed as singing the anthem from the bottom of their souls. The portrayal of the Jews' relationship to the dominant culture symbolized by the national anthem and "America" is important, I believe. The anthem and "America" strike a resonant cord in the hearts of the diners, and they are depicted as viewing America not only as their country but also as a place in which they can fulfill their potential in (relative) peace. The immigrants identify with the United States and the ideals it represents. Interestingly, their very dramatic and emotional identification with America is complicated by the fact that the dining hall is an all-Jewish space. I return to this point in the final section.

Music is representative of America in James Weldon Johnson's novel as well. The protagonist, after escaping to Europe with a millionaire patron and passing for "white," finally decides to return to the United States. He feels the need to return to his native land and make a "better future" for himself by cultivating a career in "black" classical music. Through the creation and performing of this new music, the protagonist believes he can "voice all the joys and sorrow, the hopes and ambitions, of the American Negro" (147–48). Whereas, for the Jewish immigrants described above, the national anthem and "America" serve as sites of relatively unproblematic identification with the United States, in *The Autobiography of an Ex-Colored Man*, this is not the case. The historical trajectory of the American Negro, it appears, has to be represented elsewhere, for the tyrannical hand of *racism* still smites. According to the narrator, it is ragtime, slave songs, and the like, that convey what it means to be both American and Negro.[28]

The scene that I would like discuss takes place as the ex-colored man searches for "authentic material" in the South, that is, as he is "trying to catch the spirit of the Negro in his relatively primitive state" (173). He is just about to return to one of the larger Southern cities to begin composing and performing when he is invited to spend the night in a small rural town. During the night, while he is working on his music, he hears the murmur of voices and the gallop of horses outside his window; he overhears the rumor that "some terrible crime had been committed." The narrator is agitated and cannot stay indoors, so he ventures out where he stays until the break of day. At noon, a "black man" is brought to the railroad station: "half dragged, the poor wretch made his way through the dust." Following the crowd's "suggestion" that the man be burned, a "railroad tie was sunk into the ground . . . and a chain brought and securely coiled round the victim and the stake. There he stood, a man only in form and stature, every sign of degeneracy stamped upon his countenance" (186). He is burned at the stake, and the narrator stands powerless to take his eyes from what he does not want to see (187).

It is in the aftermath of this horrific sight that the protagonist decides to renounce his dreams of a musical career and "forsake [his] race." He describes his decision as one determined not by discouragement or fear or a desire for "a larger field of opportunity," but rather by shame: "I knew it was shame at being identified with a people that could with impunity be treated worse than animals. For certainly the law would restrain and punish the malicious burning alive of animals" (191). The narrator, left alone after this trauma, rails against the United States. He is ashamed of his country, ashamed that "the great example of democracy to the world should be the only civilized, if not the only state on earth, where a human being would be burned alive. My heart turned bitter within me" (188). Unlike his Jewish counterparts in the dining scene, here the protagonist is not served choice meat but rather burnt flesh. He cannot declaim the lines, "We are not persecuted under the flag. At last we have found a home." The American Dream and the possibility of upward mobility, he is forced to acknowledge, have in many ways come at the expense of the American Negro. The protagonist's decision to abandon his quest to create "black" classical music and return to New York is a dramatization of this realization. He decides that he is "not going to be a Negro," and this *enables* him to avail himself "of every possible opportunity to make a white man's success; and that, if it can be summed up in any one word, means 'money'" (193). His apparent desire is to disprove the prevalent racist belief that "one drop of Negro blood renders a man unfit" (197). The paradox, of course, is that once he crosses over to the other side he cannot reveal — for fear of reprisal — his one drop of black blood to the outside world.

Ethnicity and Race: The Performative Difference

If race and ethnicity are indeed cultural "fictions," which have their own specific histories, how then have they come to operate as categories of identification, that is, as one of the hegemonic categories of identification through which subjects become intelligible as subjects? In this last section, I would like to suggest that we must reconceptualize race and ethnicity as particular modalities of performativity.

As I have already argued, precisely because the different categories of identification, such as race, class and gender, are not identical and have their own particular genealogies, we need to begin thinking of each category as producing specific modalities of performativity. The way in which these modalities of performativity are produced, however, cannot be reduced to the varying norms attached to each category. Rather,

I have argued that the categories operate, in large part, by producing and encouraging a certain relationship between the subject's identification and "the desire-to-be." In terms of performativity, then, both *The Autobiography of an Ex-Colored Man* and *The Rise of David Levinsky* reveal the coercive aspect of subjects' interpellation and the complex relationship between identification and the desire-to-be.

The ex-colored man is interpellated into society as "white." The protagonist's mother has never discussed the issue of race with him, and consequently he has never been told that he is "black" according to the existent one-drop rule. Rather, immersed as he is within a culture in which there is an assumption of whiteness, he too assumes he is "white." But early on, the narrator experiences a "corrective," as it were, where he is (re)interpolated into society as a "black" man even though he "looks white."

One day during his second term at school, the principal enters the protagonist's classroom, asking all of the white children to stand. The narrator stands with the rest of the "white" children, only to be told that he needs to "sit down for the present, and rise with the *others*" (16, emphasis added). He leaves school in a stupor, while a few of the boys jeer at him. This experience stamps itself in the narrator's memory (20); indeed, the ex-colored man describes this interpellation into the American race regime as a tragedy. He tells us from "that time I looked out through other eyes, my thoughts were colored, my words *dictated*, my actions by one dominating, all pervading idea which constantly increased in *force* and *weight*" (21, emphasis added). Thus, the narrator's interpellation scene underscores both the way in which whiteness serves as the unmarked norm and how race, as a category of identification, is something that historically has been coerced. Being interpellated into the race regime, the narrator claims "is the dwarfing, warping, distorting influence which operates upon each and every colored man in the United States. He is *forced* to take his outlook on all things, not from the view-point of a citizen, or a man, or even a human being, but from the view point of a colored man" (21, emphasis added). For if race is one of the axes along which differentiation and stratification revolves, then the interpellation into the dominant social order as a raced subject is crucial for the workings of power and more particularly, for the grounding of white supremacy.

James Weldon Johnson depicts his young narrator's struggle to come to terms with his new position in the social world. On the one hand,

Johnson reveals the way in which racist regimes compel and encourage subjects' to desire to live up to norms associated with whiteness. Throughout his childhood, the narrator distances himself from the other black children in his school, as he "had a very strong aversion to being classed with them" (23). His best friend is Red, a white boy, and his first love a white woman. But Johnson also shows us how in social practice this compulsion to "desire to be white" is always much more complex and conflictual. Here I would like to mention briefly a few of the ways that Johnson problematizes the hegemonic identification/desire-to-be nexus and demonstrates the way in which norms never totally determine the subject.

Racial norms, to be sure, are spawned by a particular configuration of power relations, and these norms both are the condition of possibility of viable subjects, and help produce and shape the subject's very preference and aspirations, desire and identification. This does not mean, however, that subjects are merely docile bodies, but rather, subjects can and do disidentify with dominant norms. The ex-colored man's desire-to-be, I argue, is influenced strongly by the norms of whiteness. As we have seen above, he does not associate with other black children in his adolescence. And throughout the text, norms associated with whiteness prove difficult to abjure. His multi-tiered classification of African Americans reveals his belief in "uplift," "progress" and "civilization," all terms which in the U.S. context inevitably reinscribe American Anglo-Saxon whiteness as the pinnacle of civilization.

However, as soon as he "discovers" that he is "black" and is forced to identify as such, his "desire-to-be" fluctuates. Before his interpellation into the race regime as a "black" man, his heroes are King David and Robert the Bruce, but subsequently he discovers Frederick Douglass and Alexandre Dumas. He begins to dream of "bringing glory and honor to the Negro race . . . to be a great man, a great *colored* man, to reflect credit on the race and gain fame for myself" (46, emphasis added). Later in the novel, he describes his desire to become a famous "black" composer — even after his millionaire patron offers to help him become a famous "*white*" European musician. The desire to be a famous "black" composer reveals the partial abjuration of white norms. And what this apparent embrace of his blackness points to, I believe, is that coerced identification also can have productive subject effects, in the sense that subjects can and do perform regulatory ideals in contestatory ways. By "choosing" to continue identifying as "black" and becoming a famous "black" composer, the protagonist is thwarting the hegemon's injunction to desire whiteness.[29] This is particularly powerful since the protagonist "looks white"; thus, his insistence on the desirability of blackness potentially can disrupt hegemonic discourse. On the other hand, his desire to be a famous colored composer cannot be separated totally from hegemonic norms. It is quite revealing, I believe, that the narrator tells us that he wishes to voice all the joys and sorrows of the American Negro in "*classical* musical form" (148, emphasis added).[30]

Ultimately, however, Johnson dramatically illustrates just how difficult it has been to identify concurrently as black and desire to live up to norms associated with blackness, *and maintain a nonmarginal existence* — that is, to maintain one's already precarious (by virtue of being interpellated as black) access to privilege and positions of power. In effect, by re-linking identification and desire-to-be, one (potentially) relinquishes all claims to being American, since "being American" and "becoming white," as many scholars have argued, historically have been coterminous.[31] This is dramatized powerfully in the lynching scene discussed above. The ex-colored man describes the black man who is about to be burned as having "every sign of *degeneracy* stamped upon his countenance" (186, emphasis added). If the hegemonic discourse on race has produced and reinforced a linking of specific attributes to whiteness (civilized/intelligent/moral/hardworking) and blackness (savage/instinctual/simple/licentious/lazy), then I believe we can read the description of this condemned man as the protagonist's realization of the punishment meted out to subjects who attempt to embody blackness. The condemned man, in the eyes of the narrator, has strived to embody at least some of the "degenerate" attributes the hegemon has concatenated to "blackness." It is no coincidence that the narrator decides to abandon his attempt to live up to norms associated with "blackness," that is, "black" music, at this juncture. Witnessing this brutal and inhumane act is not the only impetus for the protagonist's decision, however. Rather, the narrator's recognition that the attempt to identify with blackness *and* live up to norms that have been concatenated artificially to blackness in the service of social hierarchies, leaves one open to potentially lethal violence *as well as* to almost inevitable marginalization also informs his "choice."[32] After all, we are told that the ex-colored man wants desperately to distinguish himself and make a successful future and career for himself (147). He comes to the conclusion that the only way to access some of the things he desires is through a total disidentification with blackness. Thus, in the end, the protagonist decides to make a "white man's success," and eventually marries a woman who is "white as a lily" (198).

David Levinsky's interpellation into American society is dramatic as well, but for different reasons. The first American whom David and Gitelson—a Jew who has come to America on the same ship— encounter after leaving the docking port at Castle Garden is a policeman. In a fascinating reversal of the Althussarian interpellation scene, the immigrant hails the policeman, but the policeman does not understand the address since David speaks in Yiddish. What this interaction shows, I believe, is that although these Jews clearly can enter America, they are interpellated as foreigners, and the policeman's "witheringly dignified grimace" suggests that they are not particularly welcome foreigners (90).

A moment later, though, the two men are themselves hailed by a voice in Yiddish. It is here that David is given his first lesson in Americanization and American values. This new acquaintance reassures the two neophytes that "[i]f a fellow isn't lazy nor a fool he has no reason to be sorry he came to America" (91). That is, the two new immigrants are introduced to the American Dream—the "white man's success"— and to the notion that "Jewishness" should not constitute an obstacle to such success. With this brief but meaningful initiation, the man who has hailed the immigrants offers Gitelson a job and leaves David to his own devices. The next incident occurs just a few minutes later, following David's discovery of the Jewish Lower East Side. As he walks down the street, he hears people call him a "green one." While this annoys him, he also recognizes that the passersby are witnessing "a second birth . . . an experience which they had gone through themselves and which was one of the greatest events in their lives" (93).

Similar to the interpellation scenes in *The Autobiography of an Ex-Colored Man*, David's (re)interpellation into American society is described as something over which the protagonist does not have control. The description of David's initiation into society points to the way in which subjects only gain intelligibility by passing through, as it were, the matrix of already existing categories of identification. In addition, Abraham Cahan, like James Weldon Johnson, dramatizes just how powerful the "desire-to-be" white is, for he consistently emphasizes his character's desire to act and dress "like a genteel American" (260). These genteel Americans are both "gentile" and "white," for these two terms are interchangeable in the text just as they were during the Progressive Era. Thus, David Levinsky's desire to live up to the norms of whiteness is exposed every time he reveals his desire to be a "true American": "I was forever watching and striving to imitate the dress and the ways of well-bred American[s]" (260).

The scene of David's interpellation, however, is also revealing for what it suggests about the way "Jewish" difference was being reconstituted during this period. The policeman's incomprehension, grimace, and dismissive gesture alongside the hailing of the newcomers by a Yiddish-speaking Jew all suggest that David is interpellated into his new country as a foreigner and a Jew. What this, in turn, points to is that, due to specific but complex historical contingencies, such as the naturalization of Jews throughout the nineteenth century as "free white persons" and their subsequent economic success in certain areas, alongside the increasingly dichotomized racial discourse, by the turn of the century Jewish immigrants were initiated into American society as *both* "whites" and "Jews." The in-between racial status of the Jew, which the scenes in the first section of this chapter dramatize, can be seen as a result of the still undifferentiated and seemingly contradictory status of these two (compelled) categories of identification, since Jewishness was still being framed within a racial discourse. In other words, if you were racially a Jew, then it was questionable whether you could simultaneously be a full-blooded white.

But Abraham Cahan's text also can be read as a narrativization of the way in which "Jewishness" was beginning to be disaggregated from "race" and morphed onto "ethnicity." This process, of course, was just beginning, and this separation was not complete until the middle of the twentieth century.[33] At the end of the novel, Cahan has David boast about the hundreds if not thousands of acquaintances he has around the country—both Jews and *gentiles* (524, emphasis added). It seems he has been accepted into the elite "white" national network of cloak-and-suit manufacturers (3).[34] On the other hand, David ultimately decides against marrying a gentile woman; while he ascribes his decision to the "medieval prejudice against [the Jews], which makes so many marriages between Jew and Gentile a failure," his choice—and the text describes it as a choice—also can be seen as a continued identification with "Jewishness," despite, or perhaps because of, his relative success in approximating the dominant norms of whiteness (527).

Not only does "Jewishness" begin to emerge as a separate category of identification from race in Cahan's text, but it also appears to work differently on the level of identification. Unlike the ex-colored man, who ultimately totally disidentifies with blackness in order to make a "white" man's success, David does not renounce his "Jewish" identity in order to enter and succeed in hegemonic American society. One of the reasons for this, I believe, lies in the dominant equation of Americanness with whiteness. Due to the dominant racial discourse and other historical contingencies, the subject who was interpellated as an off-white (or not quite white or probationary white) Jew was able to "craft a social identity . . . that would not interfere with their acceptance as white."[35] And, as whites-to-be, these subjects ultimately were able and encouraged to identify fully with Americanness. For the subject who was interpellated into the United States' white racist regime as "black," however, the only way that s/he could access some of the privileges of whiteness was through the emulation of the regulatory ideals of whiteness. But, in a sense, s/he historically was not "allowed" to identify fully as an American, according to the hegemonic definition, because s/he was compelled to identify as "black." And since emulating "Americanness" historically has entailed both an identification with and a desire to live up to the norms of whiteness that have come to be associated with Americanness, the men and women interpellated as "black" have— a priori—been excluded from full membership.

Conclusion

By way of conclusion, I would like to suggest that the nascent disaggregation of "Jewishness" and "whiteness" (and thus race) that Cahan and Johnson gesture toward in their literary works is prescient. While the discrimination against different minority and immigrant groups was particularly salient in the 1920s, the changing political, social, and cultural landscape was beginning to produce a different kind of racial regime. As Matthew Jacobson claims, "The period from the 1920s to the 1960s saw a dramatic decline in the perceived differences among . . . white[s] . . . Reduced immigration . . . paired with internal black migrations altered the nation's racial alchemy . . . in effect creating 'Caucasians' where before had been so many Celts, Hebrews, Teutons, Slavs, and the like."[36]

In other words, in the aftermath of World War II, a new racial regime emerged, one that has been characterized by the sharpening of the white-black dichotomy, the emergence of a more comprehensive "white ethnicity," and the coalescing of new in-between minority groups, such as Latino/as and Asian Americans, who, according to Susan Koshy, currently are being interpellated as potential "whites-to-be."[37] The development of the category of ethnicity, then, has to be understood in relation to the changing racial landscape in America. Ethnicity as a category of identification has evolved out of a discourse of race, which itself has revolved around the poles of whiteness and blackness.[38]

I agree, then, with Matthew Jacobson's claim that the "vicissitude of Jewish whiteness is intimately related to the racial odysseys of myriad other groups—the Irish, Armenians, Italians, . . ." However, I do not want to elide the historical specificities of the different immigrant groups' experiences vis-à-vis the dominant culture. The religious dimension of "Jewishness," which is not necessarily captured under the rubric "ethnicity," has complicated "Jewish" subjects' relationship to the dominant culture. I therefore would like to underscore another point that Jacobson makes in his *Whiteness of Another Color*: "If Jewishness never faded altogether as a social distinction, it did fade considerably . . . as a *racial* one."[39] In other words, while distinctions among the "white ethnics" still exist, they are not considered racial ones.

Ethnicity, then, has emerged as a category that both unites "whites" and differentiates the various groups that have been linked under the rubric "whiteness." Although it may be true that the development of a comprehensive "white ethnicity" has meant that ethnicity has come to play a less important role in the lives and life chances of *certain* individuals or groups of European ancestry, it still remains a powerful category of identification and consequently a nexus of positive and negative power in the United States.[40] Susan Koshy convincingly argues that the invocation of ethnicity for newer immigrant groups can function as an avenue of social mobility and affiliation with whiteness.[41] And, as history teaches us, whiteness has "operated as a dynamic category whose boundaries have been progressively expanding."[42] New in-between groups are being incorporated into the social body as "white" or probational "white ethnics," thereby reorganizing the ethnic divide.[43] The social contours of ethnicity currently are changing; historically significant divisions are in some cases receding, while other divisions are developing. Therefore, it is not that ethnicity as a category of identification is necessarily disappearing, but rather that different kinds of "ethnic" differences are being produced and reinforced. Ethnicity has emerged as an alternative to or separate category from race, one which allows and encourages "ethnics" to carve out a white (and thus American) identity.

My claim in this chapter has been twofold. First, ethnicity as a category of identification evolved *out of* a discourse of race, that is, the very intelligibility of ethnicity in the United States depends on the prior construction of the black-white divide. Consequently, one cannot understand how ethnicity emerged without taking into account the black-white dichotomy. Second, ethnicity and race need to be reconceptualized as distinct modalities of performativity, since these two categories have operated differently on the level of identification and the desire-to-be. A black subject was not able to identify as white (or if he/she did, it constituted a transgression), and yet that same subject was compelled and urged to desire to live up to norms of whiteness. Jews, even though they historically were interpellated as off-white, were allowed to identify as white (and this identification did not constitute a transgression nor was it punished) while simultaneously compelled and urged to desire to emulate norms linked to whiteness. In the United States then, "being Jewish" or identifying as Jewish historically did not interfere with identifying as an American. I have argued that, historically, "being black," did.

In Nella Larsen's *Passing*, one of the characters tells the protagonist, Irene Redfield, a story about how an old and mutual acquaintance has converted to Judaism. She launches into the story of how he "was no longer a Negro . . . but had become a Jew" (169). "Jewishness" is here connected to race; the black man who "becomes a Jew" is no longer a "black" man because the Jew is *not* "black."[44] However, the three "white-enough to-pass" women who participate in the conversation are surprised and even a bit bewildered by this man's "turning into a Jew"; the social status of this black-man-turned Jew, it seems, is not a clear-cut one. Clare Kendry registers and encapsulates the ambivalent position of their old acquaintance in her reaction to the story: "It certainly sounds funny enough . . . Still, . . . [I]f he *gets along better* by turning [into a Jew]" (169, emphasis added). Although Clare never finishes the thought, the gist of this comment is clear given the context in which it is voiced — a conversation about the desirability of whiteness. On the one hand, the desire to become a Jew is odd, since "Jewishness" is not considered normative. On the other hand, becoming a "Jew" seems to carry with it certain privileges. The black-man-turned Jew, as Larsen indicates, has "something to gain" from the transformation. This scene, I believe, reminds us that the categories of race and ethnicity have had different but intimately related trajectories in the U.S. context. Perhaps this passage can be read as a literal and metaphorical exposé of the way in which the emergence of American ethnicity has depended on the *prior* racialization of "Negroes."

Chapter Five

Race and the New Woman

W HEN WE FIRST ENCOUNTER Helga Crane, the protagonist of
Nella Larsen's 1928 novel *Quicksand*, she is a teacher in the black
southern educational institution Naxos. Helga originally had trav-
eled south, we are told, with the hope of "doing good," but she very
quickly realizes that Naxos had "grown into a machine . . . cutting all
to a pattern, the white man's pattern."[1] Her disillusionment with Naxos
and her sudden decision to leave in the middle of the semester cata-
pult Helga into the harsh reality of Chicago. Yet, despite her seemingly
limited options as a black woman alone in a big metropolis, Helga not
only manages to survive in the windy city, but throughout the novel she
demonstrates a remarkable ability to negotiate between the different
constraints imposed on her in order to create spaces in which she can
live — if only for very short periods of time — with a "sense of freedom"
and contentment (46).

The protagonist of Anzia Yezierska's 1927 novel *Arrogant Beggar*,
Adele Lindner, is the child of poor Eastern-European Jewish immigrants. She refuses to accept poverty as her fate, though, and sets out
to find a place where a girl "had a right to breathe and move around
like a free human being."[2] Similar to Helga Crane, Adele endeavors to
find fulfillment in an established institution, the Hellman Home for
Working Girls. And like Helga, Adele ultimately is disenchanted by the
"soldier's routine" and hypocrisy that characterize life in the institution (26). Caught between her ties to the Jewish Lower East Side and
her desire to "rise in the world" (49), Adele also is forced to negotiate
the various constraints imposed upon her as a working-class Jewish
woman. However, despite the many parallels between the two novels,

Adele, unlike her literary counterpart, manages to find a way to thrive. At the end of *Arrogant Beggar*, she is the owner of her own restaurant-café, has created a community and is happily married. In sharp contrast, at the conclusion of *Quicksand*, Helga is living in severe poverty, has come to despise her husband, and is about to give birth to her fifth child, which, as the text suggests, will most likely kill her.

Both *Quicksand* and *Arrogant Beggar* are clearly narratives about young women who are searching for self-realization. This is already a significant fact, often overlooked in the literary criticism. The depiction of female protagonists attempting to live out the American Dream of independence, "making it on one's own," and self-fulfillment was still a relatively new phenomenon in the Jazz Age, and, as Elizabeth Ammons has argued, reflected the dramatic social changes transpiring in relation to gender roles in the early-twentieth-century United States. Ammons attributes the development of this new genre — women novelists writing about female self-determination — to the emergent ideal or norm of the New Woman.[3]

Cultural historian Kathy Peiss outlines two constitutive but sometimes conflicting aspects of the early-twentieth-century image of the New Woman: the political and professional woman and the sensual, free-spirited girl.[4] Indeed, the dramatic influx of white *middle-class* women into the paid work force during the first decades of the twentieth century testifies to the tremendous changes taking place in society's relationship to women in the public sphere.[5] And, as Lois Rudnick adds, the second generation of the New Woman, born in the 1910s, was generally more interested than her foremothers in sexual freedom and in redefining a world in which both women and men could have love and meaningful work while helping to shape a more humane social system.[6] Although many scholars have pointed to the unstable and shifting definition of the New Woman, a more open sexuality tied to some kind of professional career or public presence appears to be tied inextricably to dominant images of this ideal during the latter part of the Progressive Era and into the Jazz Age.[7]

Interestingly, the New Woman is never evoked explicitly in either Larsen's *Quicksand* or Yezierska's *Arrogant Beggar*. Yet I believe this ideal is a glaringly absent presence in both novels. I suggest that in order to make sense of the radically different narrative trajectories of Helga Crane and Adele Lindner, it is important not only to take the New Woman ideal into account, but also to examine how "race" complicates the protagonists' relation to this gender norm. Whereas Adele is "allowed" to emulate the New Woman ideal, Helga is depicted as ultimately unable to approximate this ideal because, as I will argue, it precluded black women by its very definition. In this chapter, I will begin to complicate my previous isolation of the categories of identification by looking at the ways in which norms of gender, race and class interact and contaminate one another in social praxis: I offer a theoretical discussion of this "interaction" in the next chapter.

Quicksand, I argue, underscores that middle-class black women were neither encouraged nor permitted to approximate the dominant New Woman ideal, because of its particular linkage of public space and sexuality. Instead, these women were urged to emulate another emergent ideal circulating within the black middle-class community—the New Negro Woman. This ideal, however, entailed the repression of sexuality and concatenated presence in the public space with a *de-sexualization*. Helga's tragedy accordingly can be read as her desire and ultimate inability to find a space in which she can successfully combine sexuality with a meaningful independent and public existence. While the promise of self-fulfillment "embodied" in the New Woman ideal appeared realizable for "off-white" Jewish-American woman, it was proscribed for African-American women.

The New Woman as Self-Fulfillment

As mentioned, Adele and Helga both are portrayed as desiring and attempting to "realize themselves"; yet, there is also something elusive in the way their desire is presented. Nella Larsen, for instance, depicts Helga as craving an "intangible thing" (120). This intangible thing, Helga discovers, is not exactly "leisure, attention . . . Things. Things. Things" (67), or, in other words, what she had always thought she wanted. Helga eventually recognizes that material well-being and prosperity are not enough for her and that her endless searching has only succeeded in bringing her back to "that old question of happiness" (116). Similarly, for Adele this insistent desire not only includes rising in the world and leaving poverty behind her, but also "peace—rest" (99), a state that transcends the necessities and even luxuries of everyday life. This "intangible thing" for which both protagonists seem to be searching can be read as resembling the Greek notion of happiness, *eudemonia*, a term that frequently is defined as a state of existence that combines happiness, prosperity, *and a meaningful way of being in the world.*[8]

Notions of eudemonia are context bound of course; what constitutes prosperity, fulfillment, and a meaningful existence is contingent on a variety of factors, including one's position vis-à-vis social hierarchies and the way these states of being are conceived during a particular historical period. I propose that dominant U.S. society during the Progressive Era and into the Jazz Age posited and thus understood the emulation of the New Woman ideal as one of the ways that middle-class women could achieve self-fulfillment and happiness. By combining presence in the public sphere or a "vocation" with the ability to express one's sexual desires, this norm represented the possibility of constructing a meaningful female identity based on economic, sexual, and political self-determination. In other words, by approximating this ideal, women might approach this elusive state of eudemonia.

Adele Lindner as a New Woman

Arrogant Beggar invites the reader to admire Adele for her ability to create such a meaningful existence against all odds. The first half of Yezierska's novel tracks the protagonist's growing disillusionment with the Hellman Home for Working Girls. Little by little, Adele comes to despise the "cringing, truckling" that she is forced to perform in order to stay in the good graces of the Home's patronesses (60). Despite her increasing disappointment with the institution, Adele continues to perform the role of the grateful working girl so well that she is asked to give a speech of gratitude at the Board of Directors' annual meeting. Midway through her prepared speech, however, she bursts out in an impromptu tirade of recrimination, anger, and defiance. Adele accuses the women who run the Home of hypocrisy and of treating the working girls like beggars. It is at this point in the narrative that Adele decides, abruptly, to leave the Home forever, even though she is penniless and without any kind of support network to fall back on.

Perhaps not surprisingly, her reversal of fortune is presented in Yezierska's text as something quite positive. Not only does this setback compel her to return to her poor, Jewish, Lower East Side "roots," but, more importantly, Yezierska presents this hitting rock bottom as allowing Adele to begin rebuilding her life without "borrowed feathers" (112). Her act of defiance appears to free her from the dependence and subservience that characterize the working girls' life at the Home and is portrayed as enabling her to discover her own inner strength and resources.

In addition, her friendship with Muhmenkeh, the old Jewish woman who takes Adele in during her time of greatest need, is depicted in the novel as providing Yezierska's protagonist with an alternative moral compass. Muhmenkeh, Adele tells us, represents true generosity, the right way of giving love, sympathy, and understanding (120). And, after Muhmenkeh dies, Adele is described as internalizing Muhmenkeh's ethical legacy. She resolutely decides to refashion herself, to wrench herself free from "the whining, wanting, sentimental old self" (124) and thus to make good on Muhmenkeh's bequest. Combining the skills that she has learned at the Home, Muhmenkeh's spirit of giving, and her determination to succeed, Adele single-handedly opens Muhmenkeh's Coffee Shop. Indeed, Yezierska's protagonist not only manages to create a thriving business, but is presented as offering an important service to the Jewish community: good, wholesome food at fair prices.[9]

Carol Batker convincingly argues that by "creating a wage-earning enterprise" and rejecting traditional domesticity, Adele effectively aligns herself with the New Women.[10] Adele refuses to marry Arthur Hellman (the son of the wealthy patroness who runs the Home for Working Girls), a marriage that most likely would have ensured Adele's economic dependency on her husband. Moreover, she chooses to marry her soul mate, the pianist Jean Rachmansky, and the income from her café provides the financial support and security so that Jean can cultivate his genius. While this can be seen to "reenact the immigrant ideal of a Jewish woman supporting her husband so that he can pursue learning or a secularized art," Batker persuasively contends that Jean Rachmansky, in many ways, is subsumed under Adele's professional goals rather than the other way around (88).[11] Adele's ability to combine meaningful work, a marriage based on sexual intimacy, love, and "equality," and the provision of a service to the Jewish community do seem to make the description, New Woman, a very apt and precise one for her.[12]

Jewish Women and the New Woman Ideal

Yet, if it is true, as Elizabeth Ammons, Lois Rudnick, and other scholars have argued, that the dominant New Woman norm circulating during the early twentieth century was a *racialized* ideal in which the "free-doms" associated with the New Woman were only really tolerated for white middle-class women, then Adele's ability to align herself with this ideal is actually in need of explanation.[13] After all, as I underscored in previous chapters, Jews were considered "not-quite white" or "off-white" during the early twentieth century. Jewishness was still being framed within a racial discourse, and dominant U.S. society was still questioning whether Jews were or could be full-blooded whites. Given their racial ambiguity at the time, Jews who desired access to domi-nant society and sites of power therefore were compelled to find ways of aligning themselves more closely with whiteness.

Jewish women, Lori Harrison-Kahan suggests, could not align them-selves with whiteness in the same way as Jewish men, since in order to assimilate successfully as white one needed access to the means of production.[14] "Becoming American" (i.e., white) was thus harder for Jewish women than it was for Jewish men, since gender norms and exclusionary practices still prevented women from entering the manu-facturing and business worlds. Using Yezierska's novels and short sto-ries to illustrate her claims, Harrison-Kahan also argues that due to the many obstacles standing in their way, Jewish women were more ambiv-alent about Americanization and assimilation. Adele, like Yezierska's other heroines, is thus seen as representing this ambivalence and as being caught between white aspirations and ethnic loyalties. According to Harrison-Kahan, rather than "relinquishing the Old World for the New," Adele ultimately strives to bring the two worlds together."[15]

In order to make the claim that the protagonist of *Arrogant Beggar* is caught between white aspirations and ethnic loyalties, even at the end of the narrative, Harrison-Kahan reads Adele's return to the Jew-ish Lower East side and her encounter with Muhmenkeh as a return to a more authentic Jewishness.[16] This reading, I believe, needs to be problematized, primarily because Muhmenkeh's legacy is ultimately more multifaceted and ambiguous. Muhmenkeh cannot be seen as rep-resenting a pure ethnicity, Jewishness, or "Old Worldness," since Muh-menkeh herself is an Americanized figure. When Arthur Hellman, for instance, finally discovers Adele's whereabouts following her departure from the Home, he offers to buy Muhmenkeh's entire stock of goods. Muhmenkeh refuses his "charity," and tells him, in Yiddishized English, that she "got yet my hands and feet to earn my every cent" (110). Earn-ing one's own bread is to retain one's independence and self-respect, whereas accepting charity is to succumb to an undesirable and very un-American dependence. In other words, Muhmenkeh is depicted as holding fast to a very *American* belief: the importance of "making it" on one's own. This is a crucial aspect of Muhmenkeh's legacy and, I would argue, actually serves as the basis of Adele's desire to transform herself from the "whining, wanting" self into a self-determined and independent woman — a New Woman.

It therefore seems more accurate to read this "return" to the Jewish Lower East Side as complex, and as a dramatization of the way that Jewishness and Americanness were being (re)articulated as more and more reconcilable with one another. Jewishness and Americanness are not posited as two conflicting identities but rather as compatible identifications. Being a Jewish American not only becomes a possibility in the text, but ultimately there does not seem to be much tension or opposition between "ethnic loyalties" and "white aspirations." It is not coincidental that by the end of the novel, Adele not only has accessed production successfully but has also effectively transformed the signifier Jewishness into a commodity: food that can be exchanged for money — a very American enterprise indeed.

While I agree with Harrison-Kahan that Yezierska's female protagonists initially are caught between two worlds and that gender complicated access to whiteness for Jewish women, I propose that *Arrogant Beggar* dramatizes the way that Jewishness, whiteness, *and* femaleness were being (re)configured as increasingly compatible with one another. The emulation of the New Woman ideal actually can be seen as *helping to forge* Adele's connection to and identification with white middle-class womanhood. Yezierska's text points to the way Jewish women ultimately were allowed to align themselves with whiteness by embracing this ideal.[17] The novel can, in effect, be seen to be inscribing and thereby constituting the *whiteness of Jewish women* by tracking Adele's attempt to emulate of the New Woman ideal.

The last pages of the novel depict the joyous couple, Adele and Jean, waiting to greet Shenah Gittel, Muhmenkeh's granddaughter, who is coming to America from Russia. Having succeeded in business and in love, the pair is now preparing to give Muhmenkeh's granddaughter a chance to *make it on her own* (153); in a sense, they are poised to initiate Shenah into the American Dream. Adele is described in these final scenes as filled with a "joy . . . deeper than sorrow" and a "lull of peace" (151). I maintain that Yezierska depicts her protagonist as having been "allowed" to approximate the New Woman ideal, and, as a result, as having managed to approach the coveted state of eudemonia.

Black Women and the New Negro Woman Ideal

Claudia Tate points out that Nella Larsen grants her protagonist Helga Crane "an extraordinary array of options, attributes, and advantages."[18] However, none of these various options allow Helga to find that elusive something which she is craving. Following the pioneering work of Hazel Carby and Deborah McDowell, recent critical commentary on *Quicksand* has emphasized Helga's catch-22, her being caught or having to negotiate between two seemingly contradictory proscribed roles which "Larsen sets up for black womanhood—those of the angel and the whore."[19] Drawing on these insights, I also will be focusing on Helga's sexuality. But instead of reading Helga's tragic end as a result of her inability to become a sexual *subject*, I argue that her tragedy is a result, at least in large part, of her inability to find a social space that would enable her to *link* sexuality with a meaningful independent existence, which is exactly what the New Women ideal encouraged white middle-class women to do.[20]

The New Woman still served as one of the regulatory norms circulating within hegemonic society during the Jazz Age; it was a "middle-class white ideal" that helped, on the one hand, to reinscribe the hegemony of white middle-class society and, on the other, to police its borders.[21] However, as I suggested earlier, within the African-American community, the New Woman ideal *was not* the dominant norm that middle-class women were encouraged to emulate. Rather, there was an alternative and, in a sense, a counterhegemonic norm that circulated and had currency within this specific minority community—the New Negro Woman. This alternative norm was very much informed by its hegemonic counterpart and in analogous fashion offered middle-class black women the possibility of self-realization.

Similar to the dominant New Woman ideal, the New Negro Woman was, as Darlene Clark Hine has argued, "permitted" to be independent and to act in the public sphere. But in sharp contrast to the New Woman ideal, she was *expected to renounce sexuality and to dedicate herself to the advancement of the race*: "In return for their sacrifice of sexual expression, the community gave them respect and recognition."[22] The alternative ideal, in effect, "took up" the importance of independence and self-realization for women, but responded to the specific circumstances of the black middle class.

A number of scholars have read *Quicksand* in relation to the New Negro Woman ideal and the two diametrically opposed poles of sexual subjectivity, the angel or the whore, which black women were "allowed" to access.[23] However, I suggest that we need to read Helga's elusive desire and her inability to achieve a more permanent sense of contentment first and foremost with respect to the *hegemonic* New Woman ideal. Helga's trajectory draws our attention to the immense constitutive power of dominant ideals, and the novel underscores the way that dominant ideals circumscribe subjects' desires, aspirations, opportunities, and behavior. None of the upwardly mobile African-American communities portrayed in the text are free from the influence of the dominant white society's regulatory ideals. For example, even though the "financially independent, well-connected and much sought after" Anne Grey claims that she despises "whites with a deep and burning hatred," Larsen depicts her as mimicking the clothes and manners of the dominant white middle class. And while proclaiming "loudly the undiluted good of all things Negro, she yet disliked the songs, the dances, and the softly blurred speech" of the Negro folk (48).

Anne Grey's hatred for whites and her refusal to mix with them on the one hand and her attempts to emulate "their" standards of taste and aesthetics on the other produce a tension and contradiction between dominant ideals of whiteness and the way these ideals are "taken up" by subjects. In other words, there is a difference between the way norms operate on the hegemonic level, as mechanisms that (re)produce *dominant* U.S. culture, and the way these norms are appropriated on the level of social praxis and within communities.[24] Anne certainly has been formed in the crucible of "identify as black (or else) but desire to be white," but in the "move" from norm to social praxis, something has happened. Perhaps one could argue that Anne has carried the bifurcation of identification and the desire-to-be to such an extreme that the valence attached to identification with blackness is actually transformed into something eminently desirable. Thus, while *Quicksand* gestures toward the enormous power that dominant norms wield, the novel also dramatizes that these dominant norms can be "taken up" in various and sometimes bizarre ways, and that they can be contested.

Quicksand also underscores that there are always competing norms circulating within any given community. Larsen's text illustrates how within the middle-class African-American community there are a set of conflicting norms, like the New Negro ideal, some of which are quite different from the ones circulating within the dominant white U.S. society. This is a crucial point, since in any given society, nonhegemonic communities can and do propagate different and competing norms. Within the spaces that these communities occupy, attributes or norms that are valued negatively (and even actively discouraged or punished) by the dominant society may even be affirmed as positive and desirable. The production of the New Negro Woman accordingly should be understood as a productive response to the fact that black women simply could not align themselves with the dominant ideal of the New Woman. The circulation and influence of the New Negro Woman ideal is consequently another example of the way dominant norms help shape desire, as well as of the possibility that communities will "take up," alter, or even transform dominant norms.

The New Negro Woman ideal offered middle-class black women the opportunity to take part in meaningful public work—almost always in the guise of racial uplift. But the historical equation produced by dominant white racist society of black women with hyper-sexuality prohibited the *linking* of sexual determination with an independent public presence. Thus, the ideal's de-linking of sexuality and professional life was both a reaction to the historical sexualization of the black woman's body and a means of distinguishing the middle-class New Negro woman from black working-class women, while (re)inscribing the distinction between white middle-class women and black middle-class women.

But the production of the New Negro Woman also can be seen to gesture toward the way dominant society has both compelled a certain bifurcation between identification and the desire-to-be for black subjects who wish to gain entry into mainstream society *and* engendered more constraints on the particular norms these subjects were "permitted" to emulate. Rather than compelling and encouraging these subjects to emulate the entire array of norms associated with whiteness, it may be that the dominant social order prohibited or at least made impossible certain linkages for upwardly mobile black subjects. As I have argued, middle-class black women who wished to remain respectable were compelled to eschew any linkage of sexuality and public space. This suggests that the injunction: "identify as black (or else) but desire to be white" — that is, live up to the norms linked to whiteness — needs to be complicated further. It may be that another strategy for policing the always tenuous black-white divide has been the circumscription of the kinds of norms black-identified subjects (again, those who wish to access some of the privileges of mainstream society) have been allowed to approximate. This would doubly ensure that black subjects could never "become white," or "be fully American," since alongside a compelled identification with blackness, their desire-to-be always would be informed by a different or a more limited configuration of normative attributes. For upwardly mobile black Americans, not only has identification been policed, but their "desire-to-be" also seems to have been constrained in very particular ways.

Helga Crane and the New Woman Ideal

Quicksand dramatizes Helga's inability to emulate the New Woman ideal. Like Adele, Helga abruptly leaves the security of an established institution without a support network and is forced to search for work. She is hopeful, however, that she will find something that will allow her to maintain the middle-class status to which she has grown accustomed. Dressed in a "suit of fine blue twill faultlessly tailored," she sets out to find acceptable employment (31). But as Helga walks down the Chicago streets in search of a job in her very respectable clothes, she gets accosted by men who offer her money; we are told, however, that the price of the money is "too dear" (34). Clearly, Helga either gets mistaken for a prostitute or is perceived to be sexually available simply by virtue of being a *black woman walking in public*.[25]

Even as a middle-class woman, Helga cannot appropriate the New Woman ideal without making herself vulnerable sexually. In effect, by attempting to appropriate this ideal, black women not only were unable to align themselves more closely with white middle-class womanhood and therefore with dominant norms of Americanness as Jewish women could, but, rather, by virtue of the attempt to enter public space they *were positioned* by the dominant society as the always hypersexualized lower-class black woman or the prostitute.[26] For upwardly mobile black women who were not "rebel[s] from society," the linking of sexual self-determination and public space is posited in the novel as an *impossibility*.

It is not coincidental that the two other "respectable" and admirable middle-class black women presented in *Quicksand*, Anne and the "prominent race" woman Mrs. Hayes-Rore, are widows and their status is ensured through the "money and prestige" that their husbands have bequeathed them. Both women are independent, and both women have found a vocation — they are dedicated to racial uplift; yet they are also depicted in particularly desexualized and desexualizing language. Mrs. Hayes-Rore is limned as a "plump lemon-colored woman with badly straightened hair and dirty finger-nails" (35), and Anne, though beautiful and cultivated, is portrayed as a "golden *Madonna*, grave and calm and sweet" (45, emphasis added). Through such descriptions, Anne is effectively "unsexed." In other words, within Harlem's middle-class black community, the women who are held in the most esteem are middle-class women who abjure sensuality and dedicate themselves to "racial uplift." To stray from this pattern is to risk the contumely of the community. Helga, however, ultimately cannot or is unwilling to renounce her sensuality for the advancement of the race and seems to want what the *dominant* New Woman ideal promises women: sexuality *and* esteem based on some kind of meaningful work. Helga's catch-22 is not her inability to choose between the whore and the angel, but rather the result of her desire to emulate the *dominant* New Woman ideal on the one hand, and her ultimate rejection of the New Negro Woman ideal on the other.

Of course, this inability to combine the various aspects of her life that she seems so very much to desire has a detailed history in the novel. First there is Naxos, the southern institution that offers opportunities for educated young men and women to participate in "racial uplift." Helga is described as initially having had a "keen joy and zest" in the work of helping her fellow man and woman. But rather than allowing for individual self-realization, she quickly discovers that Naxos is interested in mass production — creating a "Naxos mold." It tolerated "no innovations, no individualisms" (4). Not only is any sign of individuality or sensuality repressed, but the work of racial uplift, Helga realizes, is hypocritical. "Racial uplift," Helga begins to realize, inevitably reinscribes American Anglo-Saxon whiteness as the pinnacle of civilization. Naxos teaches its black students how to develop good taste and good sense, which translates into molding them into docile subjects who know just enough to stay in their place. Naxos, like middle-class Harlem, allows for a certain kind of meaningful existence in work and public service, but at the expense of repressing any signs of individuality or sexuality.

In Harlem, at least initially, Helga seems to bring many of the strands of her desire together; and during her first stay in New York, when she meets Anne and the Harlem crowd, Helga most closely approximates the dominant New Woman ideal. She is a successful, single, working woman, has managed to build a community, and is not interested in marrying, at least for the time being: "Her secretarial work with the Negro insurance company filled her day. Books, the theater, parties, used up the nights . . . Some day she intended to marry one of those alluring brown or yellow men who danced attendance on her" (45). She is portrayed as having a full life, and as being able, to some degree, to determine her future. We are also told that during this short period, Helga is content and happy due to a new sense of freedom (46). The question then becomes, why does Larsen portray Helga as unable to sustain this position? Why do those feelings of "discontent" and "restlessness" begin to overpower her (47)?

Perhaps part of the answer lies in her re-encounter with Robert Anderson, the former director of Naxos, who, whenever they meet, always disturbs Helga's sense of well-being. Their chance encounter in Harlem causes Helga to experience "[a] thousand indefinite longings." Helga's constant rejection of Robert is mysterious, not least because it seems to be the only real possibility presented in *Quicksand* for Helga to link sexual desire with the other aspects of life that she is depicted as craving. It appears that Helga forces herself to repress her insistent sexuality because she realizes that in order to succeed and gain admiration within the upwardly mobile black community she must not give in to her powerful desire. In many respects, this reading is corroborated toward the end of the novel: When she is finally willing to "give herself" to Robert, he shows himself in his true colors—as part of the Harlem elite that struggles against any sign of overt sexuality.

But perhaps another part of the riddle of why Helga ultimately is not fulfilled during this period of her life—and one that has not really been addressed in the critical studies of *Quicksand*—lies in the kind of work that she does while in Harlem. After all, the discontent begins well before Anderson re-enters her life. It is important to remember that during her first sojourn in New York Helga is a secretary in a black insurance firm. And while she is described as having some independence, she does not experience the "thrill" of working that she briefly experienced in Naxos or even later as a housewife trying to "help" her husband's parishioners. With neither fulfilling work nor any real possibility of expressing her sexuality while remaining respectable, it is not surprising that Helga leaves Harlem for Denmark.

In Denmark with her maternal relatives, Helga can play up her sensuality and sexuality and even maintain a certain kind of respectability. But, of course, the price she pays for this kind of existence is her objectification and loss of any kind of independent existence. We are told that one of the major reasons that Helga left America was to feel that she belonged to "herself alone" and not to a race (64), but from the very beginning of her stay in Denmark, Helga is exoticized—through an accentuation of her sexuality—due to her dark complexion; she is turned into a curio, a "peacock" and is appreciated for her difference, not as an individual but as a representative of a strange and foreign species. Had Helga married the famous but arrogant white painter Axel Olsen, she most likely would have continued to be a showcase wife, a decoration (73).[27] In many ways, she is simply reduced to her sexuality. While she manages to accumulate "things" and to enjoy prosperity and leisure in Europe, Helga realizes in the end that things do not and ultimately cannot satisfy her yearnings.

Given Helga's disillusionment with the work of racial uplift as it exists in the various black communities, her very limited professional (or, perhaps more precisely, vocational) options, and her realization that even in the white world of Denmark she does not significantly broaden her possibilities, the choice of marrying a poor black southern preacher and becoming the "preacher's wife" is perhaps not that unexpected or surprising. The prospect of doing something meaningful—God's work—along with the knowledge that as Reverend Pleasant Green's wife she can, at least in some form, finally express her sexuality appeals to Helga after her devastating meeting with Robert Anderson in which he rules out any future sexual contact between them: "[A]ll I've ever had in life has been things—except this one time . . . Things she realized, hadn't, weren't enough for her. She'd have to have something besides . . . There was God" (116–17). This is, in a sense, Helga's final and perhaps desperate attempt to bring the various strands of her desire—meaningful work and sexual self-expression—together.

As the wife of the poor southern preacher, Helga is allowed a certain amount of sexual expression: "And night came at the end of every day. Emotional, palpitating, amorous, all that was living in her sprang like rank weeds at the tingling thought of night, with a vitality so strong that it devoured all shoots of reason" (122). Yet, what becomes very clear by the end of the novel is that the *only* way Helga can access her sexuality is through a renunciation of any link to the public sphere. At this point in the narrative, Helga is confined totally to domestic space, and her short-lived belief in religion and in the significance of trying to educate the poor parishioners about beauty, which gave such a life meaning, fails her in the end. Moreover, Helga's sexuality ultimately is reduced to reproduction.

Hemmed in by the norms of the Harlem elite, which forbade the outward expression of sensuality to upwardly mobile and "respectable" middle-class women, and white supremacist culture, in which a black woman was always already over-sexed, Helga can find no way of successfully fashioning herself as a New Woman and approaching that elusive state of eudemonia. In striking and devastating irony, and in such sharp contrast to Adele Lindner, *Quicksand* ends with the very respectable and middle-class Helga Crane embodying the antithesis of the New Woman: poor, rural, domesticated, and very fertile.

Conclusion

Reading *Arrogant Beggar* and *Quicksand* through the lens of the racialized New Woman norm, I believe, helps make sense of the radically different narrative trajectories of Helga Crane and Adele Lindner. Such an analysis illuminates the very different positions and positioning of Jewish women and black women vis-à-vis this dominant ideal as well as in relation to dominant notions of Americanness during the early twentieth century. The New Woman ideal was not proscribed for upwardly mobile Jewish women, and the attempt to emulate it, I have argued, actually helped forge Jewish women's connection to and identification with white middle-class womanhood.[28] This, in turn, points yet again to the way that Jews were increasingly accessing full-blooded whiteness as well as to a certain kind of agency available to Jewish women, while simultaneously demonstrating just how powerful the desire to be a "white American" was.

Conversely, attempting to approximate the dominant New Woman ideal for black women who wished to maintain a "respectable" existence was strictly prohibited. By linking a more open sexuality with public space, upwardly mobile black women were reinscribed as "hyper-sexualized" and "promiscuous" by dominant white society and ostracized by the black middle class, which was responding to a long history of racist and sexist stereotypes. Emulating the ideal did not serve as an avenue of upward mobility for black women in any way, nor did it allow black women to align themselves more closely with the dominant norms linked to American womanhood. In sum, for black middle-class women, the New Woman did not represent a viable path to eudemonia.

Chapter Six

A Parrot of Words and
Monkey of Manners

IN THE FIRST FOUR CHAPTERS of this book, I attempted to trace the different genealogies of the categories of identification: gender, class, race, and ethnicity. As the texts I have examined suggest, *each* category creates and encourages a specific relationship between identification and what I have termed the "desire-to-be"; thus, I have proposed that each category shapes identity in a distinct way by producing a particular modality of performativity. In the following pages, however, I will continue the work I began in the last chapter and complicate my own analysis in an effort to understand some of the ways in which the different categories of identification have interacted with and reinforced one another. If previously I isolated gender, class, and race to provide an account of the differences among them, or looked at the New Woman ideal without offering a theoretical account of the way that gender, race, and class interact, in this chapter I compare the novels, revisiting some of the scenes I have already discussed as a way of examining and theorizing the complex *interrelationship* among these categories.

Background

While many theorists have argued that gender, class, and race operate in conjunction with one another, as far as I am aware, few have tried to offer a *theoretical* account of the ways in which these categories interact in social practice.[1] There are, of course, a number of important exceptions. Rose Brewer, for instance, attempts to "explain the African-

American experience through the multiple articulations of race, class, and gender" and presents an account of *class formation* through the lenses of race and gender.[2] While her essay is a convincing empirical account of how race and gender norms have affected African-American women's ability to move up the class hierarchy, it does not trace the particular histories of the categories under consideration, nor does it ultimately offer a metatheoretical framework for understanding the complex interaction among the different categories.

Kimberle Crenshaw was one of the first scholars to invoke the term "intersectionality" to highlight the imbrication of racism and sexism in the lived experiences of black women, and this notion has since became an important way of understanding the multidimensional aspects of subordination in the United States. Patricia Hill Collins, for instance, has explored how the norm of the "traditional" family naturalizes existing hierarchies in the United States; she convincingly argues that the family, as an ideal and a set of social practices, "serves as a privileged exemplar for intersectionality," since it is a site that perpetuates and normalizes multiple relations of inequality with regards to gender, race, class, sexuality, and age.[3] Like Brewer, however, Crenshaw, Collins, and other scholars of intersectionality and its successor multidimensionality tend to outline empirical structures of subordination and the multidimentional oppression of marginalized groups resulting from the intersection of various categories rather than discuss the ways in which hegemonic categories form and regulate subject formation.[4] In other words, the focus of these scholars tends to be on the *effects* of the interaction among the different categories and not on theorizing *how and in what ways* the hegemonic categories interact to help shape who we are and what we desire.

Cultural theorists Ann McClintock and Gail Bederman both have analyzed the ways in which gender, race, class, and nation have mutually constructed each other through certain nineteenth- and early-twentieth-century discourses. McClintock investigates the nineteenth-century discourse of "progress" as well as the "family of man" discourse in Britain, claiming that "the welter of distinctions of race, class, and gender were gathered into a single narrative by the image of the Family of Man."[5] She shows how both discourses drew on Darwin's theory of evolution in order to justify and reinscribe social hierarchies at home and colonization abroad. Along similar lines, Bederman discusses U.S. "civilization" discourse, which emerged at the turn of the twentieth century and which served to buttress white supremacy, gender inequality,

and middle-class privilege. Both theorists demonstrate how certain notions of gender, class, race, and nation have been reproduced by and
through such discourses and highlight the intersections among the categories of identification, asserting that—theoretically or methodologically—it is impossible to separate gender, class, or race. McClintock
claims that "gender is . . . constructed *through and by* class," while
Bederman argues that "race and gender cannot be studied as if they
were two discrete categories."[6] They go on to contend that the white,
Anglo-Saxon, middle-class man has been continuously (re)inscribed as
the most privileged subject in the United States and Britain.[7]

On the one hand, I will be following Bederman's and McClintock's
example in this chapter by tracing some of the intricate ways that the
categories of identification have been interarticulated, where articulation is understood as a form of connection that is not necessary but
which makes a unity of different elements under certain conditions.[8]
I accordingly present and interrogate specific scenes from *Arrogant Beggar, The Autobiography of an Ex-Colored Man, Passing, Quicksand, The
Rise of David Levinsky,* and *Salome of the Tenements,* which underscore
the interrelationship among gender, race, and class, showing how the
dominant norms that historically have been connected to the different
categories have overlapped and, in this way, reinforced one another. On
the other hand, my analysis differs from these scholars, since I maintain that analytically and methodologically it is imperative to trace the
different genealogies and modes of operation of the various categories,
and propose that the *very differences or irreducibility of gender, class,
and race on the level of identification and "desire-to-be"* have served to
shore up existing power relations and, in this way, have (re)produced
social stratification.[9] Perhaps it could be argued that in this chapter I am
attempting a (meta)theorization of a certain understanding of "intersectionality," one which assumes that the operations of hegemonic categories, while irreducible, are inseparable in social praxis and intersect
in complex ways to create multidimensional marginalization.

The Repetition of Norms

As I have argued repeatedly throughout this book, each category of
identification has a set of norms attached to it, and each one can be
said to constitute an "artificial unity" composed of a series of dispa-

rate attributes. This artificial unity forms a force relation, according to a Foucauldian analysis. The category of race with all of the norms linked to it, for instance, can be seen to make up one such force relation, while the category of gender makes up yet another. In this section, I argue that the early-twentieth-century novels under consideration point to the ways in which categories of identification have themselves been linked together to create "a state of power."[10] By a state of power, I mean the historical coalescing of various social hierarchies. For example, the production of the white, Anglo-Saxon, middle-class heterosexual man as the norm or standard was, I propose, the dominant "state of power" during the early twentieth century precisely because it united a series of social hierarchies. Audre Lorde defines this coalescing of various force relations as an overarching norm, or a "mythical norm," one which "each one of us knows that we do not fit." In the United States, she asserts, "this norm is . . . white . . . male, young, heterosexual, Christian, and financially secure."[11]

While each term in the link (white, middle-class, Anglo-Saxon, heterosexual) has its own regulatory injunctions or norms attached to it (e.g., civilized, hardworking), historically a further concatenation has taken place among these different categories. At the same time as dominant norms are linked to each category of identification and create an "artificial unity" made up of disparate characteristics that have no necessary connection to one another, the different categories of identification, such as gender, class, and race, are *themselves* linked in yet another artificial unity, such that heterosexuality gets linked to middle-classedness and whiteness. Various social hegemonies are crystallized through this further linking of norms, and the result is the production of a mythical or overarching norm: the white, middle-class, heterosexual, Anglo-Saxon man.

Accordingly, I suggest that one of the ways that hegemonic discourse helps produce and reinforce the "mythical norm" is through the linking of similar regulatory injunctions to the different categories of identification in order to buttress the existing configuration of power in a given historical period. More specifically, hegemonic norms that historically have been linked to gender, class, and race have certain structural similarities. If the dominant norms linked to masculinity in the early-twentieth-century United States were assertive/competitive/ambitious, as we saw in my analysis of *The Rise of David Levinsky*, the norms linked to whiteness were civilized/intelligent/moral/hardworking/clean, as

I argued in the second and fourth chapters when discussing *Passing* and *The Autobiography of an Ex-Colored Man*, and the norms linked to middle-classedness were determination/hardworking/moral upright-ness, as I proposed in the third chapter; then we begin to see how certain norms repeat themselves in their linkage to the different categories of identification. For instance, the norm of moral uprightness has been concatenated to both whiteness and to middle-classedness, while the norms of determination and willfulness concomitantly are linked to class and masculinity.

This complex repetition or overlapping of norms within the different categories of identification ensures that when a subject — who is inter-pellated into the dominant social order as male, for instance — attempts to approximate the norm of determination, he is, in effect, reinforc-ing *both* the norms connected to masculinity and the ones connected to class at one and the same time. It is in this way that the repetition of norms within different categories of identification ultimately ends up reinforcing the existing social hierarchies, and more specifically, the mythical norm. We also begin to see what Foucault means when he asserts that power is intentional (but nonsubjective), since the tactic of the overlapping of norms ensures that subjects reinforce the *over-arching* norm even while attempting to approximate the specific domi-nant norms connected to *any one* of the categories of identification.[12] Consequently, if we understand the norm of the white, Anglo-Saxon, middle-class man as the coalescing of multiple force relations, then I believe we can maintain that each category of identification has its own unique genealogy without relinquishing the claim that the different sets of norms attached to each category have served to reinforce one another.

The crucial point here is that different force relations — each one engendering and compelling a certain relationship between identifi-cation and "desire-to-be" — find support in other force relations, thus forming a chain or a system. In previous chapters, I have isolated par-ticular force relations in order to reveal the specific way that each one operates; however, in the novels (as in social praxis), these force rela-tions always operate in complex and (usually) mutually reinforcing ways. This linking together creates the *effect* of the inseparability of these multiple force relations. As Foucault argues, "Major dominations are the hegemonic effects that are sustained by all the confrontations of the force relations."[13]

My theoretical claims clearly manifest themselves in the literary texts. Abraham Cahan's depiction of David Levinsky's climb up the class ladder suggests that, by attempting to approximate the dominant norms of one category of identification, subjects simultaneously strengthen the norms associated with other categories. When David is described as doing everything he can to succeed in his cloak-manufacturing business, he not only is endeavoring to live up to norms of class, but he also can be said to be reinforcing and attempting to emulate norms of race, that is, norms linked to whiteness:

> I was forever watching and striving to imitate the dress and ways of the well-bred American merchants with whom I was, or trying to be, thrown. All this, I felt, was an essential element in achieving business success; but the ambition to *act* and *look like a gentleman* grew in me quite apart from these motives. (260, emphasis added)

Whereas in the first chapter I analyzed this passage through the lens of gender, emphasizing David's attempt to approximate norms of U.S. masculinity through bodily gestures, aspirations, and tastes, here I would like to highlight the way in which David's attempt to perform norms of class, such as the dress and ways of the well-bred American merchants, is inextricable from his attempt to act and look like a *white* gentleman. For "gentleman" and "gentile" are equivalent in Cahan's novel, while in the United States at the turn of the century, a gentleman was — by definition — a middle- or upper-middle-class, white male.

The above passage is taken from the scene in which David is invited to accompany a "full-blooded Anglo-Saxon of New England origin" (259) to an upscale restaurant. David has never entered such a restaurant before and has to be taught "proper" table manners; but he is very grateful to the rich Anglo-Saxon for initiating him into this life of luxury. Throughout the novel, David's highest respect is reserved for gentiles. Speaking of a particular cloth manufacturer, he tells us that not only did he feel inferior to the man because he (David) is Jewish, but looked up to the manufacturer since he was "a Gentile . . . an American" (502). That is, "American" can be seen to serve as the rubric under which the dominant norms associated to the different categories of identification have coalesced; "American," in effect, has served as the catchword for the overarching mythical norm.

Moreover, David confesses that he would watch "American smokers and manner of smoking as though there were a special American manner of smoking and such a thing as smoking with a foreign accent" (326). Eliminating his Talmudic gesticulations, "a habit that worried [him] like a physical defect" (327), also becomes a crucial element in his Americanization. Cahan thus illustrates how David's success as an American merchant is related to his elimination of all external characteristics that would mark him physically, not only as part of a lower and inferior class but also as a Jew, that is, as off-white.

Moving up the class hierarchy, which David Levinsky does, can be seen to facilitate one's "becoming white"; that is, there seems to be a whitening effect to climbing up the class ladder. The converse also appears to be true: the whiter one is or becomes, the more chances one has of moving up the class hierarchy. Interestingly, when David first arrives in New York, he is interpellated as a "green" one, a greenhorn. His orthodox Jewish dress and bewilderment at the sights and sounds of the Lower East Side clearly mark him as a newly arrived immigrant. In order to begin ridding himself of this color taint, David allows another "Americanized" Jew to dress him up in modern store-bought clothes. With his new clothes and haircut, David looks "quite the American," that is, less green and certainly whiter (101). As his patron informs him, transforming his appearance is the necessary first step in the path to success. And indeed, this initial make-over is only the first step in David's endless attempt to make himself over into a "true American."

It can be argued that the naturalization of Jews throughout the nineteenth century as "free white persons" alongside the increasingly dichotomized racial discourse (the black-white divide) facilitated the Jews' ability to move up the class ladder. However, as I have attempted to show, "becoming white" has been possible for in-between racial groups, and not for African Americans. Upward mobility has facilitated only certain immigrant groups' acceptance into the "white" race, although "being" interpellated as "white" or even "off white" almost always has facilitated one's move up the class ladder. The depiction of Adele Lindner forcefully illustrates both of these claims. As I argued in the previous chapter, by the end of *Arrogant Beggar*, Adele has "become whiter" by climbing the rungs of the class ladder and aligning herself with the middle-class New Woman ideal. But it was also by virtue of her almost-whiteness that she was able to move up the class hierarchy and was, in effect, permitted to emulate this ideal in the first place. By contrast, African Americans have *a priori* been barred from "becoming white," since the very intelligibility of the U.S. racial landscape has depended on maintaining the black-white divide.

In *Passing*, Nella Larsen also dramatizes the intricate way in which norms of gender, race, and class tend to reinforce one another. Returning one last time to the scene in which Irene Redfield enters the exclusive Drayton Hotel in order to escape the searing August heat, we once again encounter the complex overlapping of norms of whiteness, middle-classedness, and femininity. Just before Irene decides to hail a cab that will take her to the Drayton, a man topples over right in front of her and becomes an "inert crumpled heap on the scorching cement" (146). Irene, who feels "disagreeably damp and sticky and soiled from contact with so many sweating bodies," edges her way out of the increasing crowd (146). Once she is comfortably inside the taxi, Irene makes an attempt "to repair the damage that the heat and crowds had done to her appearance" (147). This is a fascinating moment in the text, since it so clearly gestures toward Irene's desire both to distinguish herself from the "crowd" and to live up to norms of civility or respectability, especially the norms of "womanhood." After all, to be "civilized" means to keep one's distance from the dirty, sweating masses, and to be a "woman" means to keep up one's respectable and "feminine" appearance. But civility, as we witness in this scene, is linked not only to class and gender but also closely associated with hegemonic ideals of whiteness.

Feeling that she is about to faint, Irene, as mentioned, hails a cab. The cab driver, we learn later, has assumed that Irene is white and offers to take her to the Drayton Hotel. It is here, I argue, that we begin to see how the assumption of whiteness goes hand in hand with norms of class. The fact that Irene is hailing a cab, which constitutes a very clear class marker in 1920s Chicago, *facilitates* the cab driver's assumption that Irene is white. Moreover, her well-kept appearance and her very correct behavior, as exemplified by the way in which she thanks the cab driver for his "kind helpfulness and understanding," serve as the background for her acceptance into the Drayton. Her middle-class deportment makes the hotel workers and patrons more likely to assume she is white.

It is important to note here that although the overarching norm in the United States has produced maleness as the norm or standard, compulsory heterosexuality actually requires "women" to desire to live up to norms of femininity in order to operate effectively. Hegemonic gender discourse historically has camouflaged hierarchy and the great power differential between masculinity and femininity by employing the euphemisms of difference and complementarity, since heteronormativity, unlike white supremacy or class discourse, requires two separate (but unequal) *ideals*. Dominant discourse ensures, as it were, that femininity retains a positive valence that neither blackness nor lower-classedness retain. Thus, it can be argued that a parallel — but less privileged — norm that connects whiteness and middle-classedness with femininity (in a slightly different configuration of norms) exists alongside the overarching norm.

The text that perhaps most explicitly ties norms of race and class together is James Weldon Johnson's *The Autobiography of an Ex-Colored Man*. At the end of the novel, after the protagonist has decided to pass as a white man, he tells us that he is going to avail himself of "every opportunity to make a white man's success; and that, if it can be summed up in any one word, means 'money'" (193). The irony of this sentence notwithstanding, the ex-colored man very clearly is making the connection between moving up the class hierarchy and whiteness. The sentence can be understood in at least two different ways. First, by desiring to make money, the ex-colored man is indicating that in the future he will endeavor to approximate the white man's (i.e., dominant) ideal of class status and success, thus highlighting a certain connection between norms of race and class. Or second, the narrative is pointing to how the assumption of whiteness is coupled to norms of class. In other words, accumulating wealth and approximating middle-class norms diminishes the likelihood that the ex-colored man's "great secret" (that he has been passing) will be found out, since his endeavor to emulate middle-class status will reinforce the assumption of whiteness. But, as Nella Larsen and James Weldon Johnson expose through their narratives of passing, for those subjects who have been interpellated into the social order as "black," this whitening effect is illusory and obtains only for individual light-enough-to-pass "black" subjects.

My claim that race, gender, and class reinforce one another through the repetition and overlapping of norms echoes arguments made by critics such as Gail Bederman, Patricia Hill Collins, and Ann McClintock. While these critics have underscored the interarticulation of the different categories of identification by and through specific discourses, they contend that the categories themselves — rather than the norms linked to the categories — mutually construct one another; this contention, I believe, not only fails to capture some of the more subtle ways that categories of identification reinforce each other, but actually may proscribe any attempt to ask after the specific genealogies of gender, class, and race.

Identification and Desire-to-Be

In this section, I go beyond my investigation of the *norms* linked to the different categories in order to emphasize the importance of the identification/"desire-to-be" nexus. I propose that the very *differences* or *irreducibility* of the categories of race, gender, and class on the level of identification and "desire-to-be" have also served to shore up the existing power relations, albeit in a different way from the overlapping of norms. If, for example, positive and negative power operate by helping shape the very desires and aspirations of subjects, then the concomitant privileging of whiteness — and thus the production of the desire to live up to norms associated with whiteness — alongside the barring of certain subjects from identifying with whiteness, actually serves to buttress white supremacy. After all, white supremacist regimes require both the desirability of whiteness and a patent racial hierarchy. As the various texts illustrate, a subject's very disadvantage vis-à-vis categories of identification, ironically and perhaps paradoxically, can be seen to make him/her all the more desirous of attempting to approximate the *norms* linked to the specific categories of identification. In this way, "disadvantage" may actually serve to strengthen dominant norms.

I first will present examples from *The Autobiography of an Ex-Colored Man* and *The Rise of David Levinsky* that dramatize the different operations of race and class on the level of identification and the desire-to-be. These analyses should be kept in mind when I proceed to discuss Larsen's characterization of Irene Redfield. Both sets of examples focus on the identification/"desire-to-be" nexus in order not only to show the centrality of this nexus in the production and maintenance of social hierarchies, but also to underscore that this nexus can spawn multiple and mutually reinforcing (hegemonic) effects.

Both David Levinsky and the ex-colored man express reservations at the end of the novels about their life decisions. *The Autobiography of an Ex-Colored Man* concludes with the protagonist's anguished thought that his choice to pass over into the white world might have constituted a selling of "his birthright for a mess of pottage" (211). In Cahan's novel, David cannot escape images from his past either. He tells us that, "My past and my present do not comport well. David, the poor lad swinging over a Talmud volume at the Preacher's Synagogue, seems to have more in common with my inner identity than David Levinsky, the well-known cloak manufacturer" (530). Moreover, both protagonists express regret that they did not follow an alternative path: David that he did not become "an intellectual man," a "college professor," the ex-colored man that he did not pursue a ragtime career.

What both endings gesture toward, I argue, is that race identification has had stronger psychic effects in the United States than class identification. This, in turn, points to the coercive aspect of race identification, and the punishments meted out to subjects who attempt to identify differently. *The Autobiography* can be seen to narrativize just how powerful the dominant injunction to desire to live up to norms of whiteness has been, especially in the early twentieth century. In order to make a "white man's success," the ex-colored man is forced to disidentify totally with blackness. And yet, it is not his financial success but his "passing" that is constituted, both in the novel and in the protagonist's mind, as a transgression, as something liable to bring harsh and even lethal repercussions. As I have asserted in Chapter Three, since sustained identification with the lower class has not been encouraged by the dominant social order, moving up the class hierarchy and disidentifying with one's previous class status has not been constituted a transgression in the United States. By contrast, race identification has been compelled and policed; the ex-colored man's disidentification with blackness is therefore a clear threat to the existing social hierarchies. This is especially true in the ex-colored man's case since he "looks white"; his passing over into the white world potentially could "disprove" the one-drop-of-black-blood law. As he himself muses after he has passed successfully as white and begun to succeed as a "white" business man: "Do I not disprove the theory that one drop of Negro blood renders a man unfit?" (197).

The ex-colored man's class status is described as fluctuating throughout the novel, and when, at the end of the narrative, he articulates his status as an "ordinary successful white man who has made a little money," it is not his class position that he has trouble identifying with, but rather his racial position. After all, the narrative gives sufficient hints or indications that, had the ex-colored man chosen to pursue a career as a "black" ragtime musician, he also would have been a financial success. The ex-colored man has crossed the color line, but always with the threat of being found out and punished.

The difference between class and "race" identification is also dramatized in the ending of Cahan's novel. David, I contend, sees his abandonment of or (at least partial) disidentification with more traditional Judaism as much more problematic than his upward mobility. Although he has not had to disidentify completely with Jewishness in order to "become American," he has had to emphasize his sameness with rather than his difference from gentiles. Moreover, despite David's claim that he cannot rid himself totally of his initial interpellation into the dominant social order as a poor and under-class subject, his regrets do not take the form of rejecting upward mobility or even discomfort at identifying with the middle class. In fact, Cahan, like Johnson, emphasizes how the forsaking of one's "racial" identification has constituted a transgression.[14] On the one hand, at the end of the novel, Cahan has David decide not to marry a gentile woman, even though he likes her very much. The reason for his decision, David tells us, is "not the faith of my fathers," but rather "the medieval prejudice against our people which makes so many marriages between Jew and Gentile a failure" (527). On the other hand, when speaking about his class position, Levinsky confesses that he regrets not becoming a college professor, one of the many *middle-class* occupations. It seems that there is encouragement to identify as middle class, while there is a prohibition on attempting to identify differently vis-à-vis "race." And while David does not really have to identify differently regarding "race," his interpellation as a Jew seems to have social and psychic effects that class interpellation does not.

The ex-colored man and David are interpellated into U.S. society at a disadvantage in relation to the dominant norm: David in terms of his class and "off-whiteness" and the ex-colored man in relation to race. However, due to their desire to access positions of power and privilege, the two protagonists' very disadvantage can be seen to make them all the more desirous of attempting to approximate the *norms* linked to the specific categories of identification with which they have not been allowed to identify (totally).

This is illustrated with particular force in *The Autobiography.* The novel's protagonist divides the black population in the United States into three distinct groups: the desperate class, the servant class, and the well-to-do and educated colored people. The upper class, he tells us, lives in the most isolation from their white neighbors, and this is true despite their money, education, and culture (79). When the ex-colored man describes the lives of the well-to-do and educated colored people in the United States, he tells us that they have education and money, wear nice clothes, and live in comfortable houses. In other words, they are indistinguishable from their white counterparts in every aspect of life *except* in their racial classification (80). Moreover, it is these subjects, those who could best "appreciate sympathetic co-operation" between the races, who are forced into isolation. This isolation bars them from being admitted to many sites of power that are open to subjects who have been interpellated into the dominant society as white. These well-to-do colored people described by the protagonist, however, are especially desirous of approximating regulatory ideals that historically have been associated with whiteness: "These people have their dances and dinners and card parties, their musicals, and their literary societies. The women attend social affairs dressed in good taste, and the men in dress suits which they own" (82). In fact, this group of colored people's endless effort to live up to dominant norms is "successful" enough to cause great unease among their white counterparts. The white middle class, as the ex-colored man tells us, sees these efforts to emulate dominant norms as "monkey-like imitations" (80) and adamantly refuses to mix with or accept this group.

These well-to-do black subjects are barred from identifying as white. And yet these subjects appear all the more desirous of approximating the *norms* linked to whiteness. And by approximating the norms of whiteness, these subjects, in effect, are buttressing not only norms of whiteness, but also and crucially—as one of the effects of the repetition of norms—the overarching norm(s). Creating literary societies, for instance, is related to and inextricable from the endeavor to live up to norms of civility and gentility, which, as we already have seen in the previous section, historically have been linked to race, class, *and* gender.

In Nella Larsen's novella, Irene Redfield is also preoccupied with maintaining the appearances of white, middle-class prosperity. She busies herself with mothering, social obligations, and "uplift work." She does not work for wages outside of the home. Irene attempts to be as prim, as proper, and as bourgeois as (ideals of) white middle-class ladies.[15] Larsen's description of Irene's "desire-to-be" underscores the two aspects of U.S. race discourse that I have been discussing in this section. First, the characterization of Irene, like the characterization of the ex-colored man as well as the characterization of the black middle class in *Quicksand*, emphasizes just how powerful the injunctions to desire to live up to norms of "whiteness" and the "middle class" have been. Irene, however, has been interpellated into the dominant social order as a black middle-class woman. She is compelled to identify as black, for as Angela Davis has argued, a woman of African descent has little choice but to identify as black.[16] Therefore, no matter how successful her performance of whiteness is, she is barred from ever being accepted (totally) into the white race not only due to the compelled identification with blackness, but also, as I argued in the previous chapter, due to the circumscribed array of "white" norms that black subjects were permitted to emulate; that is, unless she passes, which entails a form of disidentification with blackness and the constant threat of "being found out." Second, because of her initial interpellation as a black subject, Irene, who is depicted as especially desirous of maintaining a nonmarginal existence, compensates for this fact by making sure she approximates as much as she possibly can the norms linked to whiteness; this, in turn, reinforces the dominant norms linked to gender and class.

Subjects who are positioned as disadvantaged vis-à-vis the overarching norm and who wish to access some forms of privilege are compelled and urged to emulate the regulatory norms associated with the category in relation to which they are "disadvantaged." But more importantly, their disadvantage seems actually to spur and reinforce the desire to live up to the regulatory ideals, which has effects beyond any one category of identification. The emulation of the norms linked to one category of identification reinforces the norms linked to the other categories, as I have argued. But as the depictions of Helga Crane, David Levinsky, Irene Redfield, and the ex-colored man all dramatize, subjects who desire to live up to the dominant norms linked to one category tend to desire to live up to the dominant norms linked to the other categories. Thus we begin to see a linking of the different categories' "desire-to-be." If a subject wishes to maintain a nonmarginal existence in which s/he has access to at least some positions or sites of power, it seems that s/he is compelled and encouraged to emulate the dominant norms of not just one but all of the categories of identification. This is not surprising, of course, if we consider that the overarching norm subsumes all of these categories under its rubric. Simply put, regardless of how a subject is interpellated and forced (and encouraged) to identify, subjects are compelled and urged to desire to approximate the entire array of dominant norms.

The Assumption of Privilege

Yet another way in which the different categories of identification interact, and the last one that I will be discussing in this chapter, is through what I term the assumption of privilege. I define privilege as the *hegemonic linking or collapsing of identification and desire-to-be*. Privilege operates in such a way as to naturalize certain categories of identification; however, it is relative and always is constituted in relation to the existing social hierarchies. In a white supremacist society, a subject who is initiated into the social order as white will be able to assume privilege, since s/he is compelled and encouraged to identify as white *and* to desire to live up to the norms linked to whiteness. By sharp contrast, under this same regime, the collapse of "black" identification with the desire to live up to norms associated with blackness would in no way confer privilege (on the subject) vis-à-vis the hegemonic system. The relinking of identification as and desire-to-be black for subjects interpellated into the dominant social order as black tends to marginalize them even further (and in early twentieth century certainly left them vulnerable to potential violence). The assumption of privilege consequently must be understood as both relative and relational.

Subjects, as we have seen in the previous section, can be "privileged" vis-à-vis one category and not another. When one specific category is a site of "privilege," that is, when there is a collapse of identification and desire-to-be, there tends to be a rendering invisible of that specific category of identification. This may — and many times does — have the effect of bringing into focus the other categories of identification in relation to which a subject is not "privileged." However, the converse is also true. The singling out of the area (or areas) of one's disadvantage tends to reinforce the "naturalness" of the areas in which one is privileged. Thus, there is an interplay of "absence" and "presence," which is produced by the different configurations of identification/desire-to-be within the categories of gender, race, and class. Often when one category is pushed to the forefront, the other categories fade into the background and more easily can be "taken for granted." This "tactic" of positive and negative power, I argue, not only reinforces existing social hierarchies by producing degrees of privilege, but also operates by creating different layers of "awareness" regarding the different categories of identification. This intricate relationship among the various configurations of identification and desire-to-be also can be said to produce a "divide and conquer" effect.

A subject who is interpellated into the social order as a lower-class white male must constantly attempt to embody the norms of whiteness and masculinity, but there is a difference between this subject's relation to his whiteness and maleness, and his relationship to his lower-classedness. The difference, I argue, has to do with the collapsing of identification and the "desire-to-be."[17] For the subject who is interpellated as white and male, the identification with whiteness and maleness is coupled with the desire to live up to norms associated with these categories. That is, this subject is forced and encouraged to live up to norms of whiteness and masculinity. There is no de-linking of identification and desire-to-be, and thus the assumption of privilege is more likely to occur. The subject's continuous attempt to live up to the dominant norms of whiteness and maleness are rendered invisible in this way, and the performance of whiteness and maleness are much less likely to require "reflection" or "awareness." Because there is no gap between identification and the "desire-to-be," the dominant norms linked to these categories of identification are more likely to be taken for granted and, in this way, naturalized. The naturalization of certain hegemonic regulatory ideals has far-reaching consequences for the norms linked to other categories of identification, not only due to the overlapping of norms, but also due to the way privilege operates to render challenges to the status quo ineffective. A subject who is privileged in one respect but not in another tends to struggle to access privilege in the areas where he/she is lacking it. But by striving to access privilege in the area in which one is lacking it, one effectively reinscribes privilege in and on the sites where one does "have" it.

In *The Autobiography of an Ex-Colored Man*, the protagonist's interpellation as male serves as a site of privilege. Initiated into society as a man, he also desires to live up to the norms associated with masculinity. But his endeavors to live up to the norms of masculinity are never made explicit in the same way as his attempts to approximate whiteness (or even middle-classedness) are. Throughout the text, the ex-colored man examines questions of race and even class, and he is aware of the ways in which subjects interpellated into the U.S. racist regime must strive to approximate norms of civility and success if they wish to live nonmarginal lives. However, maleness continues to serve as his standard. There is no examination of the privilege that comes with "being a man" in the United States.

Speaking about the influence of race prejudice, the ex-colored man exclaims — echoing W. E. B. Du Bois' notion of the black man's double consciousness — that the colored man looks at everything through the prism of his relationship to society as a *colored* man. The ex-colored man draws attention to the adjective "colored," which is italicized in the narrative. The noun, "man," is, in effect, rendered neutral; he is the naturalized subject in all of the ex-colored man's discourses about race in the United States. In fact, whenever the ex-colored man discusses the "Negro" problem, he slips into the gendered pronoun, he: "The battle was first waged over the right of the Negro to be classed as a human being with a soul; later, as to whether *he* had sufficient intellect to master even the rudiments of learning; and today it is being fought out over *his* social recognition" (75, emphasis added).

When the same theoretical white male subject whom I introduced in the beginning of this section is disadvantaged vis-à-vis the hegemonic class position, a gap or dissonance appears between identification and the desire-to-be. This same subject then is made aware or conscious, on some level, of his disadvantage regarding class, and his attempts to climb the class hierarchy and approximate norms of middle-classedness cannot be "taken for granted" in the same way that his performative re-iteration of ideals of masculinity can. In the case of the ex-colored man, he is aware of his lack of privilege vis-à-vis race, while concomitantly he seems quite oblivious regarding the privileges that "being a man" — even a colored man — confer.

In order to understand better the distinction or difference between a subject's relationship to categories of identification in which there is a hegemonic collapse of identification and the "desire-to-be" and where there is a de-linking of these two loci, I would like to borrow and thus transport the concepts of pre-reflexive habitus and reflexive habitus from the sociologist Pierre Bourdieu. Moreover, I would like to describe briefly how a slightly modified notion of pre-reflexive and reflexive habitus can help us conceptualize the workings of privilege and the different modalities of performativity engendered by the different configurations of identification and "desire-to-be."

Habitus is, according to Bourdieu, the generative and unifying principle—a principle of the construction of the social world—through which an agent makes sense of his/her position in social space; but habitus is also the historical product of that agent's social position. This means that habitus is structured—it is the product of the history of a certain agent's position in social space. However, it is simultaneously structuring or generative, in the sense that while the unifying principle underlying habitus governs or structures the way a given agent perceives and acts in the world, this principle does not determine practice mechanically.

Bourdieu goes on to make a distinction between "unconscious" and more reflexive action. Moving away from a psychoanalytic understanding of the psyche, Bourdieu claims that when there is a correspondence between a habitus and a field, which he defines as "an independent social universe with its own laws of functioning," agents "perform" in the field without having to be conscious of their actions. They have a "feel for the game" (of the field), which entails a certain bodily disposition; this "feel for the game" is pre-reflexive in that it does not require calculation or reflection. In other words, habitus is not a form of consciousness but a disposition of the body that is (re)produced by and through socialization.

The field of education, for example, has its own symbolic capital (objects or attributes that accrue meaning by social agents imbuing them with value) in the form of degrees and titles. An agent who has been inculcated with the rules of the field and socialized to accept that the stakes of such a field are worth fighting for will enter the university with a "feel for the game." He or she will know what to do and how to do it without any conscious calculation. Or in Bourdieu's own words, "[Y]our mind is structured according to the structures of the world in which you play, everything will seem obvious and the question of knowing if the game is 'worth the candle' will not even be asked."[18]

In *Salome of the Tenements*, Yezierska brilliantly illustrates this "feel for the game" in her characterization of John Manning, the millionaire philanthropist. Born into the world of wealth and as an Anglo-Saxon man, Manning's habitus, or "society written in the body," is the product and conditioning of his particularly privileged position in social space. He is "the product of generations of Puritans," sprung from a "patrician race" (33, 84). Manning accordingly has a feel for the game in the dominant cultural and social fields, since his habitus is a product of those fields.[19] Without any effort or reflection on his part, he knows the right thing to do, the right thing to say in social situations, the right gestures to make; in other words, Manning has imbibed all of the social graces that make one's interaction with the social field "natural."

During Sonya and John's wedding reception for Manning's family and friends, who make up the New York social elite, Manning tells the distraught and uncomfortable Sonya to "just be natural" (122). This scene dramatically discloses both the correspondence between his habitus and the social situation in which he finds himself and the non-correspondence between Sonya's habitus and the social setting. Sonya cannot "just be natural," since "being natural" for her entails fervor and demonstrativeness—behavior unacceptable in this context; she does not have a "feel for the game." In fact, Sonya recognizes that in order to please her husband she will have to make herself "a parrot of words and a monkey of manners" (130). This lack of correspondence between habitus and field potentially can open up a space of reflexive habitus, one that can reflect on its practices and the fact that certain norms must be approximated in order to "fit in."

However, if we understand pre-reflexive habitus not only in Bourdieu's sense as the social embodied or the incorporation of certain aspects of the different social fields, but more specifically as being constituted by a coerced and encouraged identification with regulatory norms linked to the categories of identification through which subjects are interpellated into society, then perhaps we can begin to understand how certain norms and thus certain modalities of performativity are "taken for granted." That is, we may begin to understand why certain modalities of performativity are rendered invisible and naturalized by both subjects and society at large.

A subject, interpellated into white supremacist society as white, will identify as white and be compelled and encouraged to live up to norms of whiteness. This subject's habitus therefore is constituted, at least in large part, by the disposition to identify with *and* perform whiteness. Bourdieu's conception of field is temporarily reconceptualized here as hegemonic categories of identification linked to regulatory norms, that is, as the categories of identification through which subjects gain intelligibility. Since there is a correspondence or fit between the interpellated identification and the subject's desire to live up to the norms of whiteness, there is also, at least in one sense, a pre-reflexive performativity. There is no dissonance or gap between identification and desire-to-be, which, in turn, engenders a performativity less marked by possible ruptures and dissonance. The constant attempt to approximate the norms—which the subject *already* identifies with—produces and reinforces the subject's "feel for the game." Positing different "layers" of performativity may help us theorize not only how privilege operates, but also why dislodging notions of naturalness has been so difficult, as well as the different and intricate modes through which the overarching norm reproduces and reinscribes itself.

Consequently, the assumption of privilege works through the linking and thus the collapsing of identification and desire-to-be. This means that when a subject is interpellated into the dominant social order in a position of privilege vis-à-vis certain categories of identification but not in others, the attempt to access privilege through emulating the norms linked to the categories that he/she was not interpellated as privileged tends to reinforce the norms linked to those categories; it also tends to reinforce the overarching norm. But more importantly for my purposes in this section, focusing on one's "inadequacy" in one area many times leads to a naturalization of one's privilege regarding other areas. Although this is reminiscent of my argument in the previous section (and indeed I am building on my previous arguments), here I am underscoring the intricate play of presence and absence, in which certain categories fade into the background and become the unmarked "ground" for the subject's attempt to emulate norms associated with other categories of identification.

For instance, Irene's ultimate confession that race is the category "that *bound* and *suffocated* her" (225, emphasis added) renders invisible the sites where she is positioned as privileged in relation to dominant U.S. society—class, for instance. The narrative makes it very clear that Irene was born into the middle class; she comes from an upper-middle-class, college-educated black family (164). There has never been any dissonance or gap between her interpellation and identification as middle class, and her desire to live up to the norms linked to class. The rendering invisible of her privilege as a middle-class subject is dramatized in the scene where Irene suspects her husband, Brian, is having an affair with Clare Kendry. Not knowing whether to betray Clare by revealing her racial origins to Clare's racist white husband, Irene bitterly reflects that it is "enough to suffer as a woman, an individual, on one's own account, without having to suffer for the race as well" (225). In effect, Irene is pointing to the ways in which she is disadvantaged vis-à-vis the existing social hierarchies. The modality of performativity engendered by the categories through which she has been positioned at a disadvantage regarding the mythical norm is thus less likely to be pre-reflexive in the sense that she, as we can see from the passage above, is more likely to be "aware" of some elements of power or of the norms that constitute these categories of identification. For Irene, however, the noncorrespondence between the identification and the "desire-to-be" in the case of race does not in any way mean that she relinquishes her attempt to embody the dominant norms associated with either race or gender (228). But what is perhaps more interesting with respect to my argument is that Irene leaves out one crucial category, that of class. And this elision points both to Irene's privileged position regarding class and to how, when there is a collapsing of identification and desire, the category tends to be taken for granted.

Thus, we begin to see the complicated modes through which power operates to render indiscernible the norms associated with class, race, and gender (and therefore the categories themselves). In the case of Irene, norms associated with the middle class are produced as natural and normal. In the ex-colored man's case, masculinity continues to serve as the unmarked norm, even as Johnson has his protagonist critique the classist and racist aspects of (Johnson's fictive) U.S. Progressive Era society. For Irene and the ex-colored man, class and gender respectively are the sites of pre-reflexive performativity, which, in turn, serve as the unmarked background for the other modalities of performativity through which they attempt to live up to the ideals associated with the other categories of identification.

Yezierska's depiction of John Manning, who is privileged in almost every respect, exemplifies how power works to produce an "unconscious," unreflexive, or "taken-for-granted" relationship to one's privilege, but also highlights the ways in which privilege can become a "handicap" (32). On the one hand, John Manning is depicted as having a quiet self-assurance, naturalness, and complacency, which, as Pierre Bourdieu argues, comes from being situated advantageously vis-à-vis the dominant culture. On the other hand, John decides to "break away from . . . the deadly conventions of his class . . . [and] live among the Ghetto people" (32). In certain contexts and under certain circumstances, privilege may actually enable subjects to develop a more reflexive performativity.

I have tried to capture a few of the very complex ways in which the different categories of identification interact with one another and reinforce the overarching or mythical norm in this chapter. In so doing, I also have endeavored to complicate my previous argument regarding the irreducibility of gender, class, and race by demonstrating that, in social practice, gender, class, and race cannot be separated. In all five chapters, however, I have focused on the way that norms operate on the hegemonic level. I have done this, perhaps paradoxically, *in order to better understand the conditions of possibility of subversion.* I believe that only by identifying dominant norms and by trying to understand at least some of the ways in which these regulatory ideals operate as positive and negative power can we begin to "perform" more reflexively.

Epilogue

IN THIS BOOK, I have attempted to make two contributions to existing scholarly discussions — one literary and the other theoretical. Literarily, I have argued that reading modern African- and Jewish-American novels together through the lens of performativity can bring to light new aspects of this literature and, consequently, can help provide original readings of the texts. My choice of *Arrogant Beggar*, *The Autobiography of an Ex-Colored Man*, *Passing*, *Quicksand*, *The Rise of David Levinsky*, and *Salome of the Tenements* has not been coincidental. For the past years, I have been interested in looking at narratives that explicitly thematize the power of norms, and, more particularly, norms that historically have been linked to dominant notions of Americanness. Since all six novels present protagonists who attempt (at least at certain stages in the narratives) to move from margin to center by carving out a niche for themselves in mainstream U.S. society, they become powerful sites for exploring the ways in which dominant norms have helped to produce and sustain social stratification in the United States. For example, the texts reveal how and why the ambiguous in-between category of ethnicity emerged during the twentieth century in the United States. And it was my comparative approach — the juxtaposition of African- and Jewish-American narratives — that led me to conclude that the very intelligibility of ethnicity has depended upon the prior construction of the black-white divide.

Theoretically, my basic claim has been that the different categories of identification — gender, class, race, and ethnicity — operate differently on the level of identification and the desire-to-be and therefore each category produces a unique modality of performativity. I would like to suggest here that this claim is important for at least three reasons. First, by tracing the way that each category operates through a specific configuration of identification and desire-to-be, it becomes possible to account for the way performative reiteration subtends identity all of the time without reducing one category to another. The identification/ desire-to-be nexus, in other words, can help explain the "irreducibility" of the different categories, which many cultural theorists have pointed to but — as far as I am aware — spent little time explicating or mapping out. Second, my conceptualization of distinct modalities of performativity does not preclude a theorization of the ways that gender, race, class, and ethnicity interact and reinforce hegemonic norms. Rather, my argument has been that the very *differences* among the categories have served to shore up existing power relations. Finally, by revealing how each of these categories has operated differently on the level of identification and desire-to-be, it also becomes possible to unravel — and *theorize* — some of the complex modes, such as the "assumption of privilege," through which dominant norms produce and sustain social stratification. My analysis further suggests that resistance and agency cannot be understood without understanding what privilege is and how it often operates to render challenges to the status quo ineffective.

As I argued in Chapter Six, the distinction between identification and desire-to-be can help us conceptualize the elusive notion of privilege. I therefore have endeavored to outline what privilege "is" and to describe the complex ways it can and does work to undermine resistance. If it is indeed true that categories of identification operate differently, and, through an intricate interplay of presence and absence, produce degrees of privilege, then we can begin to understand — again, *theoretically* — how (and why), for example, a progressive feminist agenda can go hand in hand with a racist one. Many black feminists, such as bell hooks, have *shown* how racism informed the Woman's Movement in the United States. I believe that my conceptualization of privilege theorizes the mechanisms that have allowed for and even "promoted" the infiltration of racism into feminism's supposedly universalist and egalitarian agenda.

All of which inevitably brings me to the crucial questions of agency and the possibility of resistance. My discussion in *Performing Americanness*, for the most part, has focused on what the various novels can tell us about dominant discourses and norms, and how they help form and regulate our identification(s) and desire(s)-to-be. Paradoxically, and as I stated toward the end of the last chapter, I see my concentration on the workings of dominant norms as an attempt to better understand the conditions of possibility of subversion. I believe that only by identifying dominant norms and by trying to understand at least some of the ways in which they operate as positive and negative power can we begin to "perform" more reflexively.

Reading African- and Jewish-American texts together and focusing on the representations of dominant norms of Americanness has only strengthened my conviction that resistance is incredibly complex, dependent on an ultimately indeterminable context, and, in many ways, unpredictable. Analyzing this literature has thus led me to ask after the *conditions* of possibility of resistance. If agency does indeed emerge, at least in large part, from a subject's ability to negotiate among the different norms that make up the field of intelligibility, as the texts indeed suggest, then it follows that we must be vigilant about keeping alternative and contestatory norms in circulation. Of course, we do not know in advance what these alternative norms will be, since, as we saw in Chapter Five with the New Negro Woman ideal, the make-up of contestatory norms is always related in some way to existing and current hegemonic regulatory injunctions. Nor is this to say that we will always or necessarily wish to identify with or assume these alternative norms. But if we do want to envision a more democratic notion of "Americanness," then we must not only trace the way it has signified in the past and the exclusions it has produced, but we also need to be able to imagine, create, and promote alternative notions of Americanness, ones that are not only more inclusive but are also continuously open to contestation.

Notes

1. I put "ethnic" in quotes in order to draw attention to the inadequacy of this term. If, as I argue in Chapter Four, race and ethnicity cannot be conflated, then referring to African-American fiction as "ethnic" literature is misleading; however, the expression "racial literature" also seems to me problematic. "Ethnic" is used to simplify matters here, but will be problematized in the following pages.

2. As George Hutchinson has argued in a different context: "The issue of American national identity was . . . the dominant problematic structuring the literary field" during the first decades of the twentieth century. See Hutchinson, *The Harlem Renaissance in Black and White* (Cambridge, Mass.: Harvard University Press, 1995), 13.

3. For a concise history of this transformation from independent production to corporate capitalism, see Glenn Porter, *The Rise of Big Business: 1860–1920* (1973; reprint, Arlington Heights, Ill.: Harlan Davidson Inc., 1992).

4. See, for example, Hasia Diner's seminal book, *In the Almost Promised Land: American Jews and Black, 1915–1935* (1977; reprint, Westport, Conn.: Greenwood Press, 1995), esp. 3–27.

5. Hence the use of the epithet "Harlem Renaissance." Henry Louis Gates calls Phillis Wheatley's meeting "with eighteen of the most influential thinkers and politicians of the Massachusetts Colony" in order to verify the authorship of her poems, "the primal scene of African American letters." See Gates, "Phillis Wheatley on Trial," *New Yorker*, January 20, 2003, 82–87.

6. Hazel Carby, in her now classic *Reconstructing Womanhood: The Emergence of the Afro-American Woman Novelist* (New York: Oxford University Press, 1987), points out that the term "renaissance" has been used, almost exclusively, to refer to the literary and artistic production of intellectuals in Harlem in the years between the end of World War I and the Depression. She draws our attention to the black literary activity in Boston at the turn of the century, which was also concerned with creating a black renaissance. While Carby probably would argue against dating the "coming into its own" of a black literary culture, she likely would agree that there was more literary activity than ever before at the turn of the twentieth century.

7. A few distinctions need to be made here. On the one hand, the authors and

critics of the early twentieth century who attempted to create and define African- and Jewish-American literature had varying and occasionally conflicting conceptions of what constituted the "core" of these "ethnic" literatures. See, for example, Hutchinson, *Harlem Renaissance*, on the debates between the old guard, that is, Du Bois, and the younger generation, artists such as Claude McKay. Biological descent, of course, played a dominant role in most of these definitions. On the other hand, contemporary critics tend to define these literary traditions using some combination of thematic models, "discursive practices," and descent. For a discussion of the thematic model, see David Fine, "In the Beginning: American-Jewish Fiction: 1880–1930," in *Handbook of American-Jewish Literature*, ed. Louis Fried (Westport, Conn.: Greenwood Press, 1988), 17. For a discussion of "discursive practices," see Henry Louis Gates, Jr., *Loose Canons: Notes on the Culture Wars* (New York: Oxford University Press, 1992), esp. 79. I will be using the terms African- and Jewish-American literature simply to refer to literature written by African- and Jewish-identified Americans whose literary texts query and thematize what it means to be "black" and/or "Jewish" in the United States. As will become clear in the next few pages, I understand identification in a very specific way. I do not enter into the important debate concerning what exactly constitutes this "ethnic" literature. For two interesting discussions on this issue, see the introduction to Jules Chametzsky, John Felstiner, Hilene Flanzbaum, and Kathryn Hellerstein, eds., *Jewish American Literature: A Norton Anthology* (New York: W.W. Norton, 2001), 1–23; and Ann DuCille, *The Coupling Convention: Sex, Text, and Tradition in Black Women's Fiction* (New York: Oxford University Press, 1993), esp. 3–13.

8. See, for example, Jules Chametzky, introduction to *The Rise of David Levinsky* (1917; reprint, New York: Penguin Books, 1993), vii–xxix; and Mark Krupnick, "Jewish-American Literature," in *New Immigrant Literatures in the United States: A Sourcebook to our Multicultural Literary Heritage*, ed. Alpana Sharma Knippling (Westport, Conn.: Greenwood Press, 1996), 295–309.

9. A number of other studies do compare African- and Jewish-American literature, but they do so as part of a multi-ethnic comparative study — thus including other minority groups — and their perspective is very different. These studies usually fall into one of two overall frameworks: a presentation of a multi-ethnic literary "dialogue" or an attempt to redefine modernism and make it more inclusive of minority writers. Examples of the first category include Carol Batker, *Reforming Fictions: Native, African, and Jewish American Women's Literature and Journalism in the Progressive Era* (New York: Columbia University Press, 2000); and Gay Wilentz, *Healing Narratives: Women Writers Curing Cultural Dis-ease* (New Brunswick, N.J.: Rutgers University Press, 2000). For an example of the attempt to redefine modernism, see Delia Caparoso Konzett's *Ethnic Modernisms: Anzia Yezierska, Zora Neale Hurston, Jean Rhys, and the Aesthetics of Dislocation* (New York: Palgrave Macmillan, 2002).

10. The studies that compare African- and Jewish-American literature exclusively include Emily Miller Budick, *Blacks and Jews in Literary Conversation* (Cambridge: Cambridge University Press, 1998); Ethan Goffman, *Imagining Each Other: Blacks and Jews in Contemporary American Literature* (Albany: State University of New York Press, 2000); Adam Zachary Newton, *Facing Black and Jew: Literature as Public Space in Twentieth-Century America* (Cambridge: Cambridge University Press, 1999); and Eric Sundquist, *Strangers in the Land: Blacks, Jews, Post-Holocaust America* (Cambridge, Mass.: Harvard University Press, 2005).

11. There is one important exception that I am aware of. Martin Japtok's *Growing Up Ethnic: Nationalism and the Bildungsroman in African American and Jewish American Fiction* (Iowa City: University of Iowa Press 2005) compares early-twentieth-century African-American and Jewish-American literature. However, he concentrates on the way that each ethnic group perceives itself through literary representations, as well as the similar literary forms used by both groups to configure "ethnicity." While his book provides excellent readings of the six texts on which he chooses to focus, his framework is very different from mine, since he concentrates exclusively on the way certain African- and Jewish-American texts construct "ethnicity." Although I find his contention that these minority authors used similar literary devices convincing, he does not use performativity as a theoretical lens, which, as I argue in Chapter Four, complicates any attempt to conflate race with ethnicity.

12. This tendency is more pronounced in analyses of the Jewish-American literature. For examples of this kind of interesting but, in my view, problematic reading, see Lori Harrison-Kahan, "Drunk with the Fiery Rhythms of Jazz," *MFS: Modern Fiction Studies* 51, no. 2 (2005): 416–36; and Melanie Levinson, "'To Make Myself for a Person': 'Passing' Narratives and the Divided Self in the Work of Anzia Yezierska," *Studies in American Jewish Literature* 13 (1994): 2–9. In relation to the African-American literature, see, for example, Nell Sullivan, "Nella Larsen's *Passing* and the Fading Subject," *African American Review* 32 (1998): 373–86.

13. Stephen Knadler provides a good overview of the dichotomized debate regarding passing narratives. See Knadler, "Traumatized Racial Performativity: Passing in Nineteenth-Century African-American Testimonies," *Cultural Critique* 55 (2003): esp. 67–68.

14. Invoking Jacques Derrida's reformulation of J. L. Austin's work on performative utterances, Butler formally introduces Derrida's concepts of "iterability" and "(re)citationality" into her idea of gender performativity in *Bodies That Matter: On the Discursive Limits of "Sex"* (New York: Routledge, 1993).

15. I will be using the term "dominant social order" throughout this book as a way of describing what Butler terms "the symbolic order," that is, as the domain of *socially instituted norms* or the sedimentation of hegemonic norms and sanctioned social practices. More specifically, this domain consists of a series of hegemonic demands, sanctions, prohibitions, impossible idealizations, and threats

that wield the power to produce the field of culturally viable subjects. See Butler, *Bodies That Matter*, esp. 106.

16. The above formulation is oversimplified for the sake of brevity, since subjects are compelled to identify with certain *categories*, such as man, woman, black, or white, in order to remain viable in a given society, and these categories exist as regulatory injunctions, because they are always linked to historically specific and normative characteristics. It is this *linkage* of category to traits that helps constitute different norms. For instance, a series of traits (assertive/competitive/ambitious) that have no necessary connection to one another historically have been concatenated to normative notions of manhood in the United States; thus, being assertive has been one of the requirements or expectations of "being a real man." However, it would be mistaken to think that norms are merely repressive constructs. Rather, norms constitute and make social practices possible as they harness human energy and propel subjects to act in certain ways. This formulation is indebted to the insights of Michel Foucault in his *The History of Sexuality, Vol. I, An Introduction*, trans. Robert Hurley (New York: Vintage Books, 1990).

17. Although the language I use throughout the introduction seems to posit a subject prior to identification, I would in fact suggest that subjects emerge through this "crucible" of interpellation and subsequent identification.

18. Judith Butler, "Sovereign Performatives in the Contemporary Scene of Utterance," *Critical Inquiry* 23 (1997): 20.

19. A number of existing studies draw on the notion of performativity to analyze either African-American or Jewish-American literary texts. These include Sara Ahmed, "'She'll Wake Up One of These Days and Find She's Turned into a Nigger': Passing through Hybridity," *Theory, Culture & Society* 16 (1999): 87–105; Martin Favor, *Authentic Blackness: The Folk in the New Negro Renaissance* (Durham, N.C.: Duke University Press, 1999); Meredith Goldsmith, "'The Democracy of Beauty': Fashioning Ethnicity and Gender in the Fiction of Anzia Yezierska," *Yiddish* 11, nos. 3–4 (1999): 166–87; Knadler, "Traumatized Racial Performativity," 63–100; and Magdalena Zaborowska, "Americanization of a 'Queer Fellow': Performing Jewishness and Sexuality in Abraham's *The Rise of David Levinsky*," *American Studies in Scandinavia* 29 (1997): 18–27. Favor, for instance, invokes performative reiteration in his study of Harlem Renaissance literature. But while his text brilliantly interrogates the ways in which race, gender, and class are interarticulated, there is no in-depth theoretical discussion of performativity. Similarly, Zaborowska uses performativity as a lens through which to read *The Rise of David Levinsky*, yet her article does not provide a theoretical account of performativity, and ultimately it is not clear what exactly she means by the term.

20. One important exception is Stephen Knadler's "Traumatized Racial Performativity," which does give a theoretical account of performativity as he reads Frank Webb's 1857 novel, *The Garies and Their Friends*. His orientation is very different from mine, however, since he routes his discussion of performativity

through trauma theory and does not discuss how racial performativity differs from gender performativity.

21. Of course, the idea of a primary interpellation is a theoretical construct. Subjects are not interpellated once and for all, but rather they are interpellated continuously. The effectiveness of the primary address and subsequent identification is ensured through a process of materialization—not by a series of discrete moments, but rather by a subject's "acquisition of being through the citing of power" over time. In relation to gender, Butler calls this interpellation process the "girling" or "boying" of the subject. See Butler, *Bodies That Matter*, esp. 15, 232.

22. Michel Pecheux, *Language, Semantics, and Ideology* (New York: St. Martin's Press, 1982), 114.

23. My understanding of the ambivalent nature of identification is indebted to Judith Butler's formulations in her *Bodies That Matter* and *The Psychic Life of Power* (Stanford: Stanford University Press, 1997). Homi Bhabha's use of ambivalence in *The Location of Culture* (New York: Routledge, 1994) also has informed my understanding.

24. In Chapter Two, I detail how my understanding of identification and desire differs from Freudian and subsequent psychoanalytic conceptions of these terms.

25. For a comprehensive review of the binary terms that have been used to examine Harlem Renaissance texts, see Hutchinson, *Harlem Renaissance*, 16–23.

Chapter One: Performativity in Context (pages 16–32)

1. Abraham Cahan, *The Rise of David Levinsky* (1917; reprint, New York: Penguin Books, 1993), 3. All subsequent references to the novel come from this edition and page numbers will be given in parentheses.

2. Jules Chametzky, introduction to *The Rise of David Levinsky*, xxii.

3. See, for example, Ludgar Brinker, "The Gilded Void: Edith Wharton, Abraham Cahan, and the Turn-of-the-Century American Culture," *Yiddish* 9, nos. 3–4 (1994): 32–42; David Engel, "The 'Discrepancies' of the Modern: Towards a Revaluation of Abraham Cahan's *The Rise of David Levinsky*," *Studies in American Jewish Literature* 2 (1982): 36–60; Adam Sol, "Searching for Middle Ground in Abraham Cahan's *The Rise of David Levinsky* and Sidney Nyburg's *The Chosen People*," *Studies in American Jewish Literature* 8 (1989): 30–45; and Magdalena Zaborowska, "Americanization of a 'Queer Fellow': Performing Jewishness and Sexuality in Abraham's *The Rise of David Levinsky*," *American Studies in Scandinavia* 29 (1997): 18–27.

4. Sol, "Searching for Middle Ground," 30.

5. In Antomir, "race" operates by *neatly* bifurcating the Antomir population into gentiles and Jews, each group defining itself over and against the other. Even

geographical space is determined according to "race," rigorously keeping each group separate from the other. For example, the suburb, the Sands, is exclusively gentile. Thus, "race" discourse in Antomir can be seen to revolve around a Jew-gentile divide, which is quite different from the black-white divide that was operative in the United States, as I will argue in later chapters. "Jews," it is important to note, are considered a "racial" and not an "ethnic" group throughout the novel, since "ethnicity" as a separate and complicating category had not yet emerged. Chapter Four investigates the black-white divide as well as how and to what purposes ethnicity as a separate category emerged in the United States.

6. Daniel Boyarin, *Unheroic Conduct: The Rise of Heterosexuality and the Invention of the Jewish Man* (Berkeley: University of California Press, 1997), 2.

7. Ibid., 161.

8. Judith Butler, *Bodies That Matter: On the Discursive Limits of "Sex"* (New York: Routledge, 1993), 232.

9. Norms accumulate the force of authority and transparency through reiteration, and repetition is itself a citation of a prior set of ritualized practices, since norms are historically contingent, and their history not only "precedes but conditions their contemporary usages." See Butler, *Bodies That Matter*, 227.

10. In the next chapter, however, I will make a distinction between identification and the "desire-to-be."

11. Boyarin, *Unheroic Conduct*, 153.

12. Gail Bederman, *Manliness and Civilization: A Cultural History of Gender and Race in the United States, 1880–1917* (Chicago: University of Chicago Press, 1995), 8.

13. Boyarin, *Unheroic Conduct*, 156.

14. In a sense, David's uneven interpellation also discloses the way in which performativity operates through the process of materialization or sedimentation of norms; performativity is not constituted by a series of discrete moments, but rather the "acquisition of being through the citing of power" over time. See Butler, *Bodies That Matter*, 15.

15. Zaborowska, "Americanization of a 'Queer Fellow,'" 21–22.

16. Ibid.; emphasis added.

17. Bederman, *Manliness and Civilization*, 72.

18. Sander Gilman, *The Jew's Body* (New York: Routledge, 1991), 133.

19. Zaborowska, "Americanization of a 'Queer Fellow,'" 20. Warren Hoffman's provocative "The Rise (and Fall) of David Levinsky: Performing Jewish American Heterosexuality" also reads the novel through the lens of performativity. However, his reading focuses on sexuality rather than on gender, that is, masculinity, and he claims that the major tension in the text derives from David's inability to negotiate his homoerotic feelings for other men. While I think that Hoffman's argument that attempting to emulate heteronormativity has been a crucial aspect of "becoming" American for Jews is very important, the article seems to sug-

gest that there is a true and essential homoerotic desire: "the desire of one heart," which undercuts the claim that sexuality and gender identity are constituted by performativity. See Hoffman, "The Rise (and Fall) of David Levinsky: Performing Jewish American Heterosexuality," *MFS Modern Fiction Studies* 51, no. 2 (2005): esp. 399.

20. Judith Butler, *Gender Trouble* (New York: Routledge, 1990), 146.

21. Even though Reb Sender and Nephtali initially are set up as the most admirable characters, their portrayal too reveals the ineluctable dissonance between the norm and social practice. At first, Nephtali seems to be the masculine ideal, but soon enough David learns that his one-time idol is quickly turning apostate. By the time David leaves for America, Nephtali—although still studious—is spending most of his time reading books "written in the holy tongue on any but holy topics" (57). Reb Sender, the "kindly modest" scholar, who tries to persuade David that "only the other world has substance and reality," cannot free himself of worldly concerns (31). He harps on the fact that his wife thinks him a fool and shows more reverence for his learning than for his person. Moreover, this modest man is described as proud and sometimes boastful of his liturgical compositions, not to mention competitive when it comes to David's love.

22. Butler, *Bodies That Matter*, 237.

23. In *Bodies That Matter*, Butler expands on Foucault's discussion of the normal and the abnormal by contending that "the construction of gender operates through *exclusionary* means . . .; the human is not only produced over and against the inhuman, but through a set of foreclosures, radical erasures, that are strictly speaking, refused the possibility of cultural articulations" (8). While Foucault focuses on how power constitutes the subject as intelligible and by way of inference the normal and abnormal, Butler asserts that intelligibility not only creates the abnormal, but that intelligibility is produced primarily through exclusionary practices. Certain identities *have to be* excluded in order for the dominant social order to function as a self-sustaining system. Identification, according to Butler, always requires a violation of the other: "[S]exed positions are themselves secured through the repudiation and abjection of homosexuality and the assumption of a normative heterosexuality" (111). This logic of repudiation is the governing force of gendered identity positions, and certain exclusions actually institute the subject. In a sense, the excluded other—the radical abnormal as I would term it—is the condition of possibility of the normal.

24. Butler, *Bodies That Matter*, 124.

25. Moya Lloyd, "Performativity, Parody, Politics," *Theory, Culture & Society* 16 (1999): 210. While Lloyd argues that Butler fails to take context into account, I think Lloyd is mistaken, for the most part. In a 1999 interview with Vikki Bell, Butler contends that politics "has a character of contingency and context to it that cannot be predicted at the level of theory." Political decisions, according to Butler, "are made in the moment and they cannot be predicted from the level of theory."

Thus, planned political action is not precluded; however, Butler does warn us that it must be contextualized (and not prescriptive) and the effects of its discourse are always unpredictable. See Vikki Bell, "On Speech, Race, and Melancholia: An Interview with Judith Butler," *Theory, Culture & Society* 16 (1999): 166–67. My argument in this section is that we need to reconceptualize the notion of context.

26. Lois McNay, "Subject, Psyche and Agency: The Work of Judith Butler," *Theory, Culture & Society* 16 (1999): 179.

27. Lois McNay, *Gender and Agency: Reconfiguring the Subject in Feminist and Social Theory* (Cambridge: Polity Press, 2000), 45–46.

28. Ibid., 57.

29. Ibid., 35.

30. Bederman, *Manliness and Civilization,* 24.

31. McNay, *Gender and Agency,* 182.

Chapter Two: Passing: Race, Identification, and Desire (pages 33–52)

1. In this chapter, race will be discussed in terms of the black-white divide. I provide a fuller discussion of how the black-white dichotomy operates as a form of power in the fourth chapter.

2. W.W. Norton and Company, for example, has decided to put out Nella Larsen's *Passing* in a Norton Critical Edition.

3. See, for example, Corinne Blackmer, "The Veils of the Law: Race and Sexuality in Nella Larson's *Passing,*" *College Literature* 22, no. 3 (1995): 50–67; Michael G. Cooke, *Afro-American Literature in the Twentieth Century* (New Haven, Conn.: Yale University Press, 1984); Priscilla Ramsey, "A Study of Black Identity in 'Passing' Novels of the Nineteenth and Early Twentieth Century," *Studies in Black Literature* 7 (1976): 1–7; and Mary Helen Washington, "The Mulatta Trap: Nella Larsen's Women of the 1920s," in *Invented Lives: Narratives of Black Women, 1860–1960,* ed. Washington (New York: Anchor, 1987), 159–67.

4. Martha Cutter, "Sliding Significations: Passing as a Narrative and Textual Strategy in Nella Larsen's Fiction," in *Passing and the Fictions of Identity,* ed. Elaine Ginsberg (Durham, N.C.: Duke University Press, 1996), 75.

5. Elaine Ginsberg, "Introduction: The Politics of Passing," in *Passing and the Fictions of Identity,* 1–18.

6. Cutter, "Sliding Significations," 75.

7. See, for example, Sara Ahmed, "'She'll Wake Up One of These Days and Find She's Turned Into a Nigger': Passing through Hybridity," *Theory, Culture & Society* 16 (1999): 87–105.

8. Antonio Gramsci and Raymond Williams provide the classic definitions and discussions of hegemony. See Gramsci, *Selections from the Prison Notebooks,* ed. and trans. Quintin Hoare and Geoffrey Nowell Smith (New York: Inter-

national Publishers, 1971); and Williams, "Base and Superstructure in Marxist Cultural Theory," in *The Raymond Williams Reader*, ed. John Higgins (Oxford: Blackwell, 2001), 158–79.

9. Louis Miron and Jonathan Xavier Inda, "Race as a Kind of Speech Act," *Cultural Studies: A Research Annual* 5 (2000): 86–87.

10. Ibid., 99.

11. Ibid.

12. Frantz Fanon, *Black Skin, White Mask*, trans. Charles Lam Markmann (1952; reprint, New York: Grove Press, 1967), 109.

13. Miron and Inda, "Race," 97.

14. Miron and Inda do not provide specific examples of this concatenation. This is my intervention.

15. Nella Larsen, *Quicksand and Passing* (1928/1929; reprint, New Brunswick, N.J.: Rutgers University Press, 1986), 158–59. All subsequent references to *Passing* are from this edition and page numbers will be given in parentheses.

16. See, for example, Stuart Hall, "The Spectacle of the Other," in *Representations: Cultural Representations and Signifying Practices* (London: Sage Publications, 1997), 223–90.

17. Michel Foucault, *The History of Sexuality, Vol. I, An Introduction*, trans. Robert Hurley (New York: Vintage Books, 1990), 154.

18. In her important book, *Performance Anxieties*, Ann Pellegrini has also argued that "race is thus thinkable as a kind of speech act." Pellegrini's emphasis, however, is on displacing sexuality as the privileged site of psychoanalytic discourse by demonstrating how race also operates through complicated avenues of identification and desire. She does not investigate the specific ways in which race performativity is both similar to and different from gender performativity. See Pellegrini, *Performance Anxieties: Staging Psychoanalysis, Staging Race* (New York: Routledge, 1997), esp. 98.

19. Ahmed, "'She'll Wake Up," 93.

20. Ibid., 88.

21. This is Amy Robinson's phrase. See Robinson "Takes One to Know One: Passing and Communities of Common Interest," *Critical Inquiry* 20 (1994): 719.

22. Ibid., emphasis added.

23. F. James Davis, *Who is Black? One Nation's Definition* (University Park: Pennsylvania State University Press, 1991), 12. Davis provides an interesting historical look at the emergence of the American definition of black.

24. Pellegrini, *Performance Anxieties*, 102.

25. For another fascinating investigation of the way race definition has changed over the past four hundred years in America, see Thomas F. Gossett's *Race: The History of an Idea in America* (New York: Schocken Books, 1963).

26. Davis, *Who is Black?* 104.

27. Homi Bhabha, *The Location of Culture* (New York: Routledge 1994), 86.

28. Bhabha emphasizes the racial aspect of mimicry: "almost the same but not white."

29. Ibid., 91.

30. Ibid., 107. Mimicry, according to Bhabha, also has the potential of revealing the "differance" [sic] at the origins of colonial discourse's authority.

31. Sigmund Freud, *Group Psychology and the Analysis of the Ego: The Standard Edition*, trans. James Strachey (New York: Bantam Books, 1960), 46–47, emphasis added.

32. Ibid. As Shuli Barzilai, Diana Fuss, and others have pointed out, Freud's conception of identification is inconsistent and, at times, contradictory. See Shuli Barzilai, *Lacan and the Matter of Origins* (Stanford: Stanford University Press, 1999), esp. 112–15; and Diana Fuss, *Identification Papers* (New York: Routledge, 1995). However, I do think it fair to say that *ultimately* identification and desire are distinct forms of attachment for Freud. Identification, Freud reiterates in his 1933 *New Introductory Lectures on Psycho-analysis*, is a very important form of attachment to someone else, probably the first, and is *"not the same thing as the choice of an object."* See Freud, *New Introductory Lectures on Psycho-Analysis: The Standard Edition*, trans. James Strachey (New York: W.W. Norton & Company, 1965), 79, emphasis added. Moreover, although Freud does blur the line between normal and abnormal, there is a very definite heteronormative trajectory in Freud's notion of sexual development, in which the bifurcation of identification (the desire to be) and object-cathexis (the desire to have) plays a fundamental role. In *The Ego and the Id*, for example, Freud describes the simple *normal positive* Oedipal complex, whereby the little boy identifies with his father and develops an object-cathexis for his mother. See Freud, *The Ego and the Id*, trans. Joan Riviere and ed. James Strachey (New York: W.W. Norton & Company, 1960), 21. The dissolution and thus resolution of the simplest Oedipal complex leads to the formation of the super-ego (a further identification with the father), and the original object-cathexis is transformed into a latent desire for the opposite sex.

33. Fuss, *Identification Papers*, 11.

34. Ann Pellegrini and Diana Fuss both argue that the separation that psychoanalysis has made historically between identification and desire is a problematic one, and they both would agree that this separation is an effect of heteronormativity. Both critics also emphasize the way in which race identifications (and not just sexuality) play a crucial role in the emergence of subjectivity, and how race and gender identification are interrelated. However, Fuss and Pellegrini, following Frantz Fanon, argue that in the colonial situation, the colonized are forced to *identify with the colonizer*. See Fuss, *Identification Papers*, 145; and Pellegrini, *Performance Anxieties*, 103. Thus, while emphasizing the way politics do not "oppose the psychical but fundamentally presuppose it," they do not suggest that—for the colonized subject—an enforced bifurcation exists between identification and desire. Identification, for both Fuss and Pellegrini, remains "a violent appropria-

tion in which the Other is deposed and assimilated into the lordly domain of Self" (Fuss, *Identification Papers*, 145). I will make a case for the need to de-link identification and desire when analyzing the specific mechanisms at work in racist regimes.

35. "Desire for," in racist and heteronormative regimes like the one described in *Passing*, is incredibly complex and requires further research. Norms of heterosexuality alongside ideals privileging whiteness are inextricable when discussing how power operates to compel and encourage "desire for." For example, "being" a man implies desire for women. However, due to the undesirability of blackness under these regimes, black-identified male subjects' "desire for" historically has been influenced by ideals of whiteness. The result of both the prohibition against intermarriage—in the 1920s and well into the 1960s, laws prohibiting miscegenation were enforced—alongside the desirability of whiteness, seems to have led to black male preference for light-colored women who meet Caucasian standards of beauty. See Davis, *Who Is Black?* 39. Although Brian claims that he likes his women dark, his marriage to Irene and apparent desire for Clare, who are light enough to pass, seem to undermine his assertion. However, to complicate things even further, I would argue that black women's "desire for" is constructed differently. Given the hierarchy and power differential, women's "desire for" in heteronormative regimes is mostly elided. As objects of desire for men, women's appearance is crucial; this is not true—to the same extent—for men under such a regime. For black-identified women such as Irene who strive for a nonmarginal existence, the man's class status seems to play a crucial role in their desire for and thus needs to be taken into account. Thus it makes sense that Irene would marry Brian, for his status as a doctor gives her respectability while allowing her to approximate the "angel in the house" ideal. Here we begin to see the complicated ways in which norms of gender, race, and class are interarticulated.

36. Michel Pecheux, *Language, Semantics, and Ideology* (New York: St. Martin's Press, 1982), 11.

37. In her excellent book, *Crossing the Line: Racial Passing in Twentieth-Century U.S. Literature and Culture* (Durham, N.C.: Duke University Press, 2000), Gayle Wald speaks about the power or authority of racial discourse in the United States to ascribe identity and to assign the subject to a "stable 'place' in the racial order" (5).

38. Using Eve Sedgwick's insight in a different context, one could argue that this focus on one drop of black blood is a tool used to control the entire spectrum of race organization. In many ways, it is the very arbitrariness upon which the distinction between black and white has been made that has lent "this distinction its power to organize complicated, historical transactions of power." Therefore, difference—"white but not quite," or the one-drop rule—is a necessary part of the workings of racist hegemonies and it is maintained and guarded as a means of ensuring that the white-black hierarchy retains its force. See Sedgwick, *Between*

Men: English Literature and Male Homosocial Desire (New York: Columbia University Press, 1985), 118.

39. Robyn Wiegman, *American Anatomies: Theorizing Race and Gender* (Durham, N.C.: Duke University Press, 1995), 224.

40. The anxiety expressed by both Clare and Gertrude about the possibility of giving birth to a dark child also can be seen as part of the prohibitions operating in racist regimes. For Clare, a dark baby would have spelled disaster; it would have "given her away." For Gertrude, a dark baby would have meant possible discrimination, discrimination that she is unused to due to her light skin (and thus the assumption that she is white) and white husband. "Being found out" becomes a constant site of anxiety for "passers," as the descriptions of Rena Walden in *The House behind the Cedars* and Angela Murray in *Plum Bun* also disclose. Rena is indeed found out and it spells disaster for her, that is, her death, and the strain of passing eventually leads Angela to leave America for Europe. Moreover, to ensure success, the passer usually has to cut all connections to family and the past. Passing, as Irene Redfield points out in the text, is a "hazardous business" (157). And many passing narratives dramatize the dangers of race "transgression." See, for example, Jessie Fauset's *Plum Bun* and Charles Chesnutt's *The House behind the Cedars*.

41. Fuss, *Identification Papers*, 9.

42. Jean Laplanche and Jean-Bertrand Pontalis, *The Language of Psychoanalysis*, trans. Donald Nicholson-Smith (London: Karnac Books, 1988), 205.

43. I do not address the "unconscious nature" of identification or desire here; rather, in Chapter Six, I examine how Pierre Bourdieu's notion of pre-reflexivity might help account for some of the "psychic" effects of identification and desire.

44. Judith Butler, *The Psychic Life of Power* (Stanford: Stanford University Press, 1997), 2; second emphasis added.

45. See, for example, Butler's discussion of desire in *Bodies That Matter: On the Discursive Limits of "Sex"* (New York: Routledge, 1993).

46. Thus, while I find the Freudian distinction between identification and desire to be extremely insightful and helpful, especially when examining how categories such as gender, race, class, and ethnicity work, in this chapter—as in the book as a whole—I am attempting to reconceptualize and insert these terms into a different theoretical framework. Borrowing terms across disciplines is always a tricky business, and, yet, I believe that despite the problems that inevitably arise from such borrowings, the reconceptualization of identification and desire-to-be through a Foucauldian notion of power is crucial if we wish to understand better the ways in which hegemonic categories operate to constitute and regulate who we are as well as what we desire.

47. Once again, we see how class (and gender) is/(are) implicated in race. Attributes of whiteness are related to norms of class.

48. Fanon, *Black Skin*, 9; Hall, "Spectacle of the Other," 279.

49. See, for example, Blackmer, "Veils of Law"; Jennifer DeVere Brody, "Clare Kennedy's True Colors: Race and Class Conflict in Nella Larsen's *Passing*," *Callaloo: A Journal of African American and African Arts and Letters* 14 (1992): 1053–65; and Jacquelyn Y. McLendon, "Self-Representation as Art in the Novels of Nella Larsen," in *Redefining Autobiography in Twentieth-Century Women's Fiction: An Essay Collection*, ed. Colette Hall, Janice Morgan, and Carol Snyder (New York: Garland, 1991), 149–68.

50. McLendon, "Self-Representation," 158.

51. Blackmer, "Veils of Law," 59.

52. Hall, "Spectacle of the Other," 243.

53. For excellent discussions of the stereotype of the lascivious, over-sexed black woman, see, for example, Hazel Carby, "Policing the Black Woman's Body in an Urban Context," *Critical Inquiry* 18, no. 4 (1992): 738–55; and Deborah McDowell, Introduction to *Quicksand and Passing* (New Brunswick, N.J.: Rutgers University Press, 1986), ix–xxxv.

54. Ann DuCille, "Blues Notes on Black Sexuality: Sex and the Texts of Jessie Fauset and Nella Larsen," in *American Sexual Politics*, ed. John Fout and Maura Tantillo (Chicago: Chicago University Press, 1993), 197.

55. It also emerges in texts that do not recount incidents of passing. In Wallace Thurman's 1929 novel, *The Blacker the Berry . . .*, he underscores the protagonist's unsuccessful attempt to approximate whiteness. She is just too black, it seems, to emerge from the marginal status in which her family and society place her.

56. Butler, *Bodies That Matter*, 89, 124.

Chapter Three: American Dream Discourse and Class Performativity
(pages 53–69)

1. Jennifer Hochschild, *Facing Up to the American Dream: Race, Class and the Soul of the Nation* (Princeton, N.J.: Princeton University Press, 1995), esp. xi, 16. Robert Fossum, John Roth, and Alan DeSantis have argued that the American Dream is rather amorphous and has meant different things at different historical periods. See Alan D. DeSantis, "Selling the American Dream Myth to Black Southerners: The Chicago Defender and the Great Migration of 1915–1919," *Western Journal of Communication* 62, no. 4 (1998): 474–511; and Robert Fossum and John Roth, *The American Dream* (London: British Association for American Studies, 1981). While I agree with the assessment vis-à-vis the changing meaning of the Dream, I also believe that the promise of upper mobility through hard work has served as a relatively constant and major aspect of the Dream at least since the turn of the century. See, for example, Thomas Ferraro, *Ethnic Passages: Literary Immigrants in Twentieth-Century America* (Chicago: University of Chicago Press, 1993); Elizabeth Fox-Genovese, "Between Individualism and Fragmentation:

American Culture and the New Literary Studies of Race and Gender," *American Quarterly* 42, no. 1 (1990): 7–34; and Elizabeth Higginbotham and Lynn Weber, "Moving Up with Kin and Community: Upward Social Mobility for Black and White Women," *Gender & Society* 6, no. 3 (1992): 416–40.

2. Anzia Yezierska, *Salome of the Tenements* (1923; reprint, Urbana: University of Illinois Press, 1995), 5. All subsequent references to the novel come from this edition and page numbers will be given in parentheses.

3. Melanie Levinson, "'To Make Myself for a Person': 'Passing' Narratives and the Divided Self in the Work of Anzia Yezierska," *Studies in American Jewish Literature* 13 (1994): 9. For other examples of this kind of reading, see L. Fishbein, "Anzia Yezierska, the Sweatshop Cinderella and the Invented Life," *Studies in American Jewish Literature* 17 (1998): 137–41; Meredith Goldsmith, "'The Democracy of Beauty': Fashioning Ethnicity and Gender in the Fiction of Anzia Yezierska," *Yiddish* 11, nos. 3–4 (1999): 166–87; Rose Kamel, "'Anzia Yezierska, Get Out of Your Own Way': Selfhood and Otherness in the Autobiographical Fiction of Anzia Yezierska," *Studies in American Jewish Literature* 3 (1983): 40–50; and Edith Weinthal, "The Image of the City in Yezierska's *Bread Givers*," *Studies in American Jewish Literature* 13 (1994): 10–13.

4. Ellen Golub, "Eat Your Heart Out: The Fiction of Anzia Yezierska," *Studies in American Jewish Literature* 3 (1983): 57.

5. Martin Japtok, for instance, explores the tension between individualism and communalism in *Bread Givers*. However, he does not discuss how individualism is specifically related to U.S. class discourse or to the American Dream. See Japtok, "Justifying Individualism: Anzia Yezierska's *Bread Givers*," in *The Immigrant Experience in North American Literature: Carving out a Niche*, ed. Katherine Payant and Toby Rose (Westport, Conn.: Greenwood Press, 1999), 17–31.

6. Two qualifications need to be made from the outset. First, as I have done with gender and race, class is isolated in this chapter so that some of the specific processes that have produced classed subjectivities in America can be examined. Second, and once again reiterating the qualification I have made throughout this book, I am not attempting to describe how class actually operates on the level of social practices. That is, I am making a distinction between regulatory norms on the hegemonic level and how they operate on the level of social practices.

7. Yezierska's most famous novel, *Bread Givers* (1925), as well as her *Arrogant Beggar*, also make class an important issue. Both of these novels are similar to *Salome of the Tenements* in their narrative trajectories: Young women protagonists move up the class ladder through hard work and finally find suitable men for partners. However, I believe the characterization of the millionaire philanthropist John Manning in *Salome of the Tenements*, which does not really have a parallel in either of the other novels, makes the staging of class conflict in this text even more pronounced and urgent.

8. If class—like gender and race—is indeed one of the hegemonic categories

of identification through which subjects become intelligible as subjects, then I believe we must first examine the normative injunctions, that is, norms, that have come to be linked to class in the United States. Only then will we begin to understand the ways in which class discourse has come to materialize and naturalize certain class subjects and class relations. Rosemary Hennessey reminds us that discourse "is a material force in that it (re)produces what counts as reality." Hennessey, *Materialist Feminism and the Politics of Discourse* (New York: Routledge, 1993), 75.

9. Paul Gilroy, *Postcolonial Melancholia* (New York: Columbia University Press, 2005), 12.

10. It is important to note here that to think about class as performativity is not in any way to ignore its materiality. Following Julie Bettie, I would argue that the "materiality" of class includes both economic and cultural resources, or economic and cultural capital, which only come to have meaning by and through a particular grid of intelligibility or dominant social order. The process of materialization in class processes has to do with power's ability to naturalize and sanction certain class subjects and class relations. See Bettie, "Women without Class: *Chicas, Cholas*, Trash, and the Presence/Absence of Class Identity," *Signs* 26, no. 1 (2000): 1–35.

11. Gary Gerstle argues that American liberalism actually has been quite flexible and must be examined historically. In "The Protean Character of American Liberalism," he describes the change in liberal discourse from the Progressive Era to the New Deal period. Whereas the Progressive Era was concerned with "individual vice and virtue . . . and intent on reforming individuals and improving character," the New Deal was not so interested in remaking individuals or uniting all Americans into a single moral community. Rather, Americans of this period reserved their passion for "economic reform." Gerstle, however, reminds us that liberalism consistently has underscored emancipation, rationality, and progress. Thus, the discourse may have differed in emphasis, but one of the foundational principles of American liberalism remained intact: the basic tenet of individual rights. Both the Progressives and the New Dealers were interested in creating a space in which human nature could be nurtured: "Individuals required a humane economic and social environment in which to live, and they needed instruction in how best to express and enjoy their individuality . . . [R]ational interventions in society and culture would encourage individuals to cultivate their best human capacities." Gerstle, "The Protean Character of American Liberalism," *The American Historical Review* 99, no. 4 (1994): 1044, 1046.

12. See Gillian Brown, *Domestic Individualism: Imagining Self in Nineteenth-Century America* (Berkeley: University of California Press, 1990), esp. 1–13.

13. See Fossum and Roth, *The American Dream*; C. B. MacPherson, *The Political Theory of Possessive Individualism* (Oxford: Oxford University Press, 1962); and Ronald Takaki, *A Different Mirror: A History of Multicultural America* (Boston:

Little, Brown and Company, 1993). Takaki points out that the old republican insistence on defining people as individuals responsible for themselves and on the importance of judging people according to their individual merits or lack of them continues to hold sway in the twentieth century. See Takaki, *Iron Cages: Race and Culture in Nineteenth-Century America* (Oxford: Oxford University Press, 1990), 299.

14. See James Ceaser, "Multiculturalism and American Liberal Democracy," in *Multiculturalism and American Democracy*, ed. Arthur Melzer, Jerry Weinberger, and M. Zinman (Lawrence: University of Kansas Press, 1998), 139–57; Gerstle, "The Protean Character of American Liberalism," 1043–73; and Takaki, *Iron Cages*.

15. Michael Sandel, *Liberalism and the Limits of Justice* (Cambridge: Cambridge University Press, 1998), 19.

16. Karl Marx, *The Eighteenth Brumaire of Louis Bonaparte* (1963; reprint, New York: International Publishers, 1998), 25.

17. Manning himself embodies the tension in this class discourse. His inability to overcome his class prejudices and privilege are juxtaposed against his desire to eliminate "all artificial class barriers" and to promote human brotherhood (78, 120).

18. While I do not address the feminist aspects of *Salome of the Tenements* here, in Chapter Five I discuss Yezierska's *Arrogant Beggar*, which has a similar narrative trajectory, in relation to the New Woman ideal.

19. See Hochschild, *Facing Up*, esp. 3–39; and J. Emmett Winn, "Moralizing Upward Mobility: Investigating the Myth of Class Mobility in *Working Girl*," *The Southern Communication Journal* 66, no.1 (2000): 40–51. One could even argue that this moral overtone is linked to or inherited from the once-dominant republican ideology rooted in the Protestant ethic, with its emphasis on individual self-rule and accumulation of capital as signs of grace. See Takaki, *Iron Cages*, esp. 1–15.

20. Hochschild, *Facing Up*, 59.

21. See ibid., esp 3–39; and Takaki, *Iron Cages*.

22. Winn, "Moralizing Upward Mobility," 7.

23. Ibid.

24. Sandel, *Liberalism*, 20.

25. Ibid.

26. Although there are certainly gendered components to "being a lady," I concentrate here on the class aspects of Sonya's "performance." Nan Enstad's *Ladies of Labor, Girls of Adventure* (New York: Columbia University Press, 1999) offers a fascinating account of how Progressive Era working women performed "ladyhood" as a way of asserting their subjectivities. While Enstad's argument focuses on the way that dominant norms were appropriated, misappropriated, and "performed differently" on the level of social practices, in this chapter I am concerned

Notes

Chapter Four: Race and the Making of Ethnicity (pages 70–91)

Nella Larsen, *Quicksand and Passing* (1928/1929; reprint, New Brunswick, Rutgers University Press, 1986), 150. All subsequent references to *Passing* are this edition and page numbers will be cited parenthetically in the text.

See Werner Sollors, *Beyond Ethnicity: Consent and Descent in American re* (New York: Oxford University Press, 1986), 36.

Robyn Wiegman, *American Anatomies: Theorizing Race and Gender* (Dur-N.C.: Duke University Press, 1995), 5.

Abraham Cahan, *The Rise of David Levinsky* (1917; reprint, New York: Pen-Books, 1993), 524. All subsequent references are from this edition and page ers will be cited parenthetically in the text.

Sollors, *Beyond Ethnicity*, 170.

F. James Davis, *Who is Black? One Nation's Definition* (University Park: sylvania State University Press, 1991), 77.

Ibid., 15.

Sarah Gualtieri, "Becoming 'White': Race, Religion and the Foundations of n/Lebanese Ethnicity in the United States," *Journal of American Ethnic His-20*, no. 4 (2001): 31.

Susan Koshy, "Category Crisis: South Asian Americans and Questions of and Ethnicity," *Diaspora* 7, no. 3 (1998): 286. For example, it was in 1878 that inese applicant was first denied a naturalization request on the basis that "a on of the Mongolian race" was not a "white person" within the meaning of tatute. See Edward Rhoads, "'White Labor' vs. 'Coolie Labor': The 'Chinese stion' in Pennsylvania in the 1870s," *Journal of American Ethnic History* 21, (2002): 13.

. Eric Goldstein, "The Unstable Other: Locating the Jew in Progressive-Era rican Racial Discourse." *American Jewish History* 89, no. 4 (2002): 398.

. Susan Koshy, "Morphing Race into Ethnicity: Asian Americans and Criti-ransformations of Whiteness," *Boundary 2* 28, no. 1 (2001): 159.

. See Wiegman, *American Anatomies*, 9. This is not to say, however, that the k-white divide *was* secure. In fact, both the question of who was white and t percentage of "black" blood made one black was being negotiated constantly. Koshy, "Morphing Race"; and Teresa Zackodnik "Fixing the Color Line: The atto, Southern Courts, and Racial Identity," *American Quarterly* 53, no. 3 1): 420–51. Importantly, however, the definition of who was black was much flexible, demonstrating, I believe, how "blackness" became the axis around ch white supremacy was built. Thus, the dichotomous discourse operated as ative power, by forcing subjects into categories and wielding the threat of pun-ient over those who crossed the color line, and as positive power, by helping e the very desires and aspirations of subjects.

with outlining the constituent aspects of those domina
interested in asking how the very desire to emulate "lac
encouraged. Only then, I believe, can we ask after its su
sive) misappropriations.

27. It might seem that power should operate by el
interpellated into the dominant social order as lower
attributes associated with this class. However, as I arg
ter with regard to race, so long as the attributes associa
are coded as undesirable in class societies, only those c
embody attributes associated with the middle class ga
the benefits of privilege and power.

28. Hochschild, *Facing Up*, 35.

29. Rita Felski, "Nothing to Declare: Identity, Sham
Class," *PMLA* 115, no. 1 (2000): 38.

30. Pierre Bourdieu, *Distinction: A Social Critique*
trans. Richard Nice (Cambridge, Mass.: Harvard Unive

31. Ibid., 414–16.

32. Karl Marx and Friedrich Engels, *The German I*
(1970; reprint, New York: International Publishers, 1995)

33. Michel Foucault, *Discipline and Punish: The Birth*
Sheridan (New York: Vintage Books, 1979), 192.

34. Winn, "Moralizing Upward Mobility," 3.

35. Sonya desires a certain kind of simplicity; this
Sonya renovates her tenement apartment in order to imp
achieved the vivid simplicity for which she had longed all
breathed through the fabrics and colors with which she
(65). Ironically, as Yezierska reveals in the renovation scer
money goes into "vivid simplicity."

36. Christopher Okonkwo reads Sonya's sartorial s
commentary on Americanization, which "suppresses the
poses hegemony." In contradistinction, the Sonya Mode
the ethnic or immigrant woman." See Okonkwo, "Of Rej
the Speakerly Dress: Anzia Yezierska's *Salome of the Ten*
1 (2000): 140–42. JoAnn Pavletich, on the other hand, rec
endings of most of Yezierska's novels and notes that, "Bo
the protagonists' unproblematicized goal." But rather th
on the reinscription of the "cult of self" and individualis
Salome of the Tenements, Pavletich describes Yezierska's u
in which affective bonds come to be substitutes for polit
texts. See JoAnn A. Pavletich, "Anzia Yezierska, Immigr
Uses of Affect," *Tulsa Studies in Women's Literature* 19, no

37. Goldsmith, "Democracy of Beauty," 171.

13. Stuart Hall, "Interview with Stuart Hall: Culture and Power," *Radical Philosophy* 86 (1997): 35.

14. Koshy, "Category Crisis," 311.

15. Goldstein, "Unstable Other," 384.

16. See Karen Brodkin, *How Jews Became White Folks and What That Says about Race in America* (New Brunswick, N.J.: Rutgers University Press, 1998); Gualtieri, "Becoming 'White'"; Noel Ignatiev, *How the Irish Became White* (New York: Routledge, 1995); and David Roediger, *The Wages of Whiteness: Race and the Making of the American Working Class*, revised edition (London: Verso, 1999).

17. Koshy, "Morphing Race," 155.

18. James Weldon Johnson, *The Autobiography of an Ex-Colored Man* (1912; reprint, New York: Vintage Books, 1989), 161. All subsequent references refer to this edition and page numbers will be cited parenthetically in the text.

19. Interestingly, the narrator comments on how the Jew *looks* Jewish. Thus, unlike the narrator himself, who does not look black and therefore can "conceal" his "blackness," the Jew's Jewishness is "visible."

20. Goldstein, "Unstable Other," 396.

21. This formulation is indebted to Patricia Hill Collins, "Like One of the Family: Race, Ethnicity, and the Paradox of U.S. National Identity," *Ethnic and Racial Studies* 24, no. 1 (2001): 9.

22. This scene also illustrates how, in social practice, norms of gender and race work to reinforce one another.

23. Roediger, *Wages of Whiteness*, 127.

24. Robyn Wiegman argues that in order to understand how American racial discourse developed, we must trace the epistemic break that occurred as Europe and America entered modernity. Following Michel Foucault, Wiegman examines how natural history with its creation of taxonomy eventually gave way to a new science of man. The move from natural history to biology and comparative anatomy brought with it an emphasis on the study of the body and organicity. The move from the visible epidermal terrain that was the basis of natural history to the articulation of the interior structure of human bodies thus "extrapolated in both broader and more distinct terms the parameters of white supremacy, giving it a logic lodged fully in the body." According to Wiegman, then, it is in the context of such an epistemic break that we must analyze the development of America's binary race regime. See Wiegman, *American Anatomies*, 31.

25. Matthew Jacobson points out that in the nineteenth century, the term "race" was still used to distinguish Celts, Slavs, Hebrews, Iberics, Mediterraneans, and the like from Anglo-Saxons. Jacobson, "Becoming Caucasian: Vicissitudes of Whiteness in American Politics and Culture," *Identities* 8, no. 1 (2001): 83–104). He states that "in looking at the history of European immigration, we must admit of a system of "difference" by which one might be both white and

racially distinct from other whites" (88). This system of difference tended not only to distinguish among white immigrants but also to circumscribe life chances. Thus, this system of differences among the "white" groups worked in conjunction with the black-white dichotomy to create a complex, contingent, and fluid racial stratification. However, in the twentieth century, Caucasian was to emerge and take their place (84): "[I]n the 1920s and after, partly because the crisis over inclusive whiteness had been solved by restrictive legislation and partly in response to a new racial alchemy generated by African-American migrations to the North and West, whiteness was reconsolidated . . . the late nineteenth century's probationary white groups were now remade and granted the scientific stamp of authenticity as the unitary Caucasian race—an earlier era's Celts, Slavs, Hebrews, Iberics, and Saracens, among others, had become the Caucasians so familiar to our own visual economy and racial lexicon" (90). And so the history of race and whiteness is very much a "history of power and its disposition" (91).

26. Koshy, "Morphing Race," 190. Koshy also argues that Asian Americans today are attempting quite successfully to "morph race into ethnicity." In effect, due to a particular constellation of historical circumstances, such as the "new needs of global capital" and an attempt to revitalize the myth of the American Dream, Asian Americans increasingly are being interpellated as "whites-to-be" (187).

27. See Brodkin, *How Jews Became White Folks*, 33. Brodkin also reminds us that, at the time, law and medicine lacked the corporate context they have today, and "Jews in these professions were not corporation based. Most . . . depended upon other Jews for their clientele" (34).

28. Cristina Ruotolo makes a similar claim. See Ruotolo, "James Weldon Johnson and the Autobiography of an Ex-Colored Musician," *American Literature* 72, no. 2 (2000): 265.

29. It is important to note here that while I would like to posit the ability of subjects to negotiate between conflicting norms that circulate in any given dominant social order, I do not want to suggest that the subject has "choice" in the liberal humanist sense. As I have argued throughout this book, a subject's preliminary interpellation into the social world (paradoxically, the ex-colored man's corrective interpellation would be considered the primary one) both inaugurates the subject qua subject and imposes an initial identification with a specific gender, class, race, or ethnicity. This primary identification is, in many ways, the nexus through which a subject gains intelligibility to him/herself and to others. One could perhaps even say that this initial interpellation leaves an indelible psychic trace, one which enables and conditions all future identifications as well as negotiations among various norms. This, in turn, suggests that a subject can be conceived neither as a free-floating agent nor as a simple effect of constitutive norms or power relations. A subject's identification is *never determined* once and for all by the primary interpellation, yet all subsequent disidentifications, desires-to-

be, negotiations, and "twisting" of norms should be understood as mediated by and through this primary address. The categories of identification, such as gender, race, and class (with their respective *dominant* norms) through which the subject gains intelligibility, viability, and positionality in a given society are also what frame and "ground" the ability to negotiate among conflicting normative attributes attached to the various categories. Moreover, as the subject advances in life and negotiates among conflicting norms, the norms it "confronts" also leave a mark on the subject. Consequently, future choices are shaped not only by the norms associated with the subject's primary interpellation but also—though less indelibly—with the other norms circulating within the existing grid of intelligibility.

30. I therefore disagree with Cristina Ruotolo's claim that the protagonist desires to express whiteness and blackness together in and through his musical project. Rather, I believe the narrator desires—at this point—to emulate norms associated with blackness, which is a partial rejection of hegemonic norms. However, these contestatory norms, as I have stated above, are always in "dialogue" with the dominant ones. See Ruotolo, "James Weldon Johnson," esp. 266–67.

31. Representative examples include Valerie Babb, *Whiteness Visible: The Meaning of Whiteness in American Literature and Culture* (New York: New York University Press, 1998); James Barret and David Roediger, "Inbetween Peoples: Race, Nationality and the 'New Immigrant' Working Class," *Journal of American Ethnic History* 16 (1997): 3–44; Matthew Jacobson, *Whiteness of a Different Color* (Cambridge Mass.: Harvard University Press, 1998); and Desmond King, (2000) *Making Americans: Immigration, Race, and the Origins of the Diverse Democracy* (Cambridge, Mass.: Harvard University Press, 2000).

32. Perhaps we can read this scene as the protagonist's realization that attempts to transform the valence of certain attributes that were linked historically to blackness, such as instinctiveness and unbridled passion, would be a feat he is not up to.

33. The concluding chapter of *The Rise of David Levinsky*, for example, lays bare the fact that the separation of "Jewishness" from the discourse of race has not yet occurred. Toward the end of the novel, David meets a gentile woman, who is "of high character." But when the possibility of marrying her comes up, David rejects it. He ascribes his rejection to the "chasm of race" between them and "the medieval prejudice against [the Jewish] people" (527).

34. Here we begin to see how issues of class mobility are tied intimately to the process of "whitening." I discuss the interrelationship between class and race in the next chapter.

35. Goldstein, "Unstable Other," 409.

36. Jacobson, "Becoming Caucasian," 89.

37. Susan Koshy reminds us that other factors, such as the needs of the global economy and the United States' interests in certain part of the world, have influ-

enced the racial positioning of certain groups, both newer immigrants from East Asia and older immigrants from Middle Eastern countries. See Koshy, "Morphing Race," 187–93.

38. Arguing against Werner Sollors' claims that "ethnicity" as a word and concept first appeared in 1941, Victoria Hattam traces the term "ethnic" back to the new social theories developed in the United States between the years 1914 and 1924 by such men as Isaac Berkson, Horace Kallen, and Alfred Kroeber. Hattam, "Ethnicity: An American Genealogy," in *Not Just Black and White*, ed. Nancy Foner and George Fredrickson (New York: Russell Sage Foundation, 2004), 42–61). These theories, which were part of the larger trend in U.S. intellectual circles that underscored social interactions to explain group formations, endeavored to account for the emergence of "ethnic groups" in ways that de-emphasized the importance of biology and ancestry (i.e., race) while highlighting the importance of social conditions. Thus, although ethnicity as a concept only gained widespread currency post–World War II—when to be "ethnic" primarily meant the sharing of a common cultural background or origin—even in these turn-of-the-century social theories, the term "ethnic" was not only used but attempted to account for differences among peoples in *non-racial* terms. See Hattam, "Ethnicity," 46. See also Mary Kupiec Cayton and Peter Williams, introduction to *Encyclopedia of American Cultural and Intellectual History* (New York: Scribner's Sons, 2001); and Nancy Foner and George Fredrickson "Introduction," in *Not Just Black and White*, 1–23.

39. Jacobson, *Whiteness of a Different Color*, 197.

40. Richard Alba claims that the development of a comprehensive "white ethnicity" has meant that ethnicity has come to play a less important role in the lives and life chances of individuals and groups of European ancestry. See Alba, *Ethnic Identity: The Transformation of White America* (New Haven, Conn.: Yale University Press, 1990). See also Jonathan Warren and France Winddance Twine, "White Americans, the New Minority? Non-Blacks and the Ever-Expanding Boundaries of Whiteness," *Journal of Black Studies* 28, no. 2 (1997): 200–18.

41. This points to the ways in which the categories of identification create the conditions of intelligibility, and to how subjects can and do negotiate between different categories of identifications, which can be read as a form of agency.

42. Koshy, "Morphing Race," 185. See also Ian Haney Lopez, *White by Law: The Legal Construction of Race* (New York: New York University Press, 1996), esp. 1–35.

43. Ibid.

44. In her interesting article, "Jewishness after Mount Sinai: Jews, Blacks and the (Multi)Racial Category," Katya Gibel Azoulay describes the way in which hegemonic discourses on Jewishness and blackness have ignored or elided subjects who have both Jewish and African ancestry. *Identities* 8, no. 2 (2001): 211–246.

Chapter Five: Race and the New Woman (pages 92–107)

1. Nella Larsen, *Quicksand and Passing* (1928/1929; reprint, New Brunswick, N.J.: Rutgers University Press, 1986), 4. All subsequent references to *Quicksand* come from this edition and page numbers will be given in parentheses.

2. Anzia Yezierska, *Arrogant Beggar* (1927; reprint, Durham, N.C.: Duke University Press, 1996), 8. All subsequent references to *Arrogant Beggar* in this chapter come from this edition and page numbers will be given in parentheses.

3. Elizabeth Ammons, "The New Woman as Cultural Symbol and Social Reality: Six Women Writers' Perspectives," in *1915: The Cultural Moment*, ed. Adele Heller and Lois Rudnick (New Brunswick, N.J.: Rutgers University Press, 1991), 84.

4. Kathy Peiss, "Making Faces: The Cosmetics Industry and the Cultural Construction of Gender, 1890–1930," in *Unequal Sisters: A Multi-Cultural Reader in U.S. Women's History*, ed. Vicki Ruiz and Ellen Carol DuBois (New York: Routledge, 1994), 381.

5. The representation of middle-class women in the professions, such as law, architecture, medicine, teaching, and newspaper work, grew from 6.4 percent in 1870 to 13.3 percent in 1920, while women employed as clerks, stenographers, typists, and accountants grew from 0.8 percent in 1870 to 25.6 percent in 1920. See Ammons, "New Woman," 82.

6. Lois Rudnick, "The New Woman," in *1915*, 71.

7. See Ammons, "New Woman," 82–98; Peiss, "Making Faces," 372–95; Rudnick, "New Woman," 69–82; and Ellen Kay Trimberger, "The New Woman and the New Sexuality: Conflict and Contradiction in the Writings and Lives of Mabel Dodge and Neith Boyce," in *1915*, 98–117.

8. Aristotle, for instance, uses the term in his *Nicomachean Ethics*. Although scholars disagree about the exact definition, most definitions point to the way in which eudemonia can be reached through the good life, which I believe can be understood as a meaningful life: whether it is virtuous action or purely contemplative activity.

9. While Yezierska seems to attempt to depict her protagonist as able to "self-craft" at will, I believe that *Arrogant Beggar* as well as *Quicksand* actually illustrate how self-crafting always occurs within an existing field of constraint. In *Undoing Gender* (New York: Routledge, 2005), Judith Butler argues that "reflexivity is not only socially mediated, but socially constituted. I cannot be who I am without drawing upon the sociality of norms that precede and exceed me." A subject can "self-craft" in a sense, yet that self-crafting *always* takes place "in the context of an enabling and limiting field of constraint" (19). In other words, self-crafting always takes place within the existing social order. As I have argued throughout,

the subject can never "escape" or free itself from the identifications or the norms that have made and continuously make its existence as a subject possible. When the subject reflects or meditates on itself, that "self" has acquired "being" through the citing of norms over time; it itself has been made possible, formed in the crucible of, and is positioned in society by dominant norms. Therefore, even when a subject disidentifies with a given normative category, she/he still retains the traces of her/his initial identification as well as the other norms that have shaped and reshaped her/him over time. Negotiation therefore must be understood as a socially constituted reflexivity that is always enabled *and* circumscribed by the dominant social order. Adele's—as well as Helga's—choices and self-fashioning clearly are circumscribed by circulating regulatory norms.

10. See Carol Batker, "Literary Reformers: Crossing Class and Ethnic Boundaries in Jewish Women's Fiction of the 1920s," *MELUS* 25, no. 1 (2000): esp. 87.

11. Ibid., 88.

12. The difference in the two novels' representation of sexual intimacy is quite striking. In *Arrogant Beggar*, Adele and Jean are described as making love before marriage, and the consummation is described in triumphant and sensual terms. This stands in stark contrast to the description of Helga Crane's premarital sex, which is described in terms of "fallenness" shame and guilt.

13. See Ammons, "New Woman," 82–98; and Rudnick, "New Woman," 69–82.

14. Lori Harrison-Kahan, "Drunk with the Fiery Rhythms of Jazz," *MFS: Modern Fiction Studies* 51, no. 2 (2005): 424.

15. Ibid., 417.

16. For Harrison-Kahan, Muhmenkeh represents the "Jewish spirit." Ibid., 416.

17. This is not to say, by any means, that emulating the New Woman ideal was the only means of accessing whiteness or that all Jewish women attempted to align themselves with whiteness.

18. Claudia Tate, "Desire and Death in *Quicksand*, by Nella Larsen," *American Literary History* 7, no. 2 (1995): 240.

19. Kimberly Roberts, "The Clothes Make the Woman: The Symbolics of Prostitution in Nella Larsen's *Quicksand* and Claude McKay's *Home to Harlem*," *Tulsa Studies in Women's Literature* 16, no. 1 (1997): 112. See also Hazel Carby, *Reconstructing Womanhood: The Emergence of the Afro-American Novelist* (New York: Oxford University Press, 1982); and Deborah McDowell, Introduction to *Quicksand and Passing* (New Brunswick, N.J.: Rutgers University Press, 1986), ix–xxxv.

20. For this kind of reading, see Pamela Barnett, "'My Picture of You Is, After All, the True Helga Crane': Portraiture and Identity in Nella Larsen's *Quicksand*," *Signs* 20, no. 3 (1995): 575–600; and Kimberly Monda, "Self-Delusion and Self-Sacrifice in Nella Larsen's *Quicksand*," *African American Review* 31, no. 1 (1997): 23–39.

21. It is important to note that the New Woman ideal, as S. J. Kleinberg has argued, was increasingly under pressure in the 1920s due to the reemergence

of the "separate spheres" and domesticity discourse. See Kleinberg, *Women in the United States: 1830–1945* (London: MacMillan Press, 1999), 233–56. Elizabeth Ammons suggests, however, that the ideal of the New Woman still served as an ideal throughout the 1920s, *especially* for women in groups denied full access to the ideal to begin with, such as African-American women and Jewish women (personal correspondence). See also Ammons, "New Woman," 84.

22. Darlene Clark Hine, "Rape and the Inner Lives of Black Women in the Middle West: Preliminary Thoughts on the Culture of Dissemblance," in *Unequal Sisters*, 446.

23. See, for example, Monda, "Self-Delusion"; Roberts, "Clothes"; and Cherene Sherrard-Johnson, "'A Plea For Color': Nella Larsen's Iconography of the Mulatta," *American Literature* 76, no. 4 (2004): 833–69.

24. Judith Butler provides a brilliant theoretical discussion of this distinction as well as an argument regarding the importance of making this distinction. See Butler, *Undoing Gender*, 48.

25. Kimberly Roberts points out that Helga seems "perpetually on the verge of being mistaken for a prostitute." See Roberts, "Clothes," 111.

26. For two excellent discussions of the way in which the mass migration of blacks and black women in particular into the northern cities triggered a discourse that reinscribed the linkage between black female migrants and "sexual degeneration" and black women more generally with promiscuity, see Carby, "Policing"; and Roberts, "Clothes."

27. In fact, Helga's relatives, the social climbing Dahls, desperately want Helga to marry the famous painter, Axel Olsen. In the United States, miscegenation was, at very best, tolerated; it certainly would not have been encouraged by the upwardly mobile white middle class. This perhaps points to an interesting difference in the racial landscape of the two countries.

28. Here I can't help but think of the depiction of upwardly mobile Jewish women in *The Rise of David Levinsky* by Abraham Cahan, Yezierska's contemporary. In particular, Anna Tevkin is portrayed as a successful New Woman, and I would argue that she is described as "whiter" and less marked as "Jewish" than Fanny, the woman Levinsky leaves because he falls in love with Anna. Not surprisingly, Fanny, unlike Anna who is working in the public sphere, "is expected to be a wife, a mother, and a housekeeper" (397). Emulating the New Woman ideal aligns Anna more closely with whiteness.

Chapter Six: A Parrot of Words and Monkey of Manners (pages 108–29)

1. The number of scholars who have argued that the different categories operate in tandem is far too great for me to list here. Some representative works that have influenced my thinking include: Patricia Hill Collins, "It's All in the Family:

Intersections of Gender, Race, and Nation," *Hypatia* 13, no. 3 (1998): 62–83; Kimberle Crenshaw, "Mapping the Margins: Intersectionality, Identity, Politics, and Violence against Women of Color," *Stanford Law Review* 43, no. 6 (1991): 1241–99; and "Demarginalizing the Intersection of Race and Sex: A Black Feminist Critique of Antidiscrimination Doctrine, Feminist Theory, and Antiracist Politics," in *Feminism and Politics*, ed. Anne Phillips (Oxford: Oxford University Press, 1998), 314–43; Angela Davis, *Women, Race, and Class* (New York: Vintage Books, 1983), and *The Angela Davis Reader*, ed. Joy James (Cambridge, Mass.: Blackwell Publishers, 1998); Martin Favor, *Authentic Blackness: The Folk in the New Negro Renaissance* (Durham, N.C.: Duke University Press, 1999); bell hooks, *Feminist Theory: From Margin to Center* (Boston: South End Press, 1984); and Valerie Smith, *Not Just Race, Not Just Gender: Black Feminist Readings* (New York: Routledge, 1998).

2. Rose Brewer, "Theorizing Race, Class, and Gender: The New Scholarship of Black Feminist Intellectuals and Black Women's Labor," in *Materialist Feminism: A Reader in Class, Difference, and Women's Lives*, ed. Rosemary Hennessy and Chrys Ingraham (New York: Routledge, 1997), 236.

3. Collins, "All in the Family," 77.

4. For a good overview of the intersectionality scholarship in the social sciences, see Leslie McCall, "The Complexity of Intersectionality," *Signs* 30, no. 3 (2005): 1771–1800. For a discussion of both intersectionality and multidimensionality in relation to Critical Race Studies, see Darren Lenard Hutchinson, "Critical Race Histories: In and Out," *American University Law Review* 53, no. 6 (2004): 1188–1215. For an excellent critique of intersectionality, especially as understood by Patricia Hill Collins, see Wendy Brown, "The Impossibility of Women's Studies," *differences: A Journal of Feminist Cultural Studies* 9, no. 3 (1997): 79–101.

5. Ann McClintock, *Imperial Leather: Race, Gender and Sexuality in the Colonial Contest* (New York: Routledge, 1995), 44.

6. Ibid., 94; Gail Bederman, *Manliness and Civilization: A Cultural History of Gender and Race in the United States, 1880–1917* (Chicago: University of Chicago Press, 1995), 239.

7. In many ways, Patricia Hill Collins' argument in "It's All in the Family: Intersections of Gender, Race, and Nation" is quite similar to McClintock's and Bederman's, since she discusses how age, gender, race, and sexuality intersect in the "traditional" family discourse. She also seems opposed to investigating the different categories as if they were discrete axes of analysis. Yet Collins' emphasis, like that of other scholars of intersectionality, is on examining interlocking systems of oppression and a "matrix of domination" rather than on the "productive" nature of discourse or on the way that hegemonic categories are constructed by and through one another.

8. This is Stuart Hall's definition of articulation. See Hall, *Critical Dialogues in Cultural Studies*, ed. David Morley and Kuan-Hsing Chen (New York: Routledge, 1996), 141.

9. I therefore disagree with Bederman's and Crenshaw's claims that the categories cannot be examined in isolation. I am closer to McClintock, who argues that gender, class, and race are neither reducible nor identical with one another. They exist, she says, "in intimate, reciprocal and contradictory relations." Nonetheless, McClintock neither expands on nor investigates the ways in which these categories are irreducible to one another. See McClintock, *Imperial Leather*, 5.

10. Michel Foucault, *The History of Sexuality, Vol. I, An Introduction*, trans. Robert Hurley (New York: Vintage Books, 1990), 93.

11. Audre Lorde, "Age, Race, Class, and Sex: Women Redefining Difference," in *Dangerous Liaisons: Gender, Nation and Postcolonial Perspectives*, ed. Anne McClintock, Aamir Mufti, and Ella Shohat (Minneapolis: University of Minnesota Press, 1997), 374–81.

12. For his discussion of the intentionality but nonsubjective "nature" of power, see Foucault, *History of Sexuality*, 94.

13. Ibid., 95.

14. It should be remembered that "Jewishness" was still being framed within a discourse of race.

15. See Ann DuCille, "Blues Notes on Black Sexuality: Sex and the Texts of Jessie Fauset and Nella Larsen," in *American Sexual Politics*, ed. John Fout and Maura Tantillo (Chicago: Chicago University Press, 1993), 197. Two clarifications need to be made at this point. First, Irene seems to represent both the New Negro Woman as well as more traditional norms of femininity. On the one hand, she can be described as a New Negro Woman, given her dedication to racial uplift work and her rejection of outward signs of sexuality. On the other hand, Irene is very much shaped by traditional norms of middle-class white "ladyhood." The depiction of Irene suggests that the line between these two norms was fluid. The New Negro Woman was, in many ways, a modified version of traditional "white" femininity that allowed for a bit more female presence in the public sphere, and did not—even as an alternative norm—counter the hegemonic injunction: Identify as black but desire to be white. On the contrary, the New Negro Woman reinforced this injunction on many levels even while it circumscribed the array of "white" norms that black women were permitted to approximate. However, as I argued in the previous chapter, the way this norm was taken up on the level of social praxis did sometimes challenge or at least complicate this injunction. Second, it is important to remember that the dominant New Woman ideal was under pressure in the 1920s, and there was a resurgence of the separate spheres and domesticity discourse. Not only was the dominant New Woman ideal not accessible for black middle-class women, as I argued in the previous chapter, but the New Woman qua

ideal was under pressure during the 1920s due to the re-emergence of the domesticity discourse. Thus, this period can be seen to be marked by competing versions of the mythical norm in relation to femininity.

16. Davis, *Reader*, 319.

17. Although class operates differently on the level of identification and desire-to-be due to the lack of assumption of essence that I discussed in the second chapter, here I am not taking this difference into account. Rather, here I focus on the subject's initial disadvantage in relation to norms of class.

18. Pierre Bourdieu, *Practical Reason: On the Theory of Action* (Stanford: Stanford University Press, 1998), 77.

19. The social field, of course, is made up of various possible social positions. When I speak about the correspondence between Manning's habitus and the social field, this correspondence only applies to cases where the novel describes social situations in which the dominant social norms have currency. Manning is certainly not as comfortable in the Lower East Side restaurant where he meets Sonya at the beginning of their courtship.

Bibliography

Ahmed, Sara. "'She'll Wake Up One of These Days and Find She's Turned into a Nigger': Passing through Hybridity." *Theory, Culture & Society* 16 (1999): 87–105.

Alba, Richard. *Ethnic Identity: The Transformation of White America.* New Haven, Conn.: Yale University Press, 1990.

Allen, Amy. "Power Trouble: Performativity as Critical Theory." *Constellations* 5, no. 4 (1998): 456–71.

Althusser, Louis. "Ideology and Ideological State Apparatuses (Notes towards an Investigation)." In *Lenin and Philosophy and Other Essays,* translated by Ben Brewster, 127–86. New York: Monthly Review Press, 1971.

Ammons, Elizabeth. *Conflicting Stories.* New York: Oxford University Press, 1991.

———. "The New Woman as Cultural Symbol and Social Reality: Six Women Writers' Perspectives." In *1915: The Cultural Moment,* edited by Adele Heller and Lois Rudnick, 82–98. New Brunswick, N.J.: Rutgers University Press, 1991.

Anderson, Amanda. "Debatable Performances: Restaging Contentious Feminisms." *Social Text* 54, no. 16 (1998): 1–24.

Appiah, Kwame Anthony. "'But Would That Still Be Me?' Notes on Gender, "Race," Ethnicity, as Sources of 'Identity.'" *The Journal of Philosophy* 87, no. 10 (1990): 493–99.

———. "Is the Post in Postmodernism the Post in Postcolonial?" *Critical Inquiry* 17, no. 2 (1991): 336–57.

Austin, J. L. *How to Do Things with Words.* Edited by Marina Sbisa and J. O. Urmson. Cambridge, Mass.: Harvard University Press, 1962.

Azoulay, Katya Gibel. "Jewishness after Mount Sinai: Jews, Blacks and the (Multi)Racial Category." *Identities* 8, no. 2 (2001): 211–46.

Babb, Valerie. *Whiteness Visible: The Meaning of Whiteness in American Literature and Culture.* New York: New York University Press, 1998.

Barnett, Pamela. "'My Picture of You Is, After All, the True Helga Crane': Portraiture and Identity in Nella Larsen's *Quicksand.*" *Signs* 20, no. 3 (1995): 575–600.

Barret, James, and David Roediger. "Inbetween Peoples: Race, Nationality and the 'New Immigrant' Working Class." *Journal of American Ethnic History* 16 (1997): 3–44.

Barzilai, Shuli. *Lacan and the Matter of Origins.* Stanford: Stanford University Press, 1999.

Bashi, Vilna, and Antonio McDaniel. "A Theory of Immigration and Racial Strati-fication." *Journal of Black Studies* 27, no. 5 (1997): 668–82.

Batker, Carol. "Literary Reformers: Crossing Class and Ethnic Boundaries in Jew-ish Women's Fiction of the 1920s." *MELUS* 25, no. 1 (2000): 81–104.

———. *Reforming Fictions: Native, African, and Jewish American Women's Liter-ature and Journalism in the Progressive Era.* New York: Columbia University Press, 2000.

Bederman, Gail. *Manliness and Civilization: A Cultural History of Gender and Race in the United States, 1880–1917.* Chicago: University of Chicago Press, 1995.

Bell, Vikki. "Mimesis as Cultural Survival: Judith Butler and Anti-Semitism." *Theory, Culture & Society* 16 (1999): 133–61.

———. "On Speech, Race, and Melancholia: An Interview with Judith Butler." *Theory, Culture & Society* 16 (1999): 163–74.

———. "Performativity and Belonging: An Introduction." *Theory, Culture & Soci-ety* 16 (1999): 1–10.

Bettie, Julie. "Women without Class: *Chicas, Cholas,* Trash, and the Presence/Absence of Class Identity." *Signs* 26, no. 1 (2000): 1–35.

Bhabha, Homi. *The Location of Culture.* New York: Routledge, 1994.

Bhavnani, Kum-Kum, ed. *Feminism and Race.* New York: Oxford University Press, 2000.

Birch, Eva Lennox. *Black American Women's Writing: A Quilt of Many Colors.* New York: Harvester Wheatsheaf, 1994.

Blackmer, Corinne. "The Veils of the Law: Race and Sexuality in Nella Larson's *Passing.*" *College Literature* 22, no. 3 (1995): 50–67.

Blackmore, David. "'That Unreasonable Restless Feeling': The Homosexual Sub-texts of Nella Larsen's *Passing.*" *African American Review* 26 (1992): 475–84.

Bontemps, Arna, ed. *The Harlem Renaissance Remembered.* New York: Dodd, 1972.

Bourdieu, Pierre. *Distinction: A Social Critique of the Judgment of Taste.* Trans-lated by Richard Nice. Cambridge, Mass.: Harvard University Press, 1984.

———. *In Other Words: Essays Towards a Reflexive Sociology.* Translated by Mat-thew Adamson. Stanford: Stanford University Press, 1990.

———. *The Logic of Practice.* Translated Richard Nice. Stanford: Stanford Univer-sity Press, 1990.

———. *Practical Reason: On the Theory of Action.* Stanford: Stanford University Press, 1998.

Boyarin, Daniel. *Unheroic Conduct: The Rise of Heterosexuality and the Invention of the Jewish Man.* Berkeley: University of California Press, 1997.

Brewer, Rose. "Theorizing Race, Class, and Gender: The New Scholarship of Black Feminist Intellectuals and Black Women's Labor." In *Materialist Feminism: A*

Reader in Class, Difference, and Women's Lives, edited by Rosemary Hennessy and Chrys Ingraham, 236–248. New York: Routledge, 1997.

Brink, Andre. "Complications of Birth: Interface of Gender, Race and Class in July's People." *English in Africa* 21, nos. 1–2 (1994): 157–80.

Brinker, Ludgar. "The Gilded Void: Edith Wharton, Abraham Cahan, and the Turn-of-the-Century American Culture." *Yiddish* 9, nos. 3–4 (1994): 32–42.

Brodkin, Karen. *How Jews Became White Folks and What That Says about Race in America.* New Brunswick, N.J.: Rutgers University Press, 1998.

Brody, Jennifer DeVere. "Clare Kennedy's 'True' Colors: Race and Class Conflict in Nella Larsen's *Passing*." *Callaloo: A Journal of African American and African Arts and Letters* 14 (1992): 1053–65.

Brown, Gillian. *Domestic Individualism: Imagining Self in Nineteenth-Century America.* Berkeley: University of California Press, 1990.

Brown, Wendy. "The Impossibility of Women's Studies." *differences: A Journal of Feminist Cultural Studies* 9, no. 3 (1997): 79–101.

Budick, Emily Miller. *Blacks and Jews in Literary Conversation.* Cambridge: Cambridge University Press, 1998.

Butler, Judith. *Bodies That Matter: On the Discursive Limits of "Sex."* New York: Routledge, 1993.

———. *Gender Trouble.* New York: Routledge, 1990.

———. *The Psychic Life of Power.* Stanford: Stanford University Press, 1997.

———. "Sovereign Performatives in the Contemporary Scene of Utterance." *Critical Inquiry* 23 (197): 20.

———. *Undoing Gender.* New York: Routledge, 2005.

Cahan, Abraham. *The Rise of David Levinsky.* 1917. Reprint, New York: Penguin Books, 1993.

Carby, Hazel. *Reconstructing Womanhood: The Emergence of the Afro-American Woman Novelist.* New York: Oxford University Press, 1987.

———. "Policing the Black Woman's Body in an Urban Context." *Critical Inquiry* 18, no. 4 (1992): 738–55.

Cayton, Mary Kupiec, and Peter Williams. Introduction to *Encyclopedia of American Cultural and Intellectual History.* Edited by Mary Kupiec Cayton and Peter Williams. New York: Scribner's Sons, 2001.

Ceaser, James. "Multiculturalism and American Liberal Democracy." In *Multiculturalism and American Democracy*, edited by Arthur Melzer, Jerry Weinberger, and M. Zinman, 139–57. Lawrence: University of Kansas Press, 1998.

Chametzky, Jules. Introduction to *The Rise of David Levinsky.* 1917. Reprint, New York: Penguin Books, 1993.

Chametzky, Jules, John Felstiner, Hilene Flanzbaum, and Kathryn Hellerstein, eds. *Jewish American Literature: A Norton Anthology.* New York: W.W. Norton, 2001.

Chen, K. H., and D. Morley, eds. *Stuart Hall, Critical Dialogues in Cultural Studies*. New York: Routledge, 1996.

Chesnutt, Charles. *The House behind the Cedars*. 1900. Reprint, New York: Penguin Books, 1993.

Christian, Barbara. *Black Women Novelists: The Development of a Tradition: 1892–1976*. Westport, Conn.: Greenwood Press, 1980.

Collins, Patricia Hill. "It's All in the Family: Intersections of Gender, Race, and Nation." *Hypatia* 13, no. 3 (1998): 62–83.

———. "Like One of the Family: Race, Ethnicity, and the Paradox of U.S. National Identity." *Ethnic and Racial Studies* 24, no. 1 (2001): 3–28.

Cooke, Michael G. *Afro-American Literature in the Twentieth Century*. New Haven, Conn.: Yale University Press, 1984.

Crenshaw, Kimberle. "Mapping the Margins: Intersectionality, Identity, Politics, and Violence against Women of Color." *Stanford Law Review* 43, no. 6 (1991): 1241–99.

———. "Demarginalizing the Intersection of Race and Sex: A Black Feminist Critique of Antidiscrimination Doctrine, Feminist Theory, and Antiracist Politics." In *Feminism and Politics*, edited by Anne Phillips, 314–43. Oxford: Oxford University Press, 1998.

Cutter, Martha. "Sliding Significations: Passing as a Narrative and Textual Strategy in Nella Larsen's Fiction." In *Passing and the Fictions of Identity*, edited by Elaine Ginsberg, 75–99. Durham, N.C.: Duke University Press, 1996.

Davies, Carole Boyce. *Black Women, Writing and Identity: Migrations of the Subject*. New York: Routledge, 1994.

Davis, Angela. *The Angela Davis Reader*. Edited by Joy James. Cambridge, Mass.: Blackwell Publishers, 1998.

———. *Women, Race, and Class*. New York: Vintage Books, 1983.

Davis, F. James. *Who is Black? One Nation's Definition*. University Park, Penn.: Pennsylvania State University Press, 1991.

Derrida, Jacques. *Margins of Philosophy*. Translated by Alan Bass. Chicago: University of Chicago Press, 1982.

———. *Writing and Difference*. Translated by Alan Bass. Chicago: University of Chicago Press, 1978.

DeSantis, Alan D. "Selling the American Dream Myth to Black Southerners: The Chicago Defender and the Great Migration of 1915–1919." *Western Journal of Communication* 62, no. 4 (1998): 474–511.

Dickson, Bruce. *Black American Writing from the Nadir: The Evolution of a Literary Tradition, 1877–1915*. Baton Rouge: Louisiana State University Press, 1989.

Diner, Hasia. *In the Almost Promised Land: American Jews and Blacks, 1915–1935*. 1977. Reprint, Westport, Conn.: Greenwood Press, 1995.

Du Bois, W. E. B. *The Souls of Black Folks*. 1903. Reprint, New York: Avon Books, 1965.

DuCille, Ann. "Blues Notes on Black Sexuality: Sex and the Texts of Jessie Fauset and Nella Larsen." In *American Sexual Politics*, edited by John Fout and Maura Tantillo, 193–219. Chicago: Chicago University Press, 1993.

———. *The Coupling Convention: Sex, Text, and Tradition in Black Women's Fiction*. New York: Oxford University Press, 1993.

Engel, David. "The 'Discrepancies' of the Modern: Towards a Revaluation of Abraham Cahan's *The Rise of David Levinsky.*" *Studies in American Jewish Literature* 2 (1982): 36–60.

Enstad, Nan. *Ladies of Labor, Girls of Adventure*. New York: Columbia University Press, 1999.

Fanon, Frantz. *Black Skin, White Masks*. Translated by Charles Lam Markmann. 1952. Reprint, New York: Grove Press, 1967.

Fauset, Jessie Redmon. *Plum Bun: A Novel without a Moral*. 1929. Reprint, Boston: Beacon Press, 1990.

Favor, Martin. *Authentic Blackness: The Folk in the New Negro Renaissance*. Durham, N.C.: Duke University Press, 1999.

Felski, Rita. "Nothing to Declare: Identity, Shame, and the Lower Middle Class." *PMLA* 115, no. 1 (2000): 33–46.

Ferraro, Thomas. *Ethnic Passages: Literary Immigrants in Twentieth-Century America*. Chicago: University of Chicago Press, 1993.

Fine, David. "In the Beginning" American-Jewish Fiction: 1880–1930." In *Handbook of American-Jewish Literature*, ed. Louis Fried. Westport, Conn.: Greenwood Press, 1988.

Fishbein, L. "Anzia Yezierska, the Sweatshop Cinderella and the Invented Life." *Studies in American Jewish Literature* 17 (1998): 137–41.

Foner, Nancy, and George Fredrickson. Introduction to *Not Just Black and White: Historical and Contemporary Perspectives on Immigration, Race, and Ethnicity*, edited by Nancy Foner and George Fredrickson, 1–23. New York: Russell Sage Foundation, 2004.

Fossum, Robert, and John Roth. *The American Dream*. London: British Association for American Studies, 1981.

Foucault, Michel. *Discipline and Punish: The Birth of the Prison*. Translated by Alan Sheridan. New York: Vintage Books, 1979.

———. *The History of Sexuality, Vol. I, An Introduction*. Translated by Robert Hurley. New York: Vintage Books, 1990.

Fox-Genovese, Elizabeth. "Between Individualism and Fragmentation: American Culture and the New Literary Studies of Race and Gender." *American Quarterly* 42, no. 1 (1990): 7–34.

Fraser, Nancy. "Heterosexism, Misrecognition, and Capitalism: A Response to Judith Butler." *Social Text* 52/53, no. 15 (1997): 278–89.

Freud, Sigmund. *The Ego and the Id*. Translated by Joan Riviere and edited by James Strachey. New York: W.W. Norton & Company, 1960.

————. *Group Psychology and the Analysis of the Ego: The Standard Edition*. Translated by James Strachey. New York: Bantam Books, 1960.

————. *New Introductory Lectures on Psycho-Analysis: The Standard Edition*. Translated by James Strachey. New York: W.W. Norton & Company, 1965.

Fried, Lewis, ed. *Handbook of American-Jewish Literature*. New York: Greenwood Press, 1988.

Fuss, Diana. *Identification Papers*. New York: Routledge, 1995.

Gates, Henry Louis, Jr. *Loose Canons: Notes on the Culture Wars*. New York: Oxford University Press, 1992.

Gerstle, Gary. "The Protean Character of American Liberalism." *The American Historical Review* 99, no. 4 (1994): 1043–73.

Gibson-Graham, J. K. *The End of Capitalism (as we knew it): A Feminist Critique of Political Economy*. Oxford: Blackwell Publishers, 1996.

Giddings, Paula. *When and Where I Enter: The Impact of Black Women on Race and Sex in American*. New York: Bantam Books, 1984.

Gilman, Sander. *The Jew's Body*. New York: Routledge, 1991.

Gilroy, Paul. *Postcolonial Melancholia*. New York: Columbia University Press, 2005.

Ginsberg, Elaine. "Introduction: The Politics of Passing." In *Passing and the Fictions of Identity*, edited by Elaine Ginsberg, 1–18. Durham, N.C.: Duke University Press, 1996.

Goellnicht, Donald. "Passing as Autobiography: James Weldon Johnson's *The Autobiography of an Ex-Colored Man*." *African American Review* 30, no. 1 (1996): 17–33.

Goffman, Ethan. *Imagining Each Other: Blacks and Jews in Contemporary American Literature*. Albany: State University of New York Press, 2000.

Goldsmith, Meredith. "'The Democracy of Beauty': Fashioning Ethnicity and Gender in the Fiction of Anzia Yezierska." *Yiddish* 11, nos. 3–4 (1999): 166–87.

Goldstein, Eric. "'Different Blood Flows in Our Veins': Race and Jewish Self-Definition in Late Nineteenth Century America." *American Jewish History* 85, no. 1 (1997): 29–55.

————. "The Unstable Other: Locating the Jew in Progressive-Era American Racial Discourse." *American Jewish History* 89, no. 4 (2002): 383–409.

Goldstein, Joseph. *Jewish History in Modern Times*. Brighton: Sussex Academic Press, 1995.

Golub, Ellen. "Eat Your Heart Out: The Fiction of Anzia Yezierska." *Studies in American Jewish Literature* 3 (1983): 51–61.

Gossett, Thomas F. *Race: The History of an Idea in America*. New York: Schocken Books, 1963.

Gramsci, Antonio. *Selections from the Prison Notebooks*. Edited and translated by Quintin Hoare and Geoffrey Nowell Smith. New York: International Publishers, 1971.

Gualtieri, Sarah. "Becoming 'White': Race, Religion and the Foundations of Syrian/Lebanese Ethnicity in the United States." *Journal of American Ethnic History* 20, no. 4 (2001): 29–58.

Hall, Stuart. *Critical Dialogues in Cultural Studies.* Edited by David Morley and Kuan-Hsing Chen. New York: Routledge, 1996.

———. "Interview with Stuart Hall: Culture and Power." *Radical Philosophy* 86 (1997): 24–41.

———. "The Spectacle of the Other." In *Representations: Cultural Representations and Signifying Practices*, edited by Stuart Hall, 223–90. London: Sage Publications, 1997.

Harap, Louis. *The Image of the Jew in American Literature: From Early Republic to Mass Immigration.* Philadelphia: The Jewish Publication Society of America, 1974.

Harper, Francis. *Iola Leroy.* 1892. Reprint, Boston: Beacon Press, 1987.

Harrison-Kahan, Lori. "Drunk with the Fiery Rhythms of Jazz." *MFS: Modern Fiction Studies* 51, no. 2 (2005): 416–36.

Hattam, Victoria. "Ethnicity: An American Genealogy." In *Not Just Black and White*, edited by Nancy Foner and George Fredrickson, 42–61. New York: Russell Sage Foundation, 2004.

Hennessy, Rosemary. *Materialist Feminism and the Politics of Discourse.* New York: Routledge, 1993.

Higginbotham, Elizabeth, and Lynn Weber. "Moving Up with Kin and Community: Upward Social Mobility for Black and White Women." *Gender & Society* 6, no. 3 (1992): 416–40.

Hine, Darlene Clark. "Rape and the Inner Lives of Black Women in the Middle West: Preliminary Thoughts on the Culture of Dissemblance." In *Unequal Sisters: A Multi-Cultural Reader in U.S. Women's History*, edited by Vicki Ruiz and Ellen Carol DuBois, 342–48. New York: Routledge, 1994.

Hochschild, Jennifer. *Facing Up to the American Dream: Race, Class and the Soul of the Nation.* Princeton, N.J.: Princeton University Press, 1995.

Hoffman, Warren. "The Rise (and Fall) of David Levinsky: Performing Jewish American Heterosexuality." *MFS Modern Fiction Studies* 51, no. 2 (2005): 393–415.

hooks, bell. *Ain't I a Woman: Black Women and Feminism.* Boston: South End Press, 1981.

———. *Feminist Theory: From Margin to Center.* Boston: South End Press, 1984.

Horton, Merrill. "Blackness, Betrayal, and Childhood: Race and Identity in Nella Larsen's *Passing*." *College Language Association Journal* 29 (1994): 31–45.

Hostetler, Ann. "The Aesthetics of Race and Gender in Nella Larsen's *Quicksand*." *PMLA* 105, no. 1 (1990): 35–46.

Huggins, Nathan. *Harlem Renaissance.* New York: Oxford University Press, 1987.

Hutchinson, Darren Lenard. "Critical Race Histories: In and Out." *American University Law Review* 53, no. 6 (2004): 1188–1215.

Hutchinson, George. *The Harlem Renaissance in Black and White*. Cambridge, Mass.: Harvard University Press, 1995.

Ignatiev, Noel. *How the Irish Became White*. New York: Routledge, 1995.

Jacobson, Matthew. "Becoming Caucasian: Vicissitudes of Whiteness in American Politics and Culture." *Identities* 8, no. 1 (2001): 83–104.

———. *Whiteness of a Different Color*. Cambridge, Mass.: Harvard University Press, 1998.

Japtok, Martin. *Growing Up Ethnic: Nationalism and the Bildungsroman in African American and Jewish American Fiction*. Iowa City: University of Iowa Press, 2005.

———. "Justifying Individualism: Anzia Yezierska's *Bread Givers*." In *The Immigrant Experience in North American Literature: Carving out a Niche*, edited by Katherine Payant and Toby Rose, 17–31. Greenwich, Conn.: Greenwood Press.

Johnson, James Weldon. *The Autobiography of an Ex-Colored Man*. 1912. Reprint, New York: Vintage Books, 1989.

Kamel, Rose. "'Anzia Yezierska, Get Out of Your Own Way': Selfhood and Otherness in the Autobiographical Fiction of Anzia Yezierska." *Studies in American Jewish Literature* 3 (1983): 40–50.

King, Desmond. *Making Americans: Immigration, Race, and the Origins of the Diverse Democracy*. Cambridge, Mass.: Harvard University Press, 2000.

Kleinberg, S. J. *Women in the United States: 1830–1945*. London: MacMillan Press, 1999.

Knadler, Stephen. "Traumatized Racial Performativity: Passing in Nineteenth-Century African-American Testimonies." *Cultural Critique* 55 (2003): 63–100.

Konzett, Delia Caparoso. *Ethnic Modernisms: Anzia Yezierska, Zora Neale Hurston, Jean Rhys, and the Aesthetics of Dislocation*. New York: Palgrave Macmillan, 2002.

Koshy, Susan "Category Crisis: South Asian Americans and Questions of Race and Ethnicity." *Diaspora* 7, no. 3 (1998): 285–320.

———. "Morphing Race into Ethnicity: Asian Americans and Critical Transformations of Whiteness." *Boundary 2* 28, no. 1 (2001): 153–94.

Kress, Susan. "Women and Marriage in Abraham Cahan's Fiction." *Studies in American Jewish Literature* 3 (1983): 26–39.

Krupnick, Mark. "Jewish-American Literature." In *New Immigrant Literatures in the United States: A Sourcebook to Our Multicultural Literary Heritage*, edited by Alpana Sharma Knippling, 295–309. Westport, Conn.: Greenwood Press, 1996.

Laplanche, Jean, and Jean-Bertrand Pontalis. *The Language of Psychoanalysis*. Translated by Donald Nicholson-Smith. London: Karnac Books, 1988.

Larsen, Nella. *Quicksand and Passing*. 1928/1929. Reprint, New Brunswick, N.J.: Rutgers University Press, 1986.

Levinson, Melanie. "'To Make Myself for a Person': 'Passing' Narratives and the Divided Self in the Work of Anzia Yezierska." *Studies in American Jewish Literature* 13 (1994): 2–9.

Lloyd, Moya. "Performativity, Parody, Politics." *Theory, Culture & Society* 16 (1999): 195–213.

Lopez, Ian Haney. *White by Law: The Legal Construction of Race*. New York: New York University Press, 1996.

Lorde, Audre. "Age, Race, Class, and Sex: Women Redefining Difference." In *Dangerous Liaisons: Gender, Nation and Postcolonial Perspectives*, edited by Anne McClintock, Aamir Mufti, and Ella Shohat, 374–81. Minneapolis: University of Minnesota Press, 1997.

Lott, Eric. "Love and Theft: The Racial Unconscious of Blackface Minstrelsy." *Representations* 39 (1992): 23–50.

MacPherson, C. B. *The Political Theory of Possessive Individualism*. Oxford: Oxford University Press, 1962.

Marks, Carole. "The Great Migration: African Americans Searching for the Promised Land: 1916–1930." Available online: http://www.inmotionaame.org/texts/index.cfm?migration=8&topic=99&type=text, accessed August 2006.

Marovitz, Sanford. "The Secular Trinity of a Lonely Millionaire: Language, Sex, and Power in *The Rise of David Levinsky*." *Studies in American Jewish Literature* 2 (1982): 20–35.

Marx, Karl. *The Eighteenth Brumaire of Louis Bonaparte*. 1963. Reprint, New York: International Publishers, 1998.

Marx, Karl, and Friedrich Engels. *The German Ideology*. Edited by C. J. Arthur. 1970. Reprint, New York: International Publishers, 1995.

McCall, Leslie. "The Complexity of Intersectionality." *Signs* 30, no. 3 (2005): 1771–1800.

McClintock, Anne. *Imperial Leather: Race, Gender and Sexuality in the Colonial Contest*. New York: Routledge, 1995.

———, ed. *Dangerous Liaisons: Gender, Nation, and Postcolonial Perspectives*. Minneapolis: University of Minnesota Press, 1997.

McDowell, Deborah. Introduction to *Quicksand and Passing*. New Brunswick, N.J.: Rutgers University Press, 1986, ix–xxxv.

McLendon, Jacquelyn Y. "Self-Representation as Art in the Novels of Nella Larsen." In *Redefining Autobiography in Twentieth-Century Women's Fiction: An Essay Collection*, edited by Colette Hall, Janice Morgan, and Carol Snyder, 149–68. New York: Garland, 1991.

McNay, Lois. *Gender and Agency: Reconfiguring the Subject in Feminist and Social Theory*. Cambridge: Polity Press, 2000.

———. "Subject, Psyche and Agency: The Work of Judith Butler." *Theory, Culture & Society* 16 (1999): 175–93.

Meyer, Adam. "Not Entirely Strange, But Not Entirely Friendly Either: Jewish and Black Navigations of the Color Line." *African American Review* 38, no. 3 (2004): 441–50.

Michaels, Walter Benn. "Autobiography of an Ex-White Man: Why Race Is Not a Social Construction." *Transition* 73 (1997): 122–43.

Miron, Louis, and Jonathan Xavier Inda. "Race as a Kind of Speech Act." *Cultural Studies: A Research Annual* 5 (2000): 85–107.

Monda, Kimberly. "Self-Delusion and Self-Sacrifice in Nella Larsen's *Quicksand.*" *African American Review* 31, no. 1 (1997): 23–39.

Newton, Adam Zachary. *Facing Black and Jew: Literature as Public Space in Twentieth-Century America.* Cambridge: Cambridge University Press, 1999.

Okonkwo, Christopher N. "Of Repression, Assertion, and the Speakerly Dress: Anzia Yezierska's *Salome of the Tenements.*" *MELUS* 25, no. 1 (2000): 129–45.

Omi, Michael, and Howard Winant. *Racial Formation in the United States from the 1960s to the 1980s.* New York: Routledge, 1986.

Pavletich, JoAnn. "Anzia Yezierska, Immigrant Authority, and the Uses of Affect." *Tulsa Studies in Women's Literature* 19, no. 1 (2000): 81–104.

Pecheux, Michel. *Language, Semantics, and Ideology.* New York: St. Martin's Press, 1982.

Peiss, Kathy. "Making Faces: The Cosmetics Industry and the Cultural Construction of Gender, 1890–1930." In *Unequal Sisters: A Multi-Cultural Reader in U.S. Women's History,* edited by Vicki Ruiz and Ellen Carol DuBois, 372–95. New York: Routledge, 1994.

Pellegrini, Ann. *Performance Anxieties: Staging Psychoanalysis, Staging Race.* New York: Routledge, 1997.

Porter, Glen. *The Rise of Big Business: 1860–1920.* 1973. Reprint, Arlington Heights, Ill.: Harlan Davidson Inc., 1992.

Ramsey, Priscilla. "A Study of Black Identity in 'Passing' Novels of the Nineteenth and Early Twentieth Century." *Studies in Black Literature* 7 (1976): 1–7.

Rhoads, Edward. "'White Labor' vs. 'Coolie Labor': The 'Chinese Question' in Pennsylvania in the 1870s." *Journal of American Ethnic History* 21, no. 2 (2002): 3–32.

Roberts, Kimberly. "The Clothes Make the Woman: The Symbolics of Prostitution in Nella Larsen's *Quicksand* and Claude McKay's *Home to Harlem.*" *Tulsa Studies in Women's Literature* 16, no. 1 (1997): 107–30.

Robinson, Amy. "Takes One to Know One: Passing and Communities of Common Interest." *Critical Inquiry* 20 (1994): 715–36.

Roediger, David. *The Wages of Whiteness: Race and the Making of the American Working Class.* Revised Edition. London: Verso, 1999.

Rudnick, Lois. "The New Woman." In *1915: The Cultural Moment*, edited by Adele Heller and Lois Rudnick, 69–82. New Brunswick, N.J.: Rutgers University Press, 1991.

Ruotolo, Cristina. "James Weldon Johnson and the Autobiography of an Ex-Colored Musician." *American Literature* 72, no. 2 (2000): 249–74.

Sandel, Michael. *Democracy's Discontent: America in Search of a Public Philosophy*. Cambridge, Mass.: Harvard University Press, 1996.

———. *Liberalism and the Limits of Justice*. Cambridge: Cambridge University Press, 1998.

Sedgwick, Eve. *Between Men: English Literature and Male Homosocial Desire*. New York: Columbia University Press, 1985.

Sherrard-Johnson, Cherene. "'A Plea for Color': Nella Larsen's Iconography of the Mulatta." *American Literature* 76, no. 4 (2004): 833–69.

Singh, Amritjit. *The Novels of the Harlem Renaissance: Twelve Black Writers 1923–1933*. University Park: Pennsylvania State University Press, 1976.

Smedley, A. *Race in North America: Origin and Evolution of a Worldview*. Boulder, Colo.: Westview, 1993.

Smith, Valerie. *Not Just Race, Not Just Gender: Black Feminist Readings*. New York: Routledge, 1998.

Smith-Rosenberg, Carroll. *Disorderly Conduct: Visions of Gender in Victorian American*. New York: Oxford University Press, 1985.

Sol, Adam. "Searching for Middle Ground in Abraham Cahan's *The Rise of David Levinsky* and Sidney Nyburg's *The Chosen People*." *Studies in American Jewish Literature* 8 (1989): 30–45.

Sollors, Werner. *Beyond Ethnicity: Consent and Descent in American Culture*. New York: Oxford University Press, 1986.

Sullivan, Nell. "Nella Larsen's *Passing* and the Fading Subject." *African American Review* 32 (1998): 373–86.

Sundquist, Eric. *Strangers in the Land: Blacks, Jews, Post-Holocaust America*. Cambridge, Mass.: Harvard University Press, 2005.

Takaki, Ronald. *A Different Mirror: A History of Multicultural America*. Boston: Little, Brown and Company, 1993.

———. *Iron Cages: Race and Culture in Nineteenth-Century America*. Oxford: Oxford University Press, 1990.

Tate, Claudia. "Desire and Death in *Quicksand*, by Nella Larsen." *American Literary History* 7, no. 2 (1995): 234–60.

Thurman, Wallace. *The Blacker the Berry*. 1928. Reprint, New York: Simon & Schuster, 1996.

Trimberger, Ellen Kay. "The New Woman and the New Sexuality: Conflict and Contradiction in the Writings and Lives of Mabel Dodge and Neith Boyce." In *1915: The Cultural Moment*, edited by Adele Heller and Lois Rudnick, 98–117. New Brunswick, N.J.: Rutgers University Press, 1991.

Wald, Gayle. *Crossing the Line: Racial Passing in Twentieth-Century U.S. Literature and Culture*. Durham, N.C.: Duke University Press, 2000.

Warren, Jonathan, and France Winddance Twine. "White Americans, the New Minority? Non-Blacks and the Ever-Expanding Boundaries of Whiteness." *Journal of Black Studies* 28, no. 2 (1997): 200–18.

Washington, Mary Helen. "The Mulatta Trap: Nella Larsen's Women of the 1920s." In *Invented Lives: Narratives of Black Women, 1860–1960*, edited by Mary Helen Washington, 159–67. New York: Anchor, 1987.

Weinthal, Edith. "The Image of the City in Yezierska's *Bread Givers*." *Studies in American Jewish Literature* 13 (1994): 10–13.

Wiegman, Robyn. *American Anatomies: Theorizing Race and Gender*. Durham, N.C.: Duke University Press, 1995.

Wilentz, Gay. *Healing Narratives: Women Writers Curing Cultural Dis-ease*. New Brunswick, N.J.: Rutgers University Press, 2000.

Williams, Raymond. "Base and Superstructure in Marxist Cultural Theory." In *The Raymond Williams Reader*, edited by John Higgins, 158–79. Oxford: Blackwell, 2001.

Winn, J. Emmett. "Moralizing Upward Mobility: Investigating the Myth of Class Mobility in *Working Girl*." *The Southern Communication Journal* 66, no. 1 (2000): 40–51.

Wintz, Cary. *Black Culture and the Harlem Renaissance*. College Station: Texas A&M University Press, 1996.

Yezierska, Anzia. *Arrogant Beggar*. 1927. Reprint, Durham, N.C.: Duke University Press, 1996.

———. *Bread Givers*. 1925. Reprint, New York: Persea Books, 1975.

———. *Salome of the Tenements*. 1923. Reprint, Urbana: University of Illinois Press, 1995.

Zaborowska, Magdalena. "Americanization of a 'Queer Fellow': Performing Jewishness and Sexuality in Abraham's *The Rise of David Levinsky*." *American Studies in Scandinavia* 29 (1997): 18–27.

Zackodnik, Teresa. "Fixing the Color Line: The Mulatto, Southern Courts, and Racial Identity." *American Quarterly* 53, no. 3 (2001): 420–51.

Zinn, Howard. *A People's History of the United States: 1492–Present*. New York: HarperCollins Publishers, 1980.

Index

African Americans: African-American Jews, 154n45; African-American literature, 3–4, 133–35nn7–12; "black" aesthetic, 13; class distinctions of, 108–9, 119–20; migration to northern cities, 157n26; miscegenation laws, 143n35, 157n27; post–Civil War demographic shifts of, 2. *See also* African American women; blackness; Harlem Renaissance; New Negro Woman ideal; race

African American women: Americanness and, 102; intersectionality of racism/sexism and, 109; New Woman ideal and, 94, 97, 99–100, 102–6. *See also* African Americans; gender; New Negro Woman ideal; race

agency: "choice" as factor in identification, 85–86, 152–53n29, 153n32, 154n41; "cult of the self," 64–65, 67–68, 149n36; Jewish American whiteness and, 106; as negotiation among norms, 15, 51, 132; performativity and, 29; self-crafting and, 155–56n9. *See also* identification; identity; individualism; subjectivity

Ahmed, Sara, 38

Alba, Richard, 154n40

Althusser, Louis, 54–55

American Dream discourse: African American oppression and, 82; African American uplift and, 84, 101, 103, 105, 112; class norms and, 7, 12–13, 56–57, 111–12; defined, 53; democratization of beauty and, 59–60, 67–68, 149n36; determination as component of, 57–59, 65–66, 93; ethnicity and, 86; failure and, 58–59, 66; gender and, 97; historical variance in, 145–46n1; individualism and, 55–56, 65–66, 146n5, 147n11; non-essentialist identities and, 7; upward mobility theme, 57–60, 65–66, 79–80, 145–46n1; women's independence and self-fulfillment, 93. *See also* class

Americanization movement, 55, 149n36

American male gender ideal, 22–32

Americanness: African American women and, 102; alternative conceptions of, 15, 132; in American literature, 133n2; black-white dichotomy and, 76, 79–80, 88, 102, 113–14; dominant norms and, 101–2; as ethnic literature theme, 1; identification and, 15, 76, 86–87, 90; Jewish ethnicity and, 24, 79–80, 86–87, 90, 106, 114; Jewish women and, 97, 102, 106; national anthem and, 80–81; performativity and, 15

Ammons, Elizabeth, 93, 96, 156–57n21

Aristotle, 155n8

Arrogant Beggar (1927): as assimilationist narrative, 6; class norms in, 12; New Woman ideal in, 93–94, 96–99; overview, 92–93; status as "ethnic" work, 3, 133n1. *See also names of characters*

Asian Americans, 73, 89, 153–54n37

assimilation, 5–6, 16–17, 24–25

Austin, J. L., 135n14

authenticity: in ethnic identity, 5–6; *Ex-Colored Man* ragtime theme and, 74, 81, 118; imitation of dominant norms and, 120; Muhmenkeh character (*Arrogant Beggar*) and, 97

Autobiography of an Ex-Colored Man, The (1912): African American class structure in, 119–20; lynching scene, 48, 81–82, 85–86; male privilege in, 5, 123–24; passing in, 6, 13, 33, 48; racial identification/desire in, 11–12, 44, 119–20; resistance in, 14, 84–85; status as "ethnic" work, 3; train ride incident, 74–76. *See also* ex-colored man

Azoulay, Katya Gibel, 154n45

Bashi, Vilna, 78

Batker, Carol, 96, 134n9

Bederman, Gail, 22–23, 31, 109–10, 116–17, 159n9

Bell, Vikki, 139–40n25